Launching the Balanced Literacy Classroom

mhreadingwonders.com

Send all inquiries to:
McGraw-Hill Education
2 Penn Plaza
New York, NY 10121

ISBN: 978-0-07-673098-8
MHID: 0-07-673098-0

Printed in the United States of America.

1 2 3 4 5 6 7 8 9 ROV 21 20 19 18 17 16

Table of Contents

Table of Contents

A BALANCED LITERACY CLASSROOM: WHAT DOES IT LOOK AND SOUND LIKE?

By Kathy Rhea Bumgardner

National Literacy Consultant
North Carolina Educator
Strategies Unlimited, Inc.
Belmont, North Carolina

Creator of Think Aloud Clouds and Literacy Toolkits for Comprehension; Professional Development Videos for Instructional Best Practices in Literacy

Introduction

Balanced literacy is definitely not new in education. However, in the era of more rigorous standards for English Language Arts & Literacy and expectations for 21st century college and career ready students, many educators are questioning their current instructional strategies and practices. Questions that educators frequently need to address include the following: What does effective 21st century literacy learning look and sound like? How do we prepare students to be college and career ready? What existing practices should remain in the classroom and what needs to change with the times?

Although some adjustment must be made to meet new global economy expectations, the foundation of the balanced literacy model remains solid in preparing students for reading success in school, college, and career.

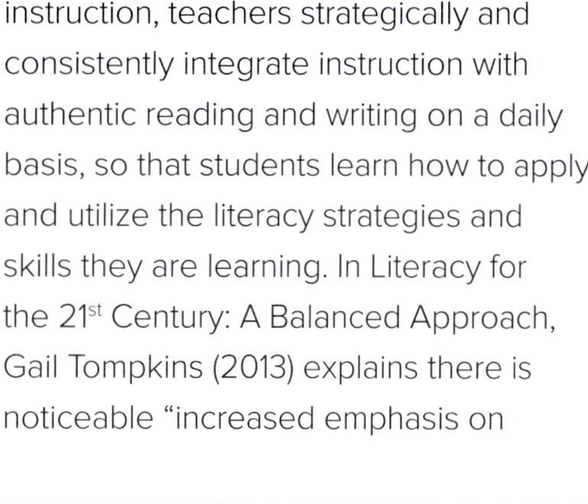

In a balanced approach to literacy instruction, teachers strategically and consistently integrate instruction with authentic reading and writing on a daily basis, so that students learn how to apply and utilize the literacy strategies and skills they are learning. In Literacy for the 21st Century: A Balanced Approach, Gail Tompkins (2013) explains there is noticeable "increased emphasis on developing strategic readers and writers" in recent years (p. 10).

A balanced approach to instructional literacy practices is grounded in the belief that ownership of literacy is central to students' lifelong success and this ownership of literacy motivates students to continue reading even when reading becomes challenging. In an era of increased emphasis on accessing

Monkey Business Images/Shutterstock.com

complex texts, a balanced literacy instructional approach ensures students are becoming proficient readers by providing multiple opportunities for modeled instruction as well as guided, collaborative, and independent practice.

A balanced approach to instructional literacy practices is grounded in the belief that ownership of literacy is central to students' lifelong success.

The Many Names and Faces of Balanced Literacy

Multiple opinions exist as to what the word balanced actually means in the term balanced literacy. At any time, in any number of school districts and classrooms across this country, various labels are used for what appears to be, in essence, the same overall balanced approach, or at least an approach that has the same basic framework and goals.

In Ann Arbor, Michigan, Ann Arbor Public Schools has a district publication, Balanced Literacy in the Ann Arbor Public Schools, that outlines a framework for balanced literacy instruction. The publication defines balanced literacy as "a set of instructional literacy practices, which encompass methods for teaching to the whole class, small groups, and individuals according to need and interest" (Hatt, Anderson, Madden, & Dickinson, 2008, p. 3).

Further, the district publication references "the inclusion of instruction in reading, writing, and word study," (Hatt et. al., 2008, p. 3) in its definition of balanced literacy. The "understanding of balance also applies to the gradual release of support from the teacher to the learner as skills become more proficient and the learner becomes more independent" (Hatt et al., 2008, p. 3).

Similarly, literature produced in Branchburg Township School District in Branchburg, New Jersey defines their district's balanced literacy instruction as a comprehensive approach to language arts instruction that "contains all of the components necessary for students to master written and oral communication" (Porowski, 2009, p. 4).

Branchburg balanced literacy components are listed as follows:

- READ-ALOUDS: Teacher Modeled Reading
- INDEPENDENT READING WORKSHOP: Daily Independent Reading
- GUIDED READING WORKSHOP: Guided Instruction in Developmentally Appropriate Books
- WRITE ALOUDS: Teacher Modeled Writing
- INDEPENDENT WRITING WORKSHOP: Daily Independent Writing
- GUIDED WRITING WORKSHOP: Guided Instruction in Developmentally Appropriate Writing
- WORD STUDY: Guided and Independent Phonics, Spelling, and Etymology

Another balanced approach is the Four-Blocks® Literacy Model. It incorporates four different approaches each day to teach children to read and write. Patricia Cunningham and Dorothy Hall developed this model. It includes:

- Guided Reading
- Working with Words
- Self-Selected Reading
- Writing

One last popular example is an instructional approach created by teachers Gail Boushey and Joan Moser, known as "The Daily 5." It is based on their own classroom teaching experiences, research, and methods they have developed for accelerating literacy and learning. The approach includes the following components:

- Read to Self
- Read to Someone
- Work on Writing
- Listen to Reading
- Word Work

Whether it is called Daily 5, reading to- , with-, and by-, reading or writing workshop, or simply balanced literacy, all the approaches are based on providing the best instruction possible in whole-group and small-group and then providing students with opportunities to work independently after a gradual release of responsibility.

A Balanced Literacy Framework Supports A Successful 21st Century Classroom

We have seen that different approaches to balanced literacy share a pattern of common components. When considering increased 21st century college career requirements, the common best-practice instructional components of balanced literacy not only hold up as viable approaches in response to the demands of more rigorous standards and expectations the components provide a balanced, scaffolded framework for helping students prepare for critical thinking, collaboration and becoming college and career reading.

Balanced literacy includes three levels of instruction:

- Whole-group (whole-class) instruction
- Differentiated small-group instruction
- Independent student work

Another tenet of balanced literacy that supports our new era of literacy instruction is the focus on progressive lessons in reading, writing, and vocabulary or word study that use a gradual release of responsibility approach. This balanced literacy lesson progression generally includes the following:

- Modeled Interactive Read-Alouds/ Modeled Writing (whole-group)
- Shared Reading and Writing (whole-group)
- Guided Reading and Writing (small-group)
- Independent Reading and Writing (small-group/individual)
- Word Study (whole-group/small-group, integrated with reading and writing)

In Neenah, Wisconsin, Neenah Joint School District is among those embracing the balanced literacy model as their chosen approach to meet the new college and career ready requirements.

The instructional components of balanced literacy provide a balanced, scaffolded framework for helping students meet more rigorous and critical requirements.

In defining their 2014–15 plan for Elementary Universal Instruction Neenah Joint School District states that they have "embraced the balanced literacy framework for instruction because it provides emerging readers and writers with opportunities to read and write every day in a variety of ways" (2014).

Neenah's balanced literacy plan gives teachers time in their first quarter for building routines to ensure a successful program that engages students in reading, writing, and speaking and listening. Also they place emphasis on "community and stamina building" (2014). This demonstrates a focus on preparing students to be collaborative and college and career ready.

Jacek Chabraszewski/Shutterstock.com

21st Century College and Career Ready Inspired Shifts in Balanced Literacy

Although the main components of balanced literacy have remained constant, 21st century college and career requirements have called for some important shifts in the implementation of these components.

1. Gradual Release and Collaboration

One example is a shift in the gradual release model of instruction. During gradual release, the teacher scaffolds each lesson to first introduce a concept or skill (I Do), then gradually releases to students the responsibility of practicing that skill, first with the teacher (We Do), then independently (You Do). In balanced literacy, this model is followed not only through the scaffolded progression of lessons (modeled, shared, guided, independent) but is also followed within the steps of each individual lesson.

More rigorous standards and the importance of collaborative practices in the global economy call for an adjustment in the gradual release model. In "Better Learning Through Structured Teaching: A Framework for the Gradual Release of Responsibility," Doug Fisher and Nancy Frey (2008) dig deeper into the methods of and reasons for the gradual release of responsibility in the instructional framework of a 21st century classroom. They note these essential and interrelated instructional phases now require an additional collaborative step in the You Do phase for a total of four phases:

- Focused Instruction: I Do
- Guided Instruction: We Do
- Collaborative Learning: You Do Together
- Independent Learning: You Do Independently

This is also reflective of the increased importance of collaborative conversations in the classroom with a direct link from collaboration to nurturing deeper comprehension. Teachers and students share a balance of equal opportunities to participate in the classroom during explicit instruction, engaged discussions, and productive group work either in whole-class or small-group activities (Archer and Hughes, 2011; Frey, Fisher, and Everlove, 2009). More rigorous demands for critical communication and collaboration in the 21st century workplace initiates the need for more intentional and consistent teacher-student and student-student communication than most classrooms experienced previously.

2. Text Complexity, Close Reading, and Informational Text

Another shift in balanced literacy instruction has occurred in the complexity of the text and the approach to reading during the shared reading lesson. Shared reading must now be done with more-complex texts alongside a protocol of close listening and reading, with a focus on text-dependent questioning and citing text evidence.

> Teachers of balanced literacy who use *Wonders Balanced Literacy* have access to a comprehensive and totally relevantly updated curriculum.

The increased text complexity of the shared read increases the importance of the read aloud lesson that precedes it. In the read aloud, students receive modeled instruction for addressing these more complex texts.

Robert Kneschke/Shutterstock.com

The current focus on informational text also calls for the inclusion, in all reading lessons, of a balance of content-rich informational texts and literature selections that are read to students, with students, and by students.

Teachers of balanced literacy who use *Wonders Balanced Literacy* have access to a cutting edge rigorous curriculum that contains a strategic and rich balance of texts, materials, and instructional supports teachers need to embrace balanced literacy and prepare students to be college and career ready.

Wonders Balanced Literacy provides teachers with texts and resources for working with students in whole-group, small-group, as well as individually, while addressing more rigorous requirements and expectations for students.

Assessment in a Balanced Literacy Classroom

Assessment provides data about students' performance that can and should be used to drive instruction. Teachers need to have multiple assessments in place to identify a student's strengths and determine what instruction the student needs next.

Assessment is a critical component of the decision-making process within balanced literacy. To support teachers in their decision-making process, data are collected systematically. The goal of this data collection is to document change over time (Clay, 2001) as well as gather evidence of learning (Shea, Murray, & Harlin, 2005).

In a balanced literacy classroom, Informal and ongoing assessments play a key role in monitoring student progress. Examples of these include anecdotal notes of teacher observations, running records and miscue analysis, retells and recounts, fluency checks, student journals and portfolios, writing samples, and student interviews.

Teacher observations of their students at work in whole groups, small groups, and independently in the classroom is one of the most valuable information sources for guiding their instructional decisions on a daily basis. Anecdotal notes enable a teacher to identify a student's learning behavior and document authentic performance to guide next steps.

It is recommended that teachers "have a clipboard with you at all times so you can document students' literacy behaviors. Putting sticky notes on the clipboard is another way to keep observations" (Poliastro & McTague, 2015, p. 24).

In today's classroom, the core principles of the balanced literacy model of instruction are still not only viable but are an effective set of instructional approaches for student reading success in school, college, and career.

The reading, writing, and word study components of *Wonders Balanced Literacy* support teaching a balanced literacy framework while guiding students to truly be college and career ready for the 21st century global economy world into which they will be living in upon graduation from high school.

References

Archer, A., & Hughes, C. (2011). Explicit instruction: Effective and efficient teaching. New York: Guilford Publications.

Boushey, G., & Moser, J. (2014). The Daily 5—Fostering literacy independence in the elementary grades. Portland, ME: Stenhouse.

Clay, M. M. (2001). Change over time in children's literacy development. Portsmouth, NH: Heinemann.

Cunningham, P., & Allington, R. (2011). Classrooms that work: They can all read and write (5th ed.). Boston, MA: Allyn & Bacon.

Cunningham, P. M., Hall, D. P., & Sigmon, C. M. (1999). The teacher's guide to the four blocks: A multimethod, multilevel framework for grades 1–3. Greensboro, NC: Carson-Dellosa.

Fisher, D., & Frey, N. (2008). Better learning through structured teaching: A framework for the gradual release of responsibility

(2nd ed.). Alexandria, VA: ASCD. Frey, N., Fisher, D., & Everlove, S. (2009).

Productive group work: How to engage students, build teamwork, and promote understanding. Alexandria, VA: ASCD.

Frey, N., & Fisher, D. (2014). Better learning through structured teaching: A framework for the gradual release of responsibility (2nd ed.). Alexandria, VA: ASCD.

Frey, N., & Fisher, D. (2014). Gradual release of responsibility. Retrieved from http://www. fisherandfrey.com/resources/

Hatt, C., Anderson, D., Madden, & Dickinson, M. (2008). Balanced literacy in the Ann Arbor Public Schools. Ann Arbor, MI: Author. Retrieved from http://www.a2schools.org/ academics/files/bal_lit_guide_sept08.pdf

Neenah Joint School District. (2014). Literacy curriculum. Neenah, WI: Author. Retrieved from http://www.neenah.k12.wi.us/ academics/literacy.cfm

National Governors Association Center for Best Practices and Council of Chief State School Officers. (2010). Common Core State Standards for English Language Arts & Literacy. Washington, DC: Authors.

Policastro, M., & McTague, B. (2015). The new balanced literacy school: Implementing Common Core. Chicago, IL: Maupin House.

Porowski, E. C. (2009). Balanced literacy instruction. Branchburg, NJ: Branchburg Township District. Retrieved from https://ltllacu.wikispaces.com/file/view/Introduction_to_the_Balanced_Literacy_Model.pdf

Lilly, E. (2014). Developing partnerships with families through children's literature. Upper Saddle River, NJ: Merrill/Prentice Hall.

Pearson, P. D., Raphael, T. E., Benson, V. L., & Madda, C. L. (2007). Balance in the literacy curriculum: Then and now. In L. B. Gambrell & L. M. Morrow (Eds.), Best practices in literacy instruction (3rd ed., pp. 30–54). New York: Guilford Press.

Shea, M., Murray, R., & Harlin, R. (2005). Drowning in data? How to collect and document student performance. Portsmouth, NH: Heinemann.

Tompkins, G. E. (2010, 2013). Literacy for the 21st century: A balanced approach (5th ed.). Upper Saddle River, NH: Pearson. 7 RD 14 M 03412

Instructional Path: Kindergarten

Follow the instructional path to guide your exploration of the text sets. For additional resources, go to **connected.mcgraw-hill.com**.

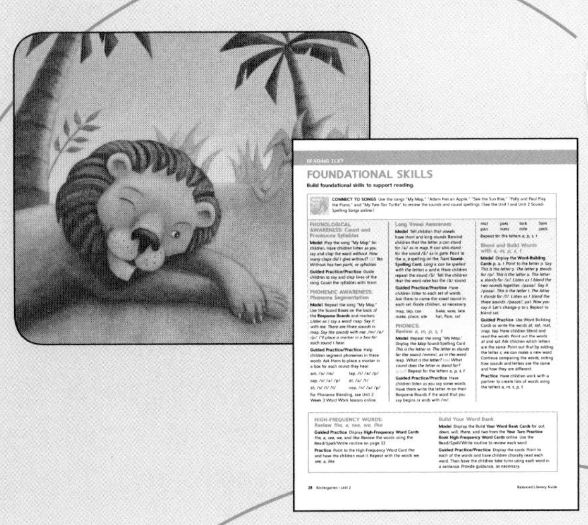

1 Introduce the Inquiry

Understanding Text

- INQUIRY: Begin the Inquiry with a song or poem.
- Listen and discuss the read alouds.

Reading Text

- Build foundational skills to support reading.

Use online photos and Think Aloud Clouds to support Read Aloud instruction. Also see online resources to support foundational skills.

2 Listen to and Read Texts

Understanding Text

- Model reading complex texts and answering text-dependent questions.
- Analyze how the author uses text, craft and structure, citing text evidence.
- INQUIRY: Expand the discussion of the Inquiry Question.
- QUICK CHECK: Use Quick Checks to determine students' needs.

Reading Text

- Apply foundational skills to read short texts.
- QUICK CHECK: Use Quick Checks to determine students' needs.

Use online resources to support reading complex texts and develop foundational skills.

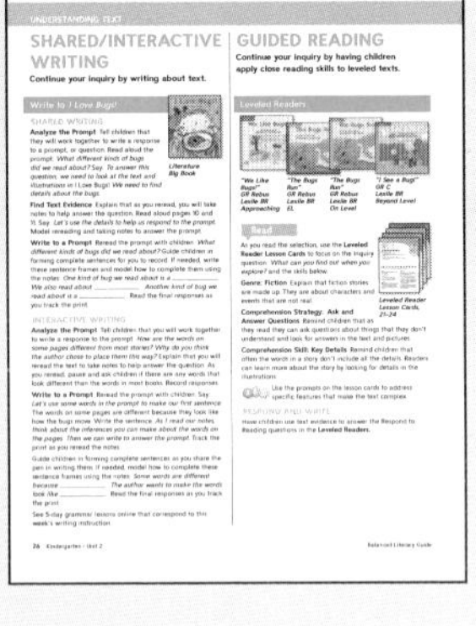

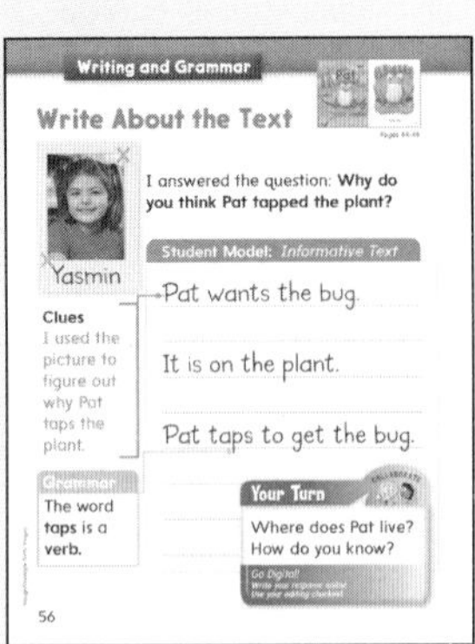

3 Write to Sources

Understanding Text

- Conduct Shared and Interactive writing lessons by using text evidence to write to the Literature Big Book.

Reading Text

- Write independently to a short text, using text evidence.
- Use the writing process to prewrite, draft, revise and edit writing.

4 Read and Write About an Extended Text

Understanding Text

- Listen to a close reading of the classroom library selection and use text evidence to answer text-dependent questions.
- Use text evidence to understand how the author uses text, craft and structure to develop a deeper understanding of the story.
- Write a short response.
- INQUIRY: Expand the discussion of the Inquiry Question.

Reading Text

- Practice foundational skills and apply skills to decodable texts in small group lessons.
- QUICK CHECKS: Use Quick Checks to determine students' needs.

5 Small Group Work

Understanding Text

- Apply close reading using leveled texts.
- INQUIRY: Expand the discussion of the Inquiry Question.

Reading Text

- Practice foundational skills and apply skills to decodable texts.
- QUICK CHECKS: Use Quick Checks to determine students' needs.

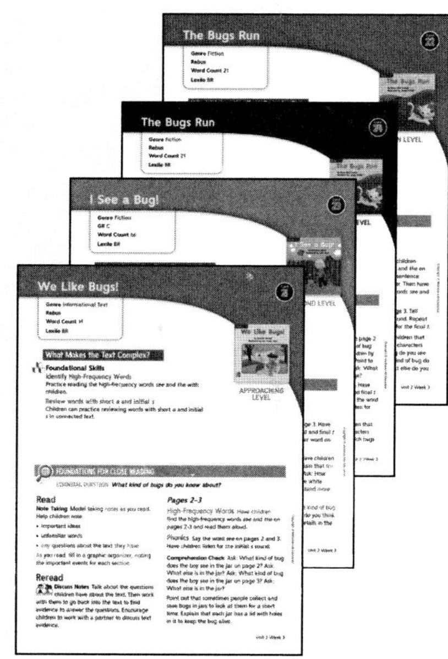

Use online resources for Approaching, Tier 2, On-Level, Beyond and English Learners to continue to differentiate instruction. Also, see online resources to support applying foundational skills in connected text.

6 Integrate Knowledge and Ideas

Integrate knowledge from multiple sources.

- Conduct a short research project to extend the learning.
- 

INQUIRY OUTCOME: Solidify understanding with a short Inquiry Outcome activity.

IN PRACTICE

Instructional Path: Grades 1-5

Follow the instructional path to guide your exploration of the text sets. For additional resources, go to connected.mcgraw-hill.com

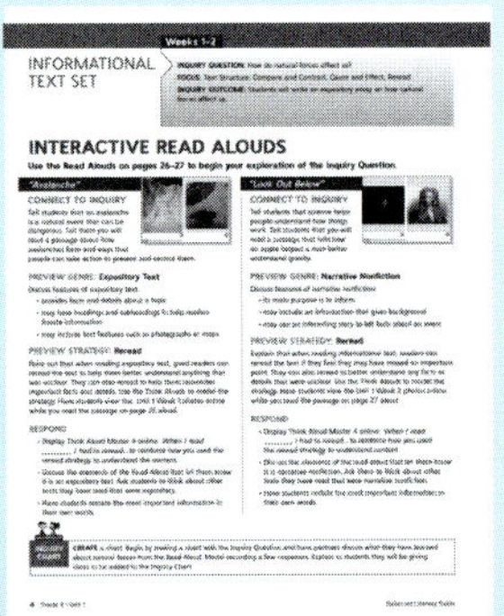
INFORMATIONAL TEXT SET

INTERACTIVE READ ALOUDS

Listen and Talk About Inquiry Topic

Guide children in collaborative discussions.

- Listen to the read aloud and discuss the stories.
- INQUIRY: Begin exploration of the Inquiry Question.

Use online photos and Think Aloud Clouds to support instruction.

2 Read Short Complex Texts

Model close reading.

- Read short complex texts, citing text evidence to answer text-dependent questions.
- Analyze how the author uses text, craft, and structure, citing text evidence.
- INQUIRY: Expand the discussion of the Inquiry Question using the texts.
- QUICK CHECK: Use quick checks to determine students' needs.

Use online resources to reinforce application of key skills to the texts.

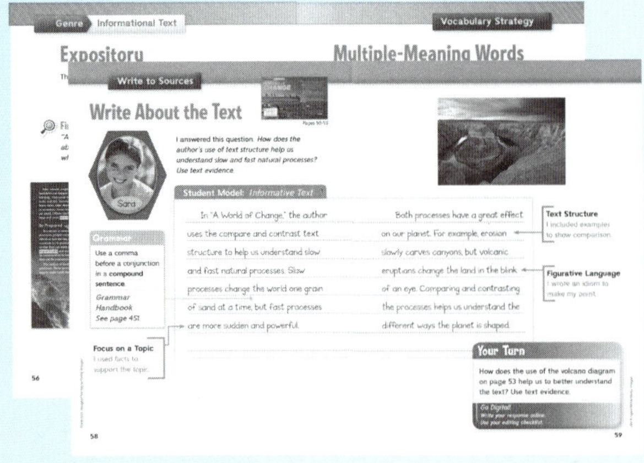

3 Write to Sources

Model writing to a source.

- Analyze a short response student model.
- Use text evidence from close reading to write to a source.

See Writer's Workspace online to support writing instruction.

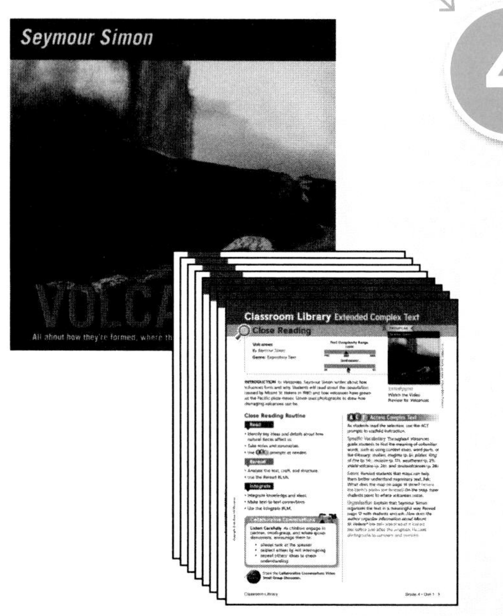

4

Read and Write About an Extended Text

Practice and apply close reading of the Classroom Library selection.

- Read an extended text, citing text evidence to answer text-dependent questions.
- Use text evidence to understand how the author uses text, craft, and structure to develop a deeper understanding of the story.
- Write a short response.
- Expand the discussion of the Inquiry Question using the extended text.

Use online resources to practice applying key skills to the text.

Small Group Work

Gradual release of support to independent work.

- Use on-level and differentiated instruction to support key skills.
- Practice close reading using leveled texts, including an Apprentice Leved Reader and corresponding online lesson.
- Move student ahead as they are ready.
- INQUIRY: Expand the discussion of the Inquiry Question using the texts.

Use online small group lessons for Approaching, Tier 2, On-Level, Beyond and English Learners to continue to differentiate instruction.

Integrate Knowledge and Ideas

Integrate knowledge from multiple sources.

- Conduct a short research project to extend the learning.
- COLLABORATE INQUIRY OUTCOME: Solidify understanding with a short Inquiry Outcome activity.

Introduction to Text Sets

Wonders Balanced Literacy offers a rich collection of curated texts that are organized around an inquiry Question. Students engage in accessing complex texts and then deepen their understanding by writing about the texts. Texts are carefully leveled to meet individual students' needs.

BUILT ON THE TEXT

Wonders Balanced Literacy is built around a rich collection of texts organized in Text Sets. A curated collection of authentic complex text, Leveled Readers, read aloud selections, and other texts make up each Text Set. These sets focus on a particular genre, key skills, and explore a unique Inquiry Question. The Text Sets are the core of *Wonders Balanced Literacy* and are the source of all of the learning, writing, and meaning making.

Each of the 10 units in Kindergarten has 3 text sets in each designed to be used over the course of a week. Grade 1 has 6 Units with 5 weekly Text Sets in each unit. In grades 2 to 5 each unit has three Text Sets, two of which are designed to be used over two weeks and the third for just one week. Each Text Set includes a variety of texts:

- Read Alouds to introduce the Inquiry Question and develop listening comprehension.
- Shared Reads for modeling and guided practice of key skills.
- Complex authentic text for group or independent reading.
- Leveled Readers for small group guided reading.
- Decodable Readers in K-2 for application of foundational skills.

Each section in this volume offers more details on the role and instructional purpose of each type of text.

Wonders Balanced Literacy is designed to be a flexible tool to help you meet the needs of your students. No two classrooms are alike and we've organized these materials so that you can easily pick and choose which lessons and texts you want to use. Each set includes a Classroom Library selection that can be used to model and guide close reading of text. Included in the program are six additional Classroom Library selections that can be used to extend Text Sets or for independent reading.

You can modify the Text Sets in a variety of ways. See Expanding Text Sets on page 130 for information on adding on to and modifying each set to better meet your students' specific instructional needs. Each additional text suggestion includes the following information to help you choose which texts to use: guided reading and lexile levels, genre, and type of read.

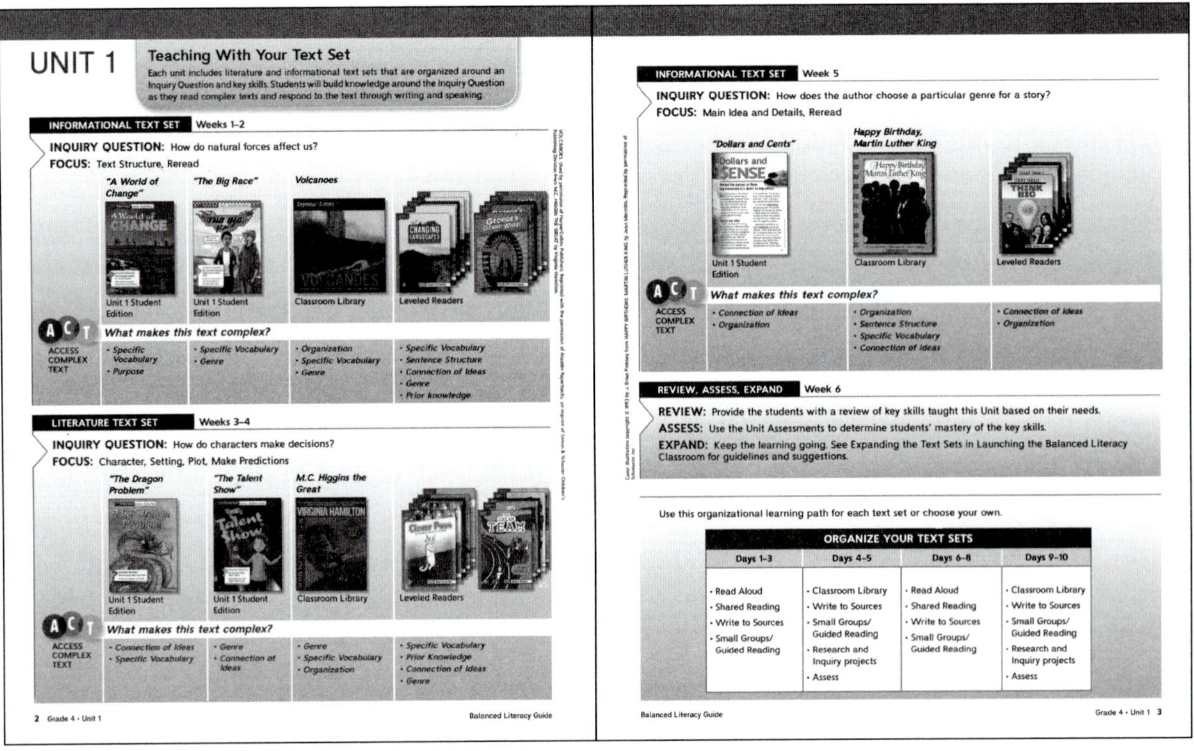
UNIT 1

Teaching With Your Text Set

Each unit includes literature and informational text sets that are organized around an Inquiry Question and key skills. Students will build knowledge around the Inquiry Question as they read complex texts and respond to the text through writing and speaking.

INFORMATIONAL TEXT SET Weeks 1–2

INQUIRY QUESTION: How do natural forces affect us?

FOCUS: Text Structure, Reread

	"A World of Change"	*"The Big Race"*	*Volcanoes*	
	Unit 1 Student Edition	Unit 1 Student Edition	Classroom Library	Leveled Readers
ACCESS COMPLEX TEXT — *What makes this text complex?*	· *Specific Vocabulary* · *Purpose*	· *Specific Vocabulary* · *Genre*	· *Organization* · *Specific Vocabulary* · *Genre*	· *Specific Vocabulary* · *Sentence Structure* · *Connection of Ideas* · *Genre* · *Prior knowledge*

LITERATURE TEXT SET Weeks 3–4

INQUIRY QUESTION: How do characters make decisions?

FOCUS: Character, Setting, Plot, Make Predictions

	"The Dragon Problem"	*"The Talent Show"*	*M.C. Higgins the Great*	
	Unit 1 Student Edition	Unit 1 Student Edition	Classroom Library	Leveled Readers
ACCESS COMPLEX TEXT — *What makes this text complex?*	· *Connection of Ideas* · *Specific Vocabulary*	· *Genre* · *Connection of Ideas*	· *Genre* · *Specific Vocabulary* · *Organization*	· *Specific Vocabulary* · *Prior Knowledge* · *Connection of Ideas* · *Genre*

2 Grade 4 · Unit 1 Balanced Literacy Guide

INFORMATIONAL TEXT SET Week 5

INQUIRY QUESTION: How does the author choose a particular genre for a story?

FOCUS: Main Idea and Details, Reread

	"Dollars and Cents"	*Happy Birthday, Martin Luther King*	
	Unit 1 Student Edition	Classroom Library	Leveled Readers
ACCESS COMPLEX TEXT — *What makes this text complex?*	· *Connection of Ideas* · *Organization*	· *Organization* · *Sentence Structure* · *Specific Vocabulary* · *Connection of Ideas*	· *Connection of Ideas* · *Organization*

REVIEW, ASSESS, EXPAND Week 6

REVIEW: Provide the students with a review of key skills taught this Unit based on their needs.

ASSESS: Use the Unit Assessments to determine students' mastery of the key skills.

EXPAND: Keep the learning going. See Expanding the Text Sets in Launching the Balanced Literacy Classroom for guidelines and suggestions.

Use this organizational learning path for each text set or choose your own.

ORGANIZE YOUR TEXT SETS

Days 1–3	Days 4–5	Days 6–8	Days 9–10
· Read Aloud · Shared Reading · Write to Sources · Small Groups/ Guided Reading	· Classroom Library · Write to Sources · Small Groups/ Guided Reading · Research and Inquiry projects · Assess	· Read Aloud · Shared Reading · Write to Sources · Small Groups/ Guided Reading	· Classroom Library · Write to Sources · Small Groups/ Guided Reading · Research and Inquiry projects · Assess

Balanced Literacy Guide Grade 4 · Unit 1 3

wavebreakmedia/Shutterstock.com

TEACHING TO THE TEXT

The instruction in *Wonders Balanced Literacy* is designed to help students access and engage in the text. The mini lessons in the Teacher Guides support students' exploration of the text by providing instruction on key skills tied to those selections. These mini lessons cover comprehension skills and strategies, foundational skills, vocabulary, and high-frequency words and are tied to the specific texts in the set so that students can apply the skills they're learning as they read. Of course sometimes students will need more support on a specific skill or work on additional skills. The Teacher Guides offer small group lessons to provide this needed review and reteaching. Additionally, the online resources provide corresponding explicit instruction, guided practice, and independent practice opportunities to support students as they engage in the Text Sets.

WRITING TO THE TEXT

After students read the selections they write about them. The writing mini lessons in the Teacher Guides teach students key writing skills as they further explore the texts they've read. Whether writing an expository piece about the topic of a selection or creating a new piece of narrative fiction using the selection as a model, students integrate what they've learned from the texts as they write. For more in depth writing process instruction there are explicit lessons online that cover a variety of genres, including narrative, opinion, and informational writing.

MAKING MEANING FROM THE TEXT

As students engage in the text they build knowledge to help them answer the Inquiry Question, the common thread which ties the entire Text Set together. After reading each selection students engage in collaborative conversations in which they deepen their understanding of the texts. Teachers record the information learned and the inferences students make on an Inquiry Chart. As students read additional texts, the chart is updated to reflect their expanded knowledge base. Students then engage in research and inquiry projects tied to what they have been reading. Finally students collaborate to integrate what they have learned from their in-depth analysis of the texts with a short Inquiry Outcome activity.

TEXT-BASED, STUDENT CENTERED

At every step of the instructional path *Wonders Balanced Literacy* offers flexibility to help you provide differentiation to meet each student's needs. A variety of text resources allows teachers to select appropriate and increasingly complex reads to meet students at their current level and to challenge them to accelerate to the next level. Explicit lessons and scaffolded small group and differentiated instruction helps teachers to find the right path for each student and to support and guide them as they navigate through more rigorous terrain on the path to reading success.

READ ALOUDS: AN IMPORTANT COMPONENT OF BALANCED LITERACY

by Kathy Rhea Bumgardner, M.Ed.

National Literacy Consultant
North Carolina Educator
Strategies Unlimited, Inc.
Belmont, North Carolina

Creator of Think Aloud Clouds and Literacy Toolkits for Comprehension Professional Development Videos for Instructional Best Practices in Literacy

Introduction

The read aloud is a strategic instructional practice in which the teacher sets aside time to read texts orally to students on a consistent basis from selected various texts. The lessons are interactive and deepen students' understanding of the text through text-dependent questions.

How important is it that teachers read aloud to their students on a daily basis? How can we ensure that, with so much to accomplish in today's 21st century classrooms, the benefits of reading aloud are worth the instructional time spent in class?

Books play an important role in students' academic and social development. Reading high-quality books increases students' overall language competence, and the process of reading, listening, questioning, and responding to a story provides a foundation for reflective and critical thinking (Pressley 2006). Children imitate their teachers, and they are eager to read the books their teachers read (Cunningham 2005).

The Value of the Read Aloud

The read aloud in today's classrooms should be a valuable and intentional part of good instruction. It can be a highly effective strategy for nurturing and developing literacy learners. It can be that match to light that love of reading fire for students.

In 1985 the report of the Commission on Reading, *Becoming a Nation of Readers*, made a lasting statement about reading aloud (p. 23). They stated: "The single most important activity for building the knowledge required for eventual success in reading is read aloud to children" (1985).

DGLimages/Shutterstock.com

Read alouds allow children to access more complex text than they can access while reading on their own as well as access more complex conepts.

In the absence of the read alouds, we may slow students' vocabulary learning; research has shown a strong positive correlation between read aloud experiences and vocabulary development (Meehan, 1999; Roberts, 2008; Sénéchal & LeFevre, 2002; Sharif, Ozuah, Dinkevich, & Mulvihill, 2003). A well-planned read aloud can repeatedly expose children to academic vocabulary that will likely show up in content textbooks.

Teachers can use read alouds to increase their student's comprehension skills, foster their critical thinking through discussion and demonstration, and develop their student's background knowledge and interest in quality literature. While reading, teachers can model oral reading fluency and encourage strategies that students can implement during independent reading.

Preparing for Successful Read Alouds: Book Choice is Crucial

Choosing short, high quality and high interest texts is the important first step for an interactive read aloud lesson. These texts should be complex due to structure, the use of language conventions, background knowledge and/or levels of meaning. Providing interaction with a variety of texts is key.

High interest informational texts should be included. When Nell Duke (2000) examined the use of informational texts in 20 first grade classrooms, she found that on average, children spent 3.6 minutes a day on informational texts, with urban schools spending 1.9 minutes a day. With the recent emphasis on a shift towards increasing informational texts, it is important to consider that balance of the genres is crucial. Encounters with high interest informational texts as well as high quality narrative read alouds give depth to the read aloud.

Next steps can be as follows:

- Pre-read and re-read the selection to determine what part of the text you will read.
- Consider your reading goals and focus.
- Identify the process and strategy information (at work in the text).
- Anticipate where background knowledge needs to be built.
- Highlight places to stop for the think alouds where you can question or make meaningful connections.
- Plan for possible discussion questions before the lesson.
- Practice reading the selection using gestures and voice intonation.
- Plan before, during, and after reading activities to enhance comprehension.

In order to deliver an effective read aloud teachers should maintain a productive quality to the pacing, tone, and setting of read aloud time to establish healthy expectations while optimizing learning potential. Teachers should consider structuring the read aloud around skill building as much as for enjoyment (Layne 2015).

Setting the stage for a read aloud by including and modeling think alouds can provide crucial scaffolding for students. The think-aloud strategy helps teachers to intentionally demonstrate for readers how to think about how they make meaning (Beers 2003).

Strategic think-alouds during the read-aloud are a way of making public the thinking that goes on inside your head as you read.

Reading aloud is still an essential tool to not only motivate readers to enjoy reading but to assist in helping students on their academic journey to be college and career ready.

References

Cunningham, P. 2005. Struggling readers: "If they don't read much, how they ever gonna get good?" *The Reading Teacher* 59 (1): 88–90.

Pressley, M. 2006. *Reading instruction that works: The case for balanced teaching*, 3rd ed. New York: Guilford.

Trelease, J., & Trelease, J. (2013) The Read-Aloud Handbook- 7th Ed. New York, NY: Penquin Books.

Richard C. Anderson, Elfrieda H. Hiebert, Judith A. Scott, and Ian A. G. Wilkinson, *Becoming a Nation of Readers: The Report of the Commission on Reading,* U. S. Department of Education (Champaign-Urbana, IL: Center for the Study of Reading, 1985), p. 23.

Layne, S. (2015) In defense of read aloud-sustaining best practice. Stenhouse Publishers (town?)

Beers, K. (2003). *When kids can't read, what teachers can do.* Portsmouth, NH: Heinemann, p. 101.

Duke, N. K. (2000). 3.6 minutes per day: The scarcity of informational texts in first grade. *Reading Research Quarterly,* 35(2), 202–224.

Meehan, M. L. (1999). *Evaluation of the Monomgalia County schools' Even Start program child vocabulary outcomes.* Charleston, WV: AEL.

Roberts, T. (2008). Home storybook reading in primary or second language preschool children: Evidence of equal effectiveness for second language vocabulary acquisition. *Reading Research Quarterly*, 43(2), 103–130.

Sénéchal, M., & LeFevre, J. A. (2002). Parental involvement in the development of children's reading skill: A five year longitudinal study. *Child Development*, 73(2), 445–460.

Sharif, I., Ozuah, P. O., Dinkevich, E. I., & Mulvihill, M. (2003). Impact of a brief literacy intervention on urban preschoolers. *Early Childhood Education Journal*, 30(3), 177–180.

IN PRACTICE

Working With Read Alouds

PURPOSE OF READ ALOUDS

Wonders Balanced Literacy provides weekly read alouds that engage students in thinking deeply about texts and help frame the discussion of the Inquiry Question. Each text set provides 1-2 interactive read aloud selections that require students to actively participate in the construction of content knowledge. In addition, Literature Big Books are provided for Kindergarten and First Grade students to help develop rich, oral language and expose students to engaging, complex text. The discussion of the read alouds help students develop critical speaking and listening skills that support literacy development in reading and writing.

Begin the Inquiry Students begin their exploration of the inquiry topic with read alouds at all grades. After listening to a read aloud, students engage in a discussion of the inquiry question as it relates to the selection. Partners collaborate to make connections and then share their ideas with the class. The teacher records the information learned on an Inquiry Chart that is used all week to build content knowledge and integrate what they have learned.

FOCUS OF READ ALOUD INSTRUCTION

Each *Wonders Balanced Literacy* read aloud lesson provides instruction, prompts and questions to develop the following areas of literacy development.

- **Oral Reading** The read alouds provide students with a model of oral reading fluency so students understand what reading fluently sounds like. Teachers read aloud the selections while students view corresponding illustrations or photographs. Additional online photographs are available to build background content knowledge, which is a critical piece of read aloud instruction.
- **Listening Comprehension** Read alouds act as a vehicle to develop critical listening comprehension skills. Text-dependent questions are provided at stopping points to develop close listening skills and build a deep understanding of the text. Students listen actively and ask questions to build on the ideas of others.
- **Speaking and Listening Skills** Students develop critical speaking and listening skills as they engage in the read aloud lessons. Students discuss the inquiry topic as it relates to the read aloud, building on each other's ideas. Students also retell the read aloud selections to build academic language.
- **Reading Strategies** Each read aloud lesson provides strategic Think Alouds in which teachers model reading strategies while reading to students.
- **Genre** Read alouds span a variety of genre including literature and informational texts. They also represent different cultures and time periods. With teacher prompts and questions, students learn to identify the features of different genres. This builds a foundation for students as they move through the text set to read other selections of the same genre.

Tyler Olsen/Shutterstock.com

LITERATURE BIG BOOKS

For Kindergarten and First Grade, Literature Big Books provide students with authentic and engaging texts. Read aloud by the teacher, this collection of big books offer selections written by award-winning authors, represent diverse cultures and cover a variety of narrative and informational text genres.

For additional support with the Literature Big Books, you may choose to use the following online resources:

- **Online Literature Big Book** which provides an audio recording that enables students the ability to follow along as the book is read aloud to them. You may choose to use this feature to for students who may need a rereading of the selection.
- **Online Interactive Lessons** that focus on comprehension strategies and genre with point of use prompts.
- **Online Retelling Cards** that students can use with a partner or small group to retell the selection. These help develop oral language skills and comprehension of the selection.
- **Online Think Aloud Cards** which prompt students with a sentence starter to promote thinking aloud and discussion of the selection.

USE THE TEACHER GUIDE LITERATURE BIG BOOK LESSONS TO:

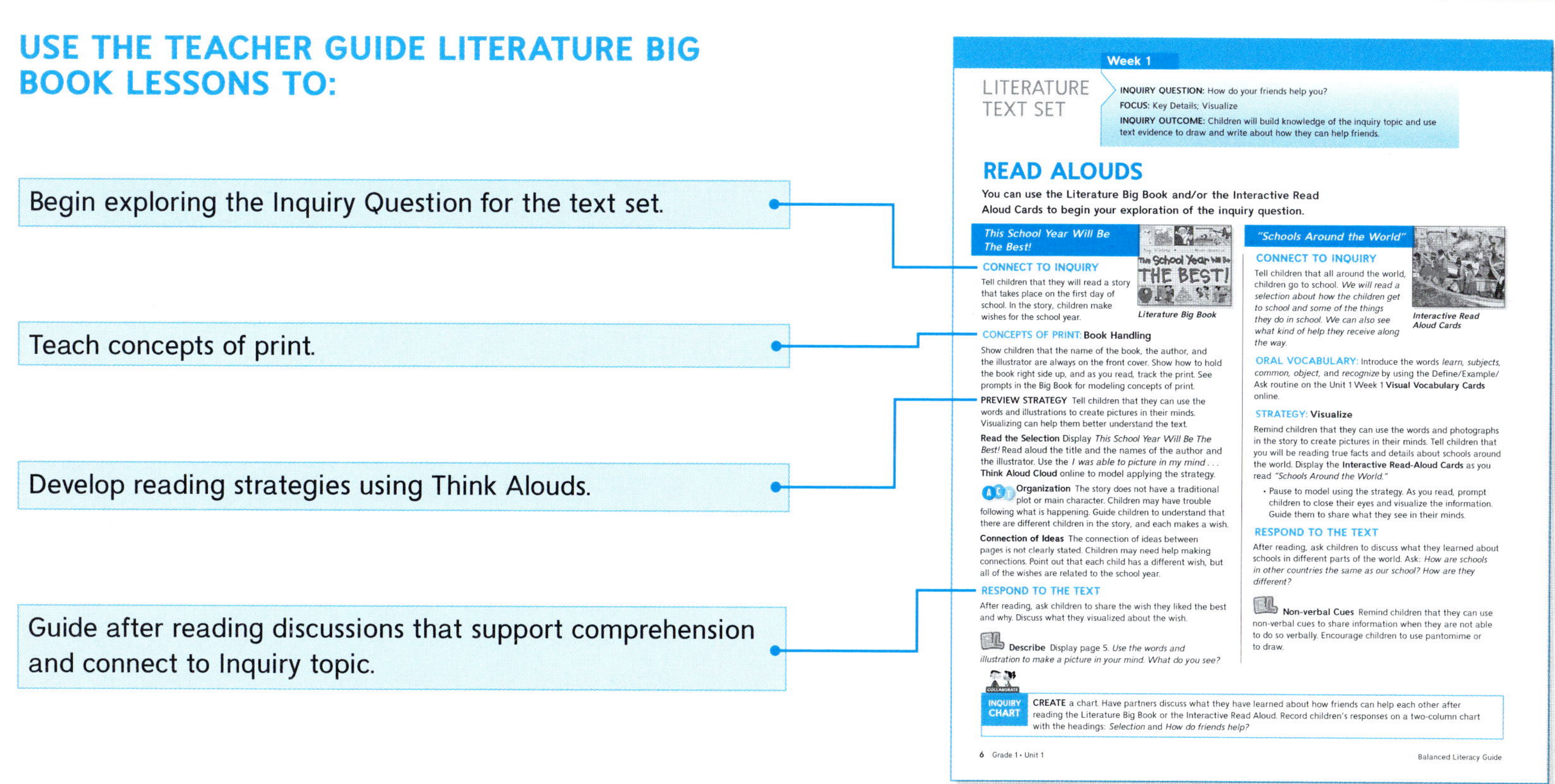

Week 1

LITERATURE TEXT SET

INQUIRY QUESTION: How do your friends help you?

FOCUS: Key Details; Visualize

INQUIRY OUTCOME: Children will build knowledge of the inquiry topic and use text evidence to draw and write about how they can help friends.

READ ALOUDS

You can use the Literature Big Book and/or the Interactive Read Aloud Cards to begin your exploration of the inquiry question.

This School Year Will Be The Best!

CONNECT TO INQUIRY

Tell children that they will read a story that takes place on the first day of school. In the story, children make wishes for the school year.

Literature Big Book

CONCEPTS OF PRINT: **Book Handling**

Show children that the name of the book, the author, and the illustrator are always on the front cover. Show how to hold the book right side up, and as you read, track the print. See prompts in the Big Book for modeling concepts of print.

PREVIEW STRATEGY Tell children that they can use the words and illustrations to create pictures in their minds. Visualizing can help them better understand the text.

Read the Selection Display *This School Year Will Be The Best!* Read aloud the title and the names of the author and the illustrator. Use the *I was able to picture in my mind . . .* **Think Aloud Cloud** online to model applying the strategy.

Organization The story does not have a traditional plot or main character. Children may have trouble following what is happening. Guide children to understand that there are different children in the story, and each makes a wish.

Connection of Ideas The connection of ideas between pages is not clearly stated. Children may need help making connections. Point out that each child has a different wish, but all of the wishes are related to the school year.

RESPOND TO THE TEXT

After reading, ask children to share the wish they liked the best and why. Discuss what they visualized about the wish.

Describe Display page 5. *Use the words and illustration to make a picture in your mind. What do you see?*

"Schools Around the World"

CONNECT TO INQUIRY

Tell children that all around the world, children go to school. *We will read a selection about how the children get to school and some of the things they do in school. We can also see what kind of help they receive along the way.*

Interactive Read Aloud Cards

ORAL VOCABULARY: Introduce the words *learn, subjects, common, object,* and *recognize* by using the Define/Example/Ask routine on the Unit 1 Week 1 **Visual Vocabulary Cards** online.

STRATEGY: **Visualize**

Remind children that they can use the words and photographs in the story to create pictures in their minds. Tell children that you will be reading true facts and details about schools around the world. Display the **Interactive Read-Aloud Cards** as you read *"Schools Around the World."*

- Pause to model using the strategy. As you read, prompt children to close their eyes and visualize the information. Guide them to share what they see in their minds.

RESPOND TO THE TEXT

After reading, ask children to discuss what they learned about schools in different parts of the world. Ask: *How are schools in other countries the same as our school? How are they different?*

Non-verbal Cues Remind children that they can use non-verbal cues to share information when they are not able to do so verbally. Encourage children to use pantomime or to draw.

COLLABORATE

INQUIRY CHART **CREATE** a chart. Have partners discuss what they have learned about how friends can help each other after reading the Literature Big Book or the Interactive Read Aloud. Record children's responses on a two-column chart with the headings: *Selection* and *How do friends help?*

6 Grade 1 • Unit 1 Balanced Literacy Guide

INTERACTIVE READ ALOUDS

The *Wonders Balanced Literacy* Interactive Read Alouds are short read alouds that are written by award-winning authors, represent diverse cultures and cover a variety of narrative and informational text genres. These selections help develop background knowledge of the Inquiry topic and kick off each text set. Read Alouds are provided in the following formats:

- Interactive Read Aloud Cards are provided for Grades Kindergarten - Second Grade
- Interactive Read Aloud selections for Third through Fifth Grades appear in the back of the Teacher Guides

For additional support with the Read Alouds, you may choose to use the following online resources:

- **Online Photos** related to the passage encourage audio-visual connections and group discussion.
- **Think Aloud Clouds** provide sentence starters to encourage students to think aloud and discuss the selection.
- **Graphic Organizers** enables students to analyze and record the characteristics of the genre of the selection.

Watch the Videos

Learn how to model academic language to support collaborative conversations. See this and other videos that will help you support your students' speaking and listening skills.

www.connected.mcgraw-hill.com

USE THE TEACHER GUIDE READ ALOUD LESSONS TO:

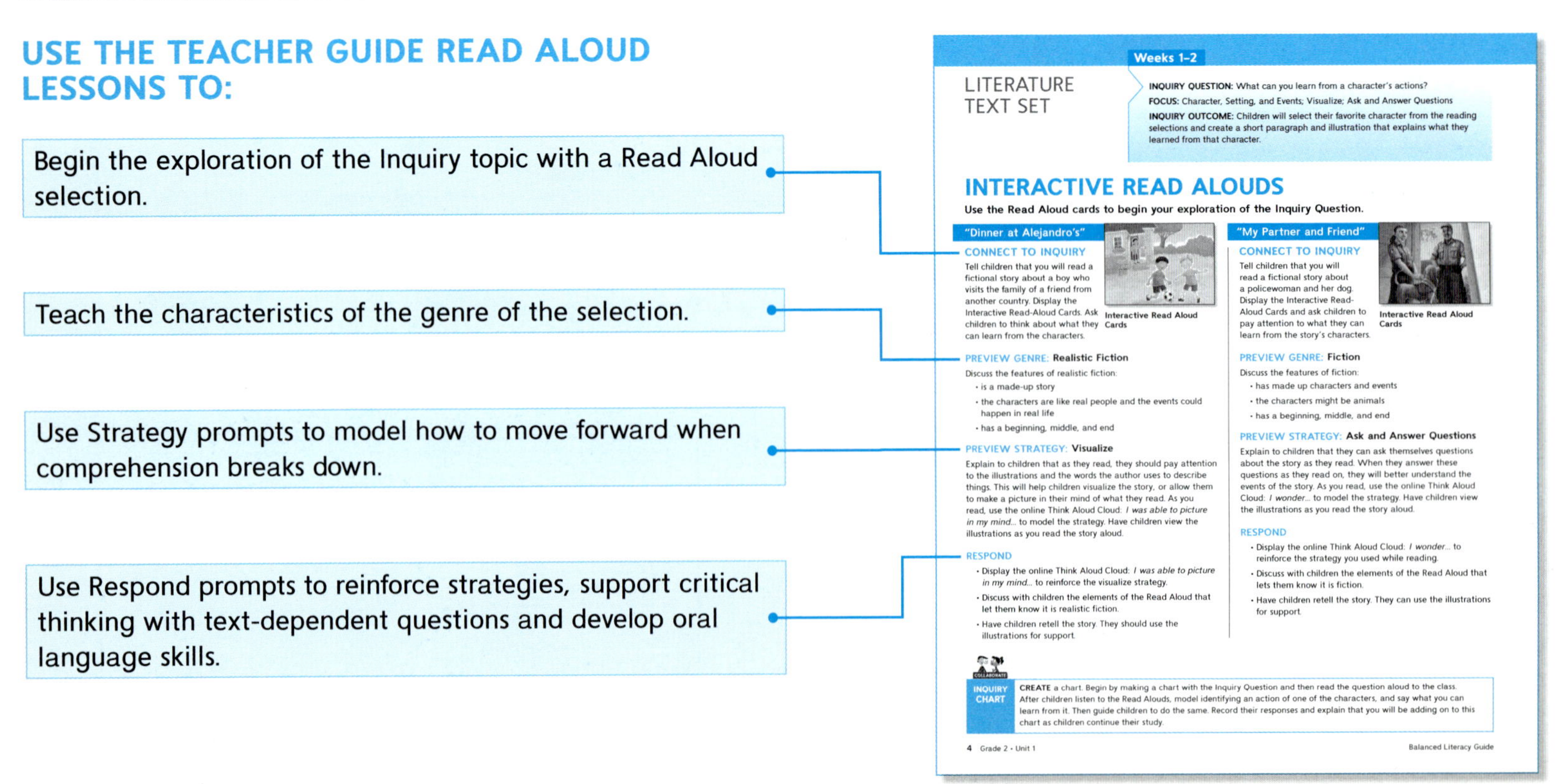

Begin the exploration of the Inquiry topic with a Read Aloud selection.

Teach the characteristics of the genre of the selection.

Use Strategy prompts to model how to move forward when comprehension breaks down.

Use Respond prompts to reinforce strategies, support critical thinking with text-dependent questions and develop oral language skills.

Weeks 1–2

LITERATURE TEXT SET

INQUIRY QUESTION: What can you learn from a character's actions?

FOCUS: Character, Setting, and Events; Visualize; Ask and Answer Questions

INQUIRY OUTCOME: Children will select their favorite character from the reading selections and create a short paragraph and illustration that explains what they learned from that character.

INTERACTIVE READ ALOUDS

Use the Read Aloud cards to begin your exploration of the Inquiry Question.

"Dinner at Alejandro's"

CONNECT TO INQUIRY

Tell children that you will read a fictional story about a boy who visits the family of a friend from another country. Display the Interactive Read-Aloud Cards. Ask children to think about what they can learn from the characters.

Interactive Read Aloud Cards

PREVIEW GENRE: **Realistic Fiction**

Discuss the features of realistic fiction:

- is a made-up story
- the characters are like real people and the events could happen in real life
- has a beginning, middle, and end

PREVIEW STRATEGY: **Visualize**

Explain to children that as they read, they should pay attention to the illustrations and the words the author uses to describe things. This will help children visualize the story, or allow them to make a picture in their mind of what they read. As you read, use the online Think Aloud Cloud: *I was able to picture in my mind...* to model the strategy. Have children view the illustrations as you read the story aloud.

RESPOND

- Display the online Think Aloud Cloud: *I was able to picture in my mind...* to reinforce the visualize strategy.
- Discuss with children the elements of the Read Aloud that let them know it is realistic fiction.
- Have children retell the story. They should use the illustrations for support.

"My Partner and Friend"

CONNECT TO INQUIRY

Tell children that you will read a fictional story about a policewoman and her dog. Display the Interactive Read-Aloud Cards and ask children to pay attention to what they can learn from the story's characters.

Interactive Read Aloud Cards

PREVIEW GENRE: **Fiction**

Discuss the features of fiction:

- has made up characters and events
- the characters might be animals
- has a beginning, middle, and end

PREVIEW STRATEGY: **Ask and Answer Questions**

Explain to children that they can ask themselves questions about the story as they read. When they answer these questions as they read on, they will better understand the events of the story. As you read, use the online Think Aloud Cloud: *I wonder...* to model the strategy. Have children view the illustrations as you read the story aloud.

RESPOND

- Display the online Think Aloud Cloud: *I wonder...* to reinforce the strategy you used while reading.
- Discuss with children the elements of the Read Aloud that lets them know it is fiction.
- Have children retell the story. They can use the illustrations for support.

COLLABORATE

INQUIRY CHART

CREATE a chart. Begin by making a chart with the Inquiry Question and then read the question aloud to the class. After children listen to the Read Alouds, model identifying an action of one of the characters, and say what you can learn from it. Then guide children to do the same. Record their responses and explain that you will be adding on to this chart as children continue their study.

4 Grade 2 • Unit 1 Balanced Literacy Guide

GUIDED READING INSTRUCTION

> "Small group guided reading provides differentiated support for students developing reading proficiency."
> *- Kathy Rhea Bumgardner, M. Ed.*

By Kathy Rhea Bumgardner, M. Ed.

National Literacy Consultant
North Carolina Educator
Strategies Unlimited, Inc.

Creator of Think Aloud Clouds and Literacy Toolkits for Comprehension; Professional Development Videos for Instructional Best Practices in Literacy

Introduction

Small-group guided reading instruction is an integral instructional component of a balanced literacy classroom. The small-group format provides differentiated support for students' developing reading proficiency. Guided reading allows teachers to help individual students learn to process increasingly challenging texts with understanding and fluency.

Guided reading also can help increase students' motivation to read. Lyons (2003) expressed the importance of motivation when she wrote, "motivation is arguably the most critical ingredient for long-term success in learning to read and write" (p. 84).

Also, small-group guided reading provides an opportunity for the teacher to lean in and listen in to assess students as they practice applying skills and strategies while reading independently.

Ford and Opitz (2001) indicate, "true guided reading is increasingly perceived as an integral part of a balanced literacy program designed to help all children become independent readers" (p. 15). The importance of formative assessment and listening in regularly as students apply skills and strategies sets balanced literacy apart from other traditional classroom approaches (Ford & Optiz, 2008).

What is Guided Reading?

The definition of small-group guided reading is subject to interpretation. Burkins and Croft (2010) identify these common elements of small-group guided reading:

- Working with small groups
- Matching student reading ability to appropriate text levels
- Providing each student in the group with the same text
- Introducing the text and setting a purpose for reading
- Listening to individual students as they read
- Prompting students to apply learned reading strategies
- Engaging students in discussions about the text

Monkey Business Images/Shutterstock.com

Guided reading focuses on processes integral to reading proficiently, such as cross-checking text meaning rather than depending solely on picture clues. For example, a student sees an illustration that features a small dog and says "dog" when the text actually says "puppy." After noticing the beginning letter p in puppy, the student is able to correct the mistake.

> Guided reading allows teachers to help individual students learn to process increasingly challenging texts.

During guided reading, teachers monitor student reading processes and check that texts are within students' grasp, allowing students to assemble their newly acquired skills into a smooth, integrated reading system (Clay, 1994).

Laguinta (2006) states, "in a truly balanced literacy program, *how* you teach is as important as *what* you teach" (p. 417). Teaching decoding and basic comprehension skills is not enough. Deep comprehension and connections to text are important as well.

Preparing for Guided Reading Instruction

Some general tasks should be considered before initiating guided reading instruction.

- **Assessment:** Use assessment tools, such as running records, retellings, teacher observations, and anecdotal notes, along with Placement and Diagnostic Assessments, DIBELS, or other recognized data, to determine the students' instructional reading levels and placement in groups.
- **Schedule:** Make a plan for working with your small groups to allow productive, flexible use of classroom time.
- **Physical Set-up:** Organize materials and set-up an area to allow small-group instruction to be as timely and productive as possible.
- **Close Read the Text:** Read and reread the texts that you will be using. Check to see what makes the leveled text complex and prepare questions for that lesson. Review anecdotal notes and formative assessments to find where students in the group may need additional support. Leveled Reader Lesson Cards include this information and are available for each of the levels in Grades K–5. Also, differentiated Leveled Reader lessons are available online for all grades.
- **Organize Independent Work:** Plan for what other students will do while you are with a small group. Independent work should be closely connected to authentic reading and writing. It should include appropriate independent reading and response. Make a plan for how you will develop and consistently monitor student accountability.

Watch the Videos

See Kathy Bumgardner conduct a lesson in the video **"Small Group Guided Reading with Individual" Coaching."**

www.connected.mcgraw-hill.com

Teaching a Guided Reading Lesson

Guided reading instruction is ultimately about the instructional choices that the teacher makes in a balanced literacy classroom. Guided reading instruction should be broken into manageable phases to allow enough time to listen in, coach, and confer with students frequently. The following is a general structure.

Before Reading (Mini Lesson)

- **Read Familiar Texts:** Use familiar texts from earlier guided reading lessons to lean in and listen in as students read. Make anecdotal notes about their progress. This step may not always be possible due to time constraints, but when time allows, it is a quick and valuable opportunity to do formative assessment of sustained learning and application of learned skills and strategies.
- **Preview:** For beginning readers, this can include a brief "picture walk" guided by the teacher encouraging students to use picture clues for meaning and decoding. For Approaching-Level readers, this can include previewing the text with the teacher providing specific directions about what students should look for in the text. For example, students may be prompted to notice the book's format, structure, a text feature or illustration.
- **Introduce**: Prepare an introduction (a gist statement) about the text to motivate focus and provide appropriate background. The introduction can include appropriate vocabulary scaffolding for sight words, vocabulary in context, and other vocabulary strategies to prepare students for challenging and possibly unknown vocabulary. The goal is to provide some background and promote interest and enthusiasm in the text without giving away too much about it.
- **Review Whole-Group Lesson:** Do a quick review of the skill or strategy taught during the related whole-group read aloud or shared read.
- **Set a Purpose:** Give students a purpose for reading the text based on the inquiry question, genre, or comprehension skill or strategy appropriate for the specific text. Restate the reading purpose as needed throughout the lesson.

During Reading

- **Encourage Independent Reading:** Assign all students to read a specific section of text independently and read to find meaning in the text. Each student is accountable for reading the text. Unlike "Round Robin" reading, students read the whole text or a portion of it softly or silently to themselves. The teacher moves through the group to monitor and coach each student.
- **Listen In and Assess:** Rotate from student-to-student as they read to themselves. Ask each student to read quietly for you and listen closely. Make anecdotal notes about strategy use or "misuse." Intervene and prompt only as needed, with broad questions like, "what will you do next?"
- **Ask Text-Dependent Questions:** At appropriate points, ask text-dependent questions. Have students reread to locate text evidence to support their thinking. Coach students as they reread and scaffold your prompts to promote deeper understanding.
- **Promote Collaborative Discussion:** Periodically prompt students to discuss specific parts of the text collaboratively while you listen in. As students discuss, prompt them as needed to locate text evidence to support their ideas. Have partners share with the small group periodically to compare and contrast responses and text evidence. Keep this brief and meaningful.
- **Support Students:** Observe each reader's behavior for evidence of strategy use and make plans for future support. Interact with individual students to assist with problem solving and locating text evidence at difficult points.

Each student is accountable for reading the text. Unlike "Round Robin" reading, students read the whole text or a portion of it softly or silently to themselves.

- **Anecdotal Notes:** While listening in as students read and discuss the text, observe and take written notes of their reading behaviors, strengths, and needs for support to guide next step instruction. Use a clipboard with mailing labels to allow you to jot down student progress notes and then later transfer the noted labels to your student files.

After Reading

- **Deepen Understanding:** Prompt students to talk about what they noticed while reading. Support their efforts to think deeply and connect ideas across the whole text. For example, a student may notice an opening illustration showing ingredients in a pantry, and by the end, the ingredients are spread around the kitchen. Another student may notice how a character is changing and point out text evidence to support that observation.
- **Reference the Text:** It is important to return to the text for one or two teaching opportunities. Students can cite text evidence or talk about how they used the strategy during reading. Pose text-dependent questions that require students to go back into the text to show where they found their answers. Use modeling to demonstrate specific examples of what this looks like and how it provides depth to their answers and thinking.
- **Review and Reflect:** Pull it all together with a review. Offer a teaching point based on observations made during reading. For example, point out that a student was able to figure out the meaning of a word in the text by using context clues. Have student reflect on and share with partners how they used strategies and solved problems as they read. Think about what the students "know" and what they "demonstrated." Then focus on what you need to teach them next.
- **Promote Collaborative Discussion:** Encourage students to collaborate and discuss with shoulder partners. Listen in on each pair. When appropriate, have students briefly write a response to the text and share their writing with the group to keep all students actively engaged in the lesson.
- **Extend the Text:** Encourage students to deepen their understanding by extending the text through writing, art, or more reading of connected text.

Scaffolding Versus Rescuing

The term scaffold as applied to learning situations by Wood, Bruner, and Ross (1976), refers to a framework and process by which teachers use support strategies to help students complete tasks they are unable to do independently at their current stage of learning.

In today's educational world, scaffolding refers to a variety of instructional techniques used to move students progressively toward understanding a learning skill or process. The end goal is students become independent and proficient readers and writers. Leading students to think for themselves and to correct their own misunderstandings is a powerful way to ensure sustainable student achievement.

wavebreakmedia/Shutterstock.com

Questions, Prompts, and Cues

Effective instructional scaffolding is key to success in small-group guided reading. In the box at right are examples of three types of scaffolds— questions, prompts, and cues—as they are applied to a lesson on how a character's feelings change from the beginning to the end of a story.

In order to provide successful scaffolding for students, strategically phrase questions so the response shows the true depth of students' understanding. Probing questions should be rich and designed with the purpose of motivating students to work towards understanding. Teachers can also guide students to craft their own guiding questions to lead themselves to deeper understanding. Providing students with robust scaffolding helps them build the reading tenacity and perseverance needed to work through "hard parts" of a complex text.

Questions, prompts, and cues can be used in sequence. Following a question with a prompt can help students engage in more focused, critical thinking. Offering additional cues for support helps shift students' attention to something they may have missed that can enhance their understanding. These are teaching moments when teachers can reference anchor charts, graphic organizers, and other visuals to encourage students to apply previous skills and strategies taught, while not giving them the answers.

Scaffolding can easily become a rescue if the teacher leads or gives students answers without wait time. Questioning can be a strong and effective scaffold for students if they have appropriate time and support in their quest for answers.

When working with a small, guided reading group, avoid reading the text for the students consistently. Instead, provide students with the scaffolded support and time to become proficient in their own reading.

Question	"How is the character feeling right now? What are the words in the text that best show you how the character was feeling at this point in the text?"
Prompt	"Reread that section aloud and, when you read the character's dialogue, make your voice sound the way you think the character would speak."
Cue	"What do you notice in the illustration? What does the expression on the character's face tell you?"

Level Up: Supporting Students to Become College and Career Ready

In balanced literacy as with any model for effective reading instruction, accelerating students to proficient levels of reading is paramount to becoming college and career ready.

Small-group guided reading is done in differentiated reading groups. Students read and learn at their tested reading level. The goal is to help students accelerate their reading skills and to provide opportunities for them to reach or exceed grade-level expectations and standards for reading proficiency.

The five sets of leveled texts part of *Wonders Balanced Literacy* includes strategic instructional support and scaffolding that allow the teacher to help students increase their reading proficiency during small-group guided reading. As students make progress in reading fluently and answering text-dependent questions at a particular level, the teacher can use Level Up lessons online to accelerate students to more complex texts.

Using Assessment to Drive Instruction

The key to effective, scaffolded instruction is knowing where students are, knowing where they need to be, and then building a bridge between those two points. This requires being able to use efficient, effective, ongoing assessment tools and adjust plans accordingly (Fountas & Pinnell, 1996).

The balanced literacy model of instruction relies on consistent formative assessment to inform instructional planning. Ongoing assessments begin with teacher observations of students during whole group, small group, and independent learning. It is especially important to assess the ongoing needs of small, differentiated groups so that instruction targets students at their level of need.

Assessment and evaluation of student performance and instructional practices can be recorded both informally while observing individuals in class and formally by completing running records, reading inventories, strategy checklists, and other state- or district-mandated assessments.

In *Guiding Readers and Writers*, Fountas and Pinnell (2006) write that assessment "involves collecting information about or evidence of your students' learning, is a continual and integral part of quality teaching. In fact, teaching without continual assessment is akin to teaching without the children" (p. 189). Teachers should prepare for ongoing assessments by having ready the available forms and methods for tracking data throughout the school day. Teachers should use that data to guide instruction.

Ongoing assessment supports instruction by allowing teachers to do the following:

- Find out what students already know and what they need to learn.
- Plan effectively and set a teaching purpose that it is intentional and productive.
- Determine and adjust differentiated student groupings for instruction.
- Identify which instructional materials are best suited for each student or group.

When can teachers fit this in? One golden opportunity for formative assessment occurs at the beginning of a small-group guided reading lesson. Have students do a "warm reread" of a previously read text as you listed in, or have students write known words or letters. Scheduled assessments can be planned with grade-level groups as directed by schools and districts and should be considered an integral part of reading instruction.

Conclusion

Guided reading is a step-by-step exercise that teachers use to engage students in practicing reading skills. This is an important opportunity for teachers to provide intentional and intense instruction which develops students' proficiency in reading accurately and closely.

For students who are experiencing difficulty, as well as for advanced readers who need to be challenged, small-group guided instruction is a key component for raising student achievement.

References

Burkins, J. M., & Croft, M. M. (2010). Preventing misguided reading: New strategies for guided reading teachers. Newark, DE: International Reading Association.

Clay, M. (1994). Reading recovery: A guidebook for teachers in training. Portsmouth, NH: Heinemann.

Ford, M. P., & Opitz, M. F. (2008). A national survey of guided reading practices: What we can learn from primary teachers. Literacy Research and Instruction, 47 (4), 309–331.

Ford, M. P., & Opitz, M. F. (2001). Reaching readers: Flexible and innovative strategies for guided reading. Portsmouth, NH: Heinemann.

Fountas, I. C., & Pinnell, G. S. (1996). Guided reading: Good first teaching for all children. Portsmouth, NH: Heinemann.

Fountas, I. C., & Pinnell, G. S. (2006). Guided readers and writers grades 3–6. Portsmouth, NH: Heinemann.

Iaquinta, A. (2006). Guided reading: A research-based response to the challenges of early reading instruction. *Early Childhood Education Journal*, 33 (6), 413–418.

Lyons, C. A. (2003). Teaching struggling readers: How to use brain-based research to maximize learning. Portsmouth, NH: Heinemann.

Wood, D., Bruner, J., & Ross, G. (1976). The role of tutoring in problem solving. *Journal of Child Psychology and Child Psychiatry*, 1 7, 89–100.

IN PRACTICE

Working with Leveled Texts

Small group guided reading lessons provide individualized time to target the instructional needs of students.

OVERVIEW OF GUIDED READING

The *Wonders Balanced Literacy* program provides small group instruction with leveled texts in each text set. The goal is to differentiate to accelerate with our Leveled Readers. Five levels of content (Apprentice*, Approaching, On-Level, Beyond and EL) provide connection points to level up students whenever they're ready – whether that's in the middle of a week, unit, or any other time. All levels have the same theme and enable your students to use and develop the same skills. They also feature text-dependent questions, paired readings that cross genres, and opportunities for writing to sources, ensuring that students are getting the most out of each text.

Guided reading and lexile levels are provided for each book, which helps teacher to assign the appropriate level to their individual students.

**Apprentice Leveled Readers are available for grades 2-5 only.*

SET UP SMALL GROUPS

Use the results of the **Fluency Benchmark** online assessment and the **Placement and Diagnostic Assessment** book online to cluster students in groups at the beginning of the school year. You may also use the **Running Records** assessment tool online to evaluate students' reading comprehension and to determine their guided reading level. As the year progresses, continue to monitor students' reading through the use of running records and text-based questioning.

CHOOSE LEVELED READERS

Use the **Leveled Readers At-a-Glance** to search for leveled readers by guided reading level, lexile level, genre, or applicable skills. For digital access, use the Leveled Reader Database online to search for leveled readers by theme, genre, skill and text features.

GUIDED READING

Teacher Guides provide guided reading lessons for use with the Leveled Readers, the goal of which is to help students learn strategies to apply independently. Each leveled reader has a corresponding **Leveled Reader Lesson Card*** which provides guided reteaching of skills and strategies, as outlined below.

**Apprentice Leveled Reader lessons are available online.*

LEVELED READERS LESSON CARDS FOCUS ON:

- **Close Reading Routine** In the lessons, students focus on close reading by reading and rereading the text for specific purposes. They cite accurate and relevant text evidence to support their responses to text-dependent questions, statements, and opinions about the text. They engage in collaborative discussion about the text.
- **ACT: Access Complex Text** The lesson cards identify features that may make the Leveled Reader texts complex for students. Scaffolded instruction is provided to help students access meaning of specific complex parts of text. Instruction on the following features of text is provided as appropriate to the text: **purpose, genre, organization, connection of ideas, sentence structure, specific vocabulary** and **prior knowledge.**
- **Connect to Inquiry** After reading their leveled texts, the teacher guide lessons ask students to connect what they have learned back to the Inquiry Question. Students have collaborative discussions and begin to make connections across texts, integrating what they have learned.

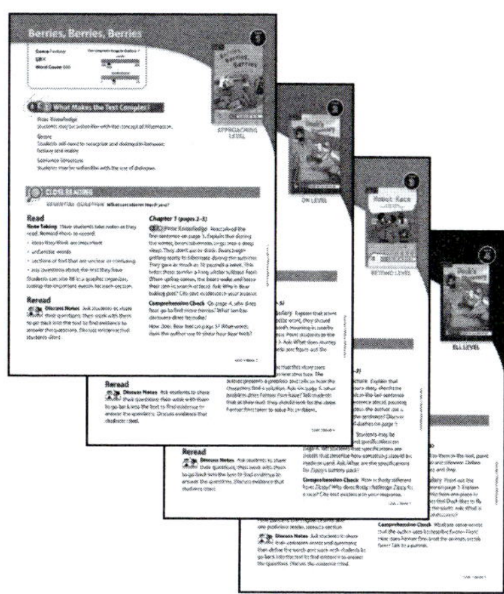

LEVEL UP WITH LEVELED READERS

Level Up Lesson Cards online provide scaffolded small group and differentiated instruction to help teachers support and guide students as they move on to more complex texts. If students can read their leveled text fluently and answer comprehension questions, teachers can work with the next level up to accelerate students' reading.

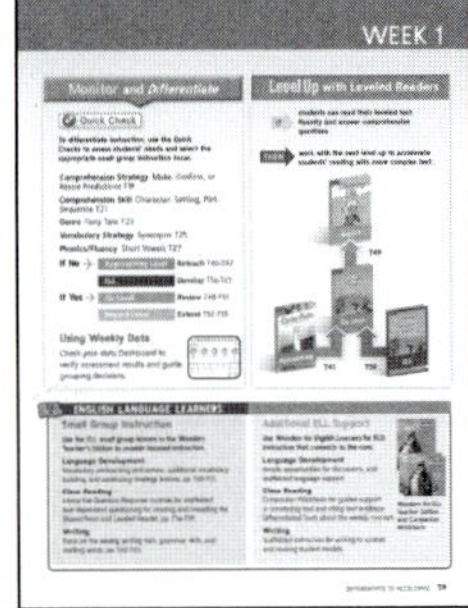

FLEXIBLE SMALL GROUPS

Be sure to continually monitor student progress through teacher observations during whole group, small group and independent work. In addition to using the Level Up Lesson Cards, you may also choose to use the Running Records online assessment tool to determine students' reading comprehension and to assign them authentic literature that is at their appropriate level. Based on how your students are progressing, you will need to adjust your guided reading small groups.

AUTHENTIC TEXT OPTION

You may choose to use authentic texts for guided reading lessons. Choose from the following materials:

- **Classroom Library** titles are provided each grade along with corresponding lessons for all titles in Grades K-5.
- **Literature eBooks** online provide rich, authentic text at appropriate grade levels.

For students that need additional practice reading books on their level, see the Expanding Text Set charts on pages 130-177 to help you find texts that can be added to your text sets.

CLOSE READING IN ELEMENTARY CLASSROOMS

"Close reading is an effective instructional practice to help students read and understand increasingly complex texts."
- *Dr. Douglas Fisher*

By Dr. Douglas Fisher

San Diego State University
Co-Director, Center for the Advancement of Reading, California State University
Author of *Language Arts Workshop: Purposeful Reading and Writing Instruction, Reading for Information in Elementary School;* coauthor of *Close Reading and Writing from Sources, Rigorous Reading: 5 Access Points for Comprehending Complex Text,* and *Text-Dependent Questions, Grades K-5* with N. Frey

In recent years, many literacy educators have focused their attention on the practice of close reading. Close reading is the instructional practice of having students critically examine a text, especially through multiple readings. It has been utilized most commonly at the secondary and college levels, usually within the context of rhetorical reading and writing courses. Adler and Van Doren (1940/1972) explain in their seminal text, *How to Read a Book,* that readers should "x-ray the book" in order to find "the skeleton hidden between its covers" (p. 75). The intent in analytic reading is to identify these deep structures in order to plumb the explicit and implicit meanings of the text. Paul and Elder (2003) explain that this practice encourages students to:

- Identify their purpose for reading
- Determine the author's purpose for writing the piece
- Develop schema
- Understand systems of thought in the disciplines

The overarching goal of close reading is to cause students to engage in critical thinking with a text. Notice how all of the above elements coincide with well researched elements of effective reading instruction. What is lacking, however, is specific research on the effectiveness of close reading for elementary students. It is fair to say that our collective understanding of this practice will grow as empirical studies are conducted with this population. Until that occurs, it is useful to examine these elements within the context of what we currently know about reading instruction for young students. Each element will be followed by suggestions for instruction in a close reading.

Identifying a Purpose for Reading

Even emergent readers understand that different pieces of text are used for different purposes. They see a parent consult a cookbook to locate a recipe for preparing a meal. A caregiver provides important read-aloud time as they read a well-loved picture book for the fiftieth time. Their teacher consults a map of the zoo as she leads her class on a field trip to study African animals. In each case, the reading demand is shaped by the reader's purpose. The recipe reader is reading for details, while the bedtime story reader is reading for comfort and enjoyment. The map of the zoo requires skimming and scanning of the layout in order to locate the elephant enclosure. In each case, the reader adjusts one's reading based on purpose.

Understanding one's purpose for reading is a metacognitive process that supports a reader's comprehension of text (Paris, Wasik, & Turner, 1991). Students apply their sense of purpose for reading in order to locate information. Reading for pleasure activates a student's expectations about how she will evaluate the text. On the other hand, if her purpose is to seek technical information, she is going to judge that reading in a completely different way. Understanding one's purpose for reading allows the learner to judge goodness of fit. In other words, was this the right text for the job? Purpose plays a key factor in motivation for reading (Guthrie & Wigfield, 2000). In their study of assessing motivation for reading, Baker and Wigfield (1999) stated, "Engaged readers are motivated to read for different purposes, utilize knowledge gained from previous experience to generate new understandings, and participate in meaningful social interactions around reading" (p. 453).

> The overarching goal of close reading is to cause students to engage in critical thinking with a text.

Teachers can build students' understanding of purposes for reading by establishing it clearly for them. A statement of the purposes establishes a learning target for students and increases the likelihood that they will reach the target, in particular because it serves as a priming mechanism (Gagné & Briggs, 1974). These statements include the content and language (reading, writing, speaking, listening) purposes (Fisher & Frey, 2011). "We're going to read this article so we can figure out how honeybees carry the pollen from one flower to another. You'll use this information in your table groups to develop a scientific illustration of how this occurs," a fourth grade teacher tells his students. In doing so, he signals students to the content purpose (to figure out how honeybees carry pollen) and the language purpose (to create a scientific illustration). Teachers can use a think-aloud approach (Davey, 1983) as they model metacognitive reading processes during interactive read-alouds and shared reading.

Determining the Author's Purpose

Think of purpose as two sides of the same coin. On one side is the reader's purpose: Why am I reading this? What do I want to get out of this text? On the opposite side is the author's purpose: What does the author want me to know? Why has this been written, and for whom? A reader who can ascertain the author's purpose is able to begin analyzing the text. An author's purpose typically addresses one or more of these:

- To entertain
- To persuade
- To inform

The Rand Reading Study Group (2002) identified determining the author's purpose as a key element of reading comprehension. The report notes that understanding the author's message is essential for determining the discourse structure, including "text genre, the distinction between given (old) and new information in the discourse context, the points (main messages) that the author intends to convey, the topic structure, the pragmatic goals or plans of the communicative exchange, and the function of the speech acts (e.g., assertion, question, directive, evaluation)" (p. 98).

> Teachers can build students' understanding of purposes for reading by establishing it clearly for them.

While this may initially sound too complex for elementary readers, in practice it is not. A durable model of promoting children's understanding of author's purpose and its relationship to discourse structures is through the use of Questioning the Author (Beck, McKeown, Hamilton, & Kucan, 1997). The researchers who developed this instructional routine advise that students query the text systematically:

- Query 1: Initiating discussion (What is the author talking about?)
- Query 2: Focusing on the message and linking information (What information has the author added that connects or fits with _______?)
- Query 3: Identify difficulties with the way the author has presented information (Did the author explain that clearly? Why or why not?)
- Query 4: Encourage students to refer to the text (Did the author give us the answer to that?)

Developing Schema

Schema theory is at the core of teaching and learning, especially in reading comprehension (Spires, Gallini, & Riggsbee, 1992). The deeper one's schema, or organized pattern or structure of knowledge about a topic, the easier it is to comprehend a text about the subject (Mannes, 1994). When one's schema on a topic has significant gaps, the reader must devote cognitive resources to constructing a mental model on which to attach this new information (Kintsch & van Dijk, 1978). This causes a delay in the comprehension of a piece of text. It is likely that you find yourself doing this all the time, perhaps even with this paper. When the information in a text is dense, and when the reader has gaps in schema, the information isn't fully understood immediately. You have to pause to figure out how this new information relates to previously understood concepts. In other words, you are actively constructing a mental model. A chief way you accomplish this is by rereading. You slow down your pace, review a previous passage, and look back to the text in order to find information.

Text-dependent questions are used in reading instruction to promote the habit of rereading text in order to build schema (Fisher & Frey, in press; Pearson & Johnson, 1978). These questions do not rely on outside sources, but rather are designed to cause students to return to the text. This is especially important when text is being used for the purpose of building knowledge. Out-of-school reading is often devoted to topics the reader already knows quite a bit about. But in classrooms, much of the text students encounter will be about topics that are less familiar. Text-dependent questions signal to readers that the information is complex and readers are expected to linger over the details in order to build those mental models. These questions move through a progression from part to whole, from word and sentence level, to paragraph and then across the entire text. As well, these questions move from explicitly stated information to those that require inferential and critical reading. These include (Fisher & Frey, in press):

- *General understanding questions* that draw on the overall view of the piece, especially the main ideas.
- *Key detail questions* are the who/what/when/ where/why/how questions that are essential to understanding the meaning of the passage.
- *Vocabulary and text structure questions* bridge explicit with implicit meanings, especially in focusing on words and phrases, as well as the way the author has organized the information. Text structure questions may include text features, and discourse structures (problem/solution, cause/effect, compare/contrast, etc.).
- *Author's purpose questions* draw the reader's attention to genre, point of view, multiple perspectives, and critical literacies, such as speculating on alternative accounts of the same event.
- *Inferential questions* challenge students to examine the implicitly stated ideas, arguments, or key details in the text.
- *Opinion and intertextual questions* allow students to use their foundational knowledge of one text to assert their opinions or to make connections to other texts, using the target text to support their claims.

wavebreakmedia/Shutterstock.com

Understanding Systems of Thought in the Disciplines

A final element of analytical reading is in understanding that each discipline has unique characteristics, especially in its systems of thought, that inform the texts of the discipline. For example, narrative structures, primarily fictional, dominate English language arts content. On the other hand, science texts use an explanatory text structure that contains a high number of technical vocabulary words. Moreover, these texts assume a tremendous level of background knowledge in order to understand new information. Paul and Elder (2003) call this text structure a "map of knowledge" and define these as the primary and secondary ideas that help us understand a system of thought. "When we understand core historical ideas, we can begin to think historically. When we understand core scientific ideas, we can begin to think scientifically. Core or primary ideas are the key to every system of knowledge. They are the key to truly learning any subject. They are the key to retaining what we learn for lifelong use" (Paul & Elder, 2008, p. 3).

These core and secondary ideas are evidenced at the grammatical level. Fang and Schleppegrell (2011, pp. 588–589) describe each:

- *Science* texts contain "technical vocabulary and dense sentences that require the reader to draw on multiple concepts simultaneously."
- *Social studies* texts contain "nominalizations (nouns derived from adjectives and verbs) that reference abstract ideas, and the presence of evaluative judgments."
- *Mathematics* texts "switch between both natural language and mathematical language and symbols, requiring readers to make similar shifts in the grammars of both."

While these informational texts utilize narrative structures more frequently at the elementary level to explain concepts and events, they can still tax a young reader's understanding. Consider this opening passage from Gibbons's (1996) *Recycle! A Handbook for Kids*:

> More and more garbage! Every day people throw more trash away. As the world population increases, more people throw trash away. Garbage trucks come to pick it up, but where does all this trash go? (p. 1)

Both the vocabulary demand and the conceptual understandings that go along with it are high. The Lexile level, a quantitative measure of text complexity, is 840L, suggesting that this picture book requires adult direction rather than independent reading. However, selecting which vocabulary will need direct teaching, and which can be learned through multiple readings of the text, can be challenging. It is useful to have a selection criteria (Frey & Fisher, 2010; Graves, 2006; Marzano & Pickering, 2005; Nagy, 1988). The first step is to identify worthy words:

- *Representative*: Is it critical to understanding?
- *Repeatability*: Will it be used again?
- *Transportable*: Is it needed for discussions or writing?

The next two questions narrow the list further, identifying words that students can figure out:

- *Contextual analysis*: Can they use context to figure it out?
- *Structural analysis*: Can they use structure (affixes, root, base) to figure it out?

Once these words are eliminated, what remains are the general academic and content-specific words and phrases that require direct instruction. The final question concerns the number:

- *Cognitive load*: Have I exceeded the number they can learn?

Considerations for Developing a Close Reading

There are several considerations useful in engaging students in a close reading. First, select short, worthy passages. Because close reading can be time-consuming, it is often best to select shorter pieces of

Lyubov Kobyakova/Shutterstock.com

text for instruction. If the selection is too long, students will not have time to reread and respond to questions that guide their thinking and will miss have opportunities to interact with others about the content. Second, close-reading lessons should be designed so students reread the text. Rereading to develop a depth of understanding is one of the key features of a close-reading lesson. Anyone who has ever read a text for the second or third time knows that understanding is improved when you know the basic outline of the text (Rasinski, 1990). One of the ways to ensure that students reread the text is to establish different purposes for each reading and to teach students to look for evidence for their responses to text-dependent questions. As noted previously, text-dependent questions should be used to guide students back to the text and provide them an opportunity to analyze the text more deeply. Third, students should learn to "read with a pencil." They don't literally have to use a pencil, but they do need to learn to annotate or make notes as they read. They must become detectives while reading, learning to look for clues as they uncover the structure and meaning of a text. Fourth, students should learn to note the parts that were confusing. This is helpful for several reasons, including the metacognitive awareness that comes from recognizing when meaning is lost. Also, noting confusing parts can guide teacher actions, modeling, and reteaching so that students have opportunities to apply what they learn in future close-reading lessons or extended reading. Finally, as part of close reading, students should interact with their peers and the teacher in discussions about the text. In these discussions, students should practice their skills in argumentation, making claims, offering counterclaims, providing evidence, and agreeing and disagreeing. Interacting with others to determine the meaning of the text is an important aspect of close reading.

Analytic Reading Is Worth the Effort

The practice of close reading invites students to read repeatedly and is guided by discussion of text-dependent questions. When practices such as close reading are consistently implemented, students become better equipped to handle increasingly difficult texts. Over time, and with practice, they will apply the approaches used in a close reading to the extended reading that they do independently. Close reading is a practice that deserves increased attention in elementary school classrooms as students are expected to read and understand increasingly complex texts.

Watch the Videos

See Dr. Douglas Fisher's video in which he discusses **"The Characteristics of an Effective Close Reading Lesson."**

www.connected.mcgraw-hill.com

References

Adler, M. J., & Van Doren, C. (1940/1972). *How to read a book.* New York: Touchstone. Baker, L., & Wigfield, A. (1999). Dimensions of Children's Motivation for Reading and Their Relations to Reading Activity and Reading Achievement. *Reading Research Quarterly,* 34, 452–477.

Beck, I. L., McKeown, M. G., Hamilton, R. L., & Kucan, L. (1997). *Questioning the Author: An Approach for Enhancing Student Engagement with Text.* Newark, DE: International Reading Association.

Davey, B. (1983). Think-aloud: Modeling the Cognitive Processes of Reading Comprehension. *Journal of Reading,* 27(1), 44–47.

Fisher, D., & Frey, N. (2011). The Purposeful Classroom: How to Structure Lessons with Learning Goals in Mind. Alexandria, VA: ASCD.

Fisher, D., & Frey, N. (in press). *Common Core Language Arts in a PLC at Work: Grades 3–5.* Bloomington, IN: Solution Tree.

Frey, N., & Fisher, D. (2009). *Learning Words Inside and Out: Vocabulary Instruction That Boosts Achievement in All Subject Areas.* Portsmouth, NH: Heinemann.

Gagné, R. M., & Briggs, L. J. (1974). *Principles of Instructional Design.* New York, NY: Holt, Rinehart & Winston.

Gibbons, G. (1996). *Recycle! A Handbook for kkids.* New York; Little, Brown.

Graves, M. F. (2006). *The Vocabulary Book: Learning and Instruction.* New York: Teachers College.

Guthrie, J.T., & Wigfield, A. (2000). Engagement and Motivation in Reading. In M.L. Kamil, P.B. Mosenthal, P.D. Pearson, & R. Barr (Eds.), *Handbook of Reading Research: Volume III* (pp. 403–422). New York: Erlbaum.

Kintsch, W., & van Dijk, T.A. (1978). Toward a Model of Text Comprehension and Production. *Psychological Review,* 85, 363–394.

Mannes, S. (1994). Strategic Processing of Text. *Journal of Educational Psychology,* 86(4), 577–588.

Marzano, R. J., & Pickering, D. J. (2005). *Building Academic Vocabulary: Teacher's Manual.* Alexandria, VA: Association for Supervision and Curriculum Development.

Nagy, W. E. (1988). *Teaching Vocabulary to Improve Reading Comprehension.* Newark, DE: International Reading Association.

Paris, S. G., Wasik, B. A., & Turner, J. C. (1991). The Development of Strategic Readers. In R. Barr, M. L. Kamil, P. Mosenthal, & P. D. Pearson (Eds.), *Handbook of Reading Research* (pp. 609–640). White Plains, NY: Longman.

Paul, R., & Elder, L. (2003). Critical Thinking . . . and the Art of Close Reading (Part 1). *Journal of Developmental Education,* 27(2), 36–37, 39.

Paul, R., & Elder, L. (2008). *The thinker's guide to how to read a paragraph: The art of close reading.* Dillon Beach, CA: The Foundation for Critical Thinking. Retrieved at www.criticalthinking.org/files/How%20to%20Read%208.11.08.pdf

Pearson, P. D., & Johnson, D. D. (1978). *Teaching Reading Comprehension.* New York: Holt, Rinehart, and Winston.

RAND Reading Study Group. (2002). *Reading for Understanding: Toward an R&D Program in Reading Comprehension.* Retrieved from http://www.rand.org/multi/achievementforall/reading/readreport. Html

Rasinski, T.V. (1990). Effects of Repeated Reading and Listening-while-reading on Reading Fluency. *Journal of Educational Research*, 83, 147–150.

Spires, H. A., Gallini, J., & Riggsbee, J. (1992). Effects of Schema-based and Structure-based Cues on Expository Prose Comprehension of Fourth Graders. *The Journal of Experimental Education*, 60(4), 307–320.

Accessing Complex Text

AUTHOR'S INSIGHT

"The ability to independently access increasingly complex text is an essential factor in students' academic success and their college and career readiness."

–Dr. Timothy Shanahan, University of Illinois at Chicago

WHAT IS TEXT COMPLEXITY?

Text complexity is defined as those characteristics that make a specific text more challenging than another. To prepare for college and careers, students must read texts of increasing complexity as they progress through grades K-12. They must be able to independently read and respond to texts of varied text complexity from a broad range of genres and topics.

Wonders Balanced Literacy uses a three-pronged model to identify how easy or challenging a specific text is to read.

1. **Quantitative** measures are "countable" features such as word length, sentence length, and word frequency that can be quantified, often calculated by a computer. Lexile is an example of a quantitative measure.
2. **Qualitative** measures include purpose, specific vocabulary, organization, coherence, and connection of ideas. These variables are often more difficult to quantify and are therefore qualitative.
3. **Reader and Task** measures are related to the individual reader and his or her task for reading. Motivation and experience are important dimensions of reader and task measures.

WHAT ARE THE BENEFITS?

Using appropriate complex text and providing instruction and modeling on the strategies to access complex texts enable students to:

- Become proficient independent readers of text of increasing complexity and a wide range of genre and topics.
- Develop proficiency with the types of complex texts they will encounter as they progress through grades K-12.
- Become prepared to be successful and competent readers as they encounter a wide range of texts in their college careers.
- Meet success in their careers.

Watch the Videos

See Dr. Tim Shanahan discuss **"Scaffolding Instruction with Complex Texts."**

www.connected.mcgraw-hill.com

TYPES OF COMPLEXITY

Tell students that this year they will encounter complex texts in a variety of genres that require them to read carefully and think deeply about what they are reading. They will need to determine the meaning of unfamiliar words, and connect and make inferences about information and ideas as they go.

Purpose The purpose of a text may be more complicated than simply to inform, entertain, or persuade. Students will need to determine where to focus their attention at any given time—on the characters, the setting, or the plot. They will need to recognize that the author has a perspective, or point of view, and may be more sympathetic to some characters than others.

Genre Different genres incorporate different literary elements and devices. Readers need to attend to these to comprehend the text fully. Students need to understand the "rules" for fictional genres. For example, they should recognize that folktales have a message and the characters' actions reveal that message.

Organization Students may need to understand how a text is organized in order to find evidence within the text. In narratives, students may find that stories do not follow a linear sequence. Stories may include literary devices such as foreshadowing and flashbacks that interrupt the sequence.

Connection of Ideas When reading complex fictional texts, students need to make inferences and synthesize information throughout the text. They must recognize that the characters' actions and motivations may be implied rather than explicit.

Sentence Structure Complex sentence structures, such as dialogue or formal and informal language, may be challenging for students and require close reading.

Specific Vocabulary Fiction texts may include idioms, similes, metaphors, regionalisms, and concept words that require students to use a dictionary, context clues, or knowledge of word parts.

Prior Knowledge Complex fiction texts may assume a level of prior knowledge that students may not have. Students may need more cultural/historical background, as well as an understanding of human emotions, to comprehend characters' feelings and actions.

SHARED READING AND WRITING

Continue your inquiry by closely reading a short complex text in the Student Edition.

"A World of Change"

Read

Model the Vocabulary Routine
Introduce the words: *alter, collapse, crises, destruction, hazard, severe, substantial, and unpredictable* by using the Vocabulary Routine found on the Unit 1 **Visual Vocabulary Cards** online.

Unit 1 Student Edition

CONNECT TO INQUIRY

Tell students that they will read about natural disasters and how people respond to them. Read page 51 and model how to take notes on key ideas and details.

Paragraph 1: Ask: *How are the natural changes that affect Earth different? How are they the same?* Model citing text evidence. (The speed of the changes vary. Some take place over many years and some are fast. But the author says that both fast and slow changes have a great effect on the planet.)

Paragraph 2: Continue modeling citing text evidence.

ACT SPECIFIC VOCABULARY Explain that some words come from names in Greek or Roman myth. Point to the words volcanic and *volcanoes* on page 52. Tell students that these words come from the name of the Roman god of fire, Vulcan. Ask: *How is Vulcan related to what you know about volcanoes?* (Both are related to fire.)

Reread

EXPLAIN/MODEL Explain that authors sometimes organize a text by comparing and contrasting things in a text. An author may use signal words such as same, *but, both,* and *like* to signal comparisons. Model identifying similarities and differences between slow and fast natural processes on pages 51-52. Fill out Graphic Organizer 67 online.

GUIDED PRACTICE Have partners complete the graphic organizer for the section "Fast and Powerful" on page 52 to compare and contrast volcanoes and landslides.

Quick Check *Are students able to identify similarities and differences between volcanoes and landslides?* If No, see Small Group Comprehension lesson page 10. If Yes, continue with lesson.

Write to "A World of Change."

Writing Fluency Have students discuss the prompt: *Write about natural disasters in* a "A World of Change." When students finish sharing ideas, have them write continuously for five minutes in their Writer's Notebook. Encourage students to keep writing.

COLLABORATE Afterwards, have partners compare ideas and make sure that they both have a clear understanding of the topic.

Write to a Prompt

Analyze the Prompt Read aloud the first paragraph on page 58 of the **Student Edition.** Ask: *What is the prompt asking?* (How the author structures the text.) Say: *Let's reread to see how the text is structured. We can note text evidence.*

Analyze Text Evidence Display Graphic Organizer 5 in Writer's Workspace online. Say: *Let's see how Sara took notes to write her entry. She wrote down facts about natural processes and noted the Grand Canyon is an example of erosion.* Guide the class through the rest of Sara's notes.

Analyze the Student Model Explain how Sara used text evidence from her notes to write a response to the prompt.

- **Focus on a Topic** Good readers pay attention to facts about the topic. Sara used text evidence that explains how our planet changes in her response. Trait: Ideas
- **Text Structure** In "A World of Change" the author compares and contrasts the ways change happens on our planet. Sara used text evidence to show how these natural processes were compared. Trait: Ideas
- **Figurative Language** Sara used the idiom "in the blink of an eye" to help the reader understand how quickly a natural disaster can happen. Trait: Word Choice

For additional practice focusing on a topic, assign **Your Turn Practice Book** online page 29. Also, see the 5-day Grammar lessons online that connect to this week's writing instruction.

Your Turn Read and discuss the Your Turn writing prompt on page 59 of the **Student Edition**. Have students answer the prompt making sure to include these elements in their writing: Focus on a Topic, Text Structure, and Figurative Language.

COLLABORATE

INQUIRY CHART **EXPAND** the Inquiry Chart. After reading the selection, have partners discuss how natural forces affect us. Have them think about what effects these natural forces have on our world. Add students' ideas to the Inquiry Chart.

Balanced Literacy Guide Grade 4 • Unit 1 5

Use ACT prompts to scaffold instruction as students develop strategies to read a short complex text.

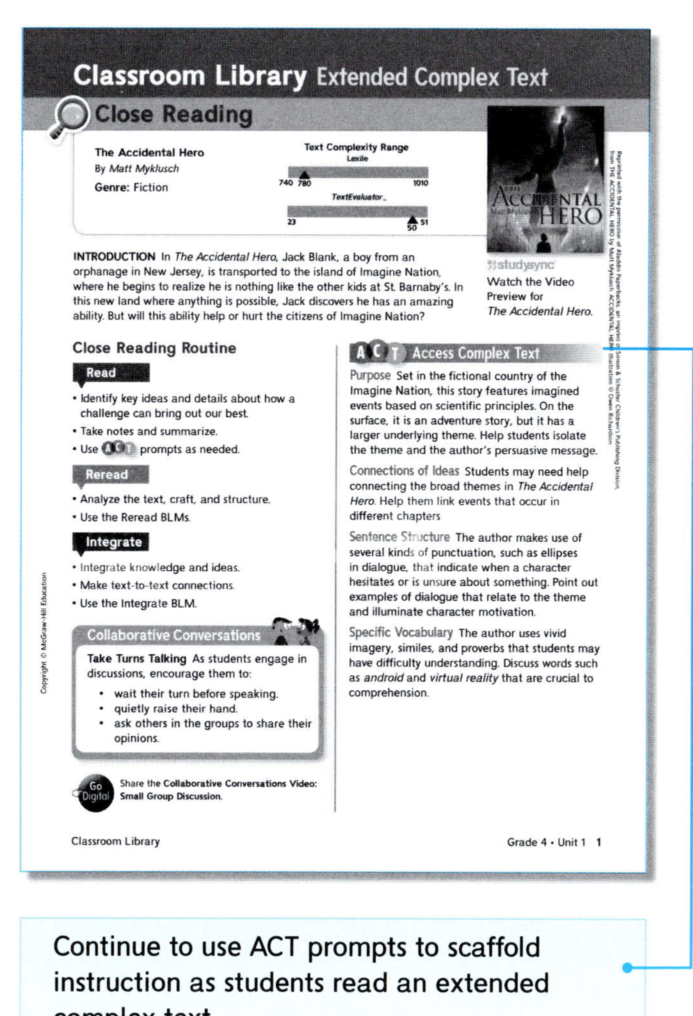
Classroom Library Extended Complex Text

Close Reading

The Accidental Hero
By *Matt Myklusch*
Genre: Fiction

Text Complexity Range	
Lexile	740 – 1010 (780)
TextEvaluator	23 – 51 (50)

INTRODUCTION In *The Accidental Hero*, Jack Blank, a boy from an orphanage in New Jersey, is transported to the island of Imagine Nation, where he begins to realize he is nothing like the other kids at St. Barnaby's. In this new land where anything is possible, Jack discovers he has an amazing ability. But will this ability help or hurt the citizens of Imagine Nation?

studysync Watch the Video Preview for *The Accidental Hero.*

Reprinted with the permission of Aladdin Paperbacks, an imprint of Simon & Schuster Children's Publishing Division, from THE ACCIDENTAL HERO by Matt Myklusch. ACCIDENTAL HERO illustration © Owen Richardson

Close Reading Routine

Read

- Identify key ideas and details about how a challenge can bring out our best.
- Take notes and summarize.
- Use ACT prompts as needed.

Reread

- Analyze the text, craft, and structure.
- Use the Reread BLMs.

Integrate

- Integrate knowledge and ideas.
- Make text-to-text connections.
- Use the Integrate BLM.

Collaborative Conversations

Take Turns Talking As students engage in discussions, encourage them to:

- wait their turn before speaking.
- quietly raise their hand.
- ask others in the groups to share their opinions.

Go Digital Share the **Collaborative Conversations Video: Small Group Discussion.**

ACT Access Complex Text

Purpose Set in the fictional country of the Imagine Nation, this story features imagined events based on scientific principles. On the surface, it is an adventure story, but it has a larger underlying theme. Help students isolate the theme and the author's persuasive message.

Connections of Ideas Students may need help connecting the broad themes in *The Accidental Hero*. Help them link events that occur in different chapters

Sentence Structure The author makes use of several kinds of punctuation, such as ellipses in dialogue, that indicate when a character hesitates or is unsure about something. Point out examples of dialogue that relate to the theme and illuminate character motivation.

Specific Vocabulary The author uses vivid imagery, similes, and proverbs that students may have difficulty understanding. Discuss words such as *android* and *virtual reality* that are crucial to comprehension.

Copyright © McGraw-Hill Education

Classroom Library Grade 4 • Unit 1 1

Continue to use ACT prompts to scaffold instruction as students read an extended complex text.

Close Reading Routine

AUTHOR'S INSIGHT

"Close reading is the instructional practice of having students critically examine a text, especially through multiple readings. The overarching goal of close reading is to cause students to engage in critical thinking with a text."

–Dr. Douglas Fisher, San Diego State University

Read What does the text say?

Assign the Reading

Begin by reading the text aloud to students, and gradually have students read chunks or passages of text on their own. You may wish to have them partner-read before they move to independently reading the text.

Take Notes

Students generate questions and take notes about aspects of the text that might be confusing for them. Have students note:

- key ideas and details.
- difficult vocabulary words or phrases.
- details that are not clear.
- information that they do not understand.

Students complete a graphic organizer to take notes on important information.

Reread How does the author say it?

Ask Text-Dependent Questions

Students reread shorter passages from the text and cite text evidence to answer deeper questions about craft and structure. Students should:

- work with partners or small groups to talk about and identify text evidence.
- generate questions about the text.

Integrate What does the text mean?

Students reread to integrate knowledge and ideas and make text-to-text connections. Students should:

- work with partners or small groups to identify and discuss connections.
- use text evidence to write a response.

Watch the Videos

See Kathy Bumgardner lead a lesson in **"Whole-Group Reading: Shared/Close Reading."**

www.connected.mcgraw-hill.com

IN PRACTICE

Working with Complex Texts

SHORT READ: SHARED READ

Purpose of the Shared Reads

The Shared Reads provide focused instruction on reading short complex texts. Teachers model close reading and focus on improving comprehension. The close reading routine works well with short, meaningful passages to be reread multiple times.

Wonders Balanced Literacy provides short reads with each text set to support close reading. In Kindergarten and early Grade 1, the focus of the short texts is on foundational skills, which includes building students' understanding of phonics and high-frequency words. From the middle of Grade 1 on, the short reads are complex in regards to these characteristics: purpose, genre, organization, connection of ideas, sentence structure, specific vocabulary, and prior knowledge. *Wonders Balanced Literacy* provides modeled, scaffolded instruction using close reading to help students read carefully and think deeply.

How to Use the Shared Reads

The Shared Reads are ideal for modeling the close reading routine and rereading multiple times with different purposes.

The Connect to Inquiry prompts from the Shared Read lessons connect the text to the inquiry topic. Use these prompts to:

- model searching for text evidence and answering questions.
- model taking notes about key details and confusing parts.
- model using the comprehension skills and strategies.
- model using your notes to identify the author's purpose and main idea of the text.

Modeling these skills with the Shared Read will help prepare students for extended complex texts and independent reading.

USE THE TEACHER GUIDE LESSON TO:

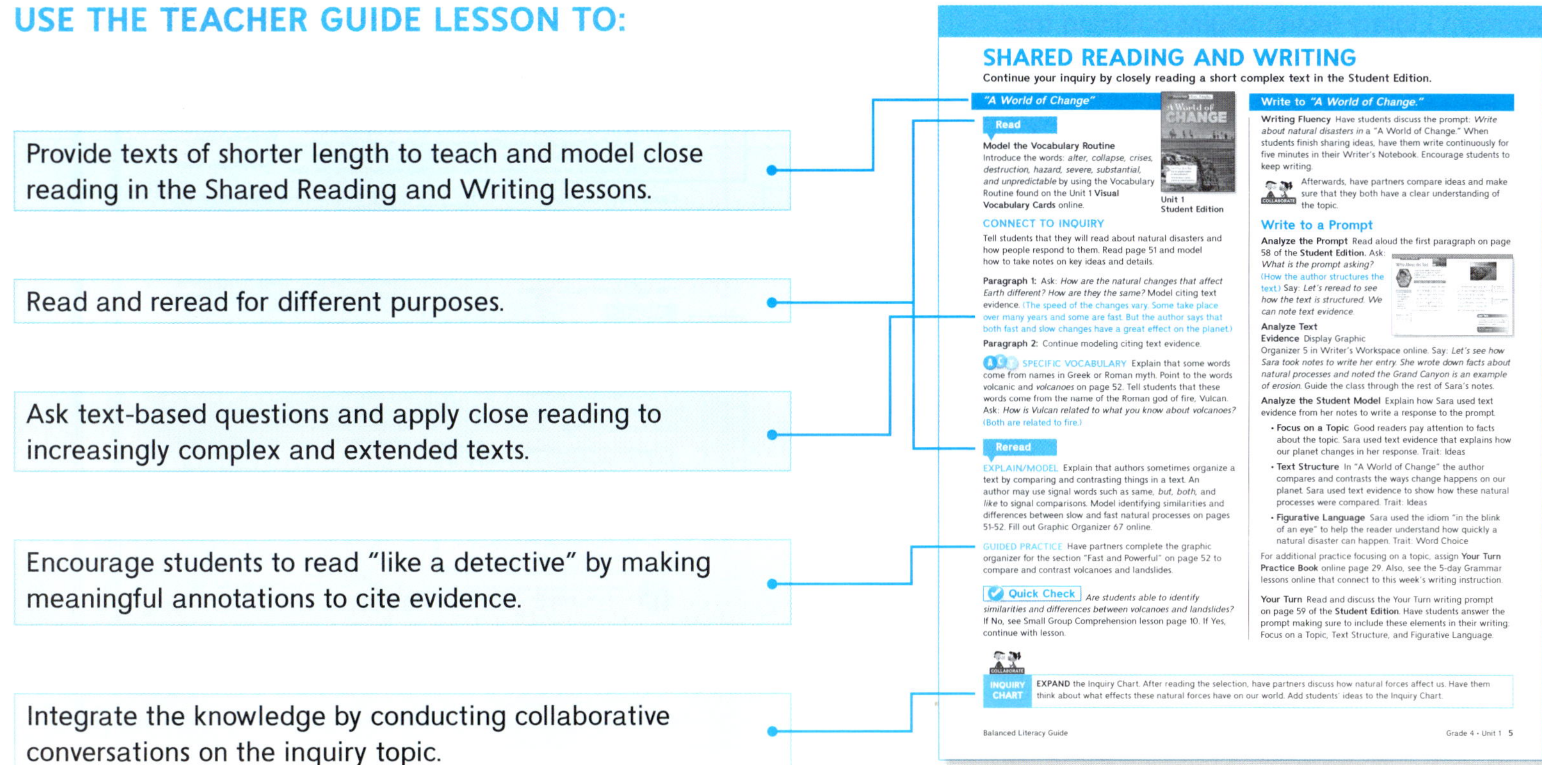

SHARED READING AND WRITING

Continue your inquiry by closely reading a short complex text in the Student Edition.

"A World of Change"

Read

Model the Vocabulary Routine
Introduce the words: *alter, collapse, crises, destruction, hazard, severe, substantial, and unpredictable* by using the Vocabulary Routine found on the Unit 1 **Visual Vocabulary Cards** online.

Unit 1 Student Edition

CONNECT TO INQUIRY

Tell students that they will read about natural disasters and how people respond to them. Read page 51 and model how to take notes on key ideas and details.

Paragraph 1: Ask: *How are the natural changes that affect Earth different? How are they the same?* Model citing text evidence. (The speed of the changes vary. Some take place over many years and some are fast. But the author says that both fast and slow changes have a great effect on the planet.)

Paragraph 2: Continue modeling citing text evidence.

SPECIFIC VOCABULARY Explain that some words come from names in Greek or Roman myth. Point to the words volcanic and *volcanoes* on page 52. Tell students that these words come from the name of the Roman god of fire, Vulcan. Ask: *How is Vulcan related to what you know about volcanoes?* (Both are related to fire.)

Reread

EXPLAIN/MODEL Explain that authors sometimes organize a text by comparing and contrasting things in a text. An author may use signal words such as same, *but, both,* and *like* to signal comparisons. Model identifying similarities and differences between slow and fast natural processes on pages 51-52. Fill out Graphic Organizer 67 online.

GUIDED PRACTICE Have partners complete the graphic organizer for the section "Fast and Powerful" on page 52 to compare and contrast volcanoes and landslides.

Quick Check *Are students able to identify similarities and differences between volcanoes and landslides?* If No, see Small Group Comprehension lesson page 10. If Yes, continue with lesson.

Write to *"A World of Change."*

Writing Fluency Have students discuss the prompt: *Write about natural disasters in* a "A World of Change." When students finish sharing ideas, have them write continuously for five minutes in their Writer's Notebook. Encourage students to keep writing.

COLLABORATE Afterwards, have partners compare ideas and make sure that they both have a clear understanding of the topic.

Write to a Prompt

Analyze the Prompt Read aloud the first paragraph on page 58 of the **Student Edition.** Ask: *What is the prompt asking?* (How the author structures the text.) Say: *Let's reread to see how the text is structured. We can note text evidence.*

Analyze Text Evidence Display Graphic Organizer 5 in Writer's Workspace online. Say: *Let's see how Sara took notes to write her entry. She wrote down facts about natural processes and noted the Grand Canyon is an example of erosion.* Guide the class through the rest of Sara's notes.

Analyze the Student Model Explain how Sara used text evidence from her notes to write a response to the prompt.

- **Focus on a Topic** Good readers pay attention to facts about the topic. Sara used text evidence that explains how our planet changes in her response. Trait: Ideas
- **Text Structure** In "A World of Change" the author compares and contrasts the ways change happens on our planet. Sara used text evidence to show how these natural processes were compared. Trait: Ideas
- **Figurative Language** Sara used the idiom "in the blink of an eye" to help the reader understand how quickly a natural disaster can happen. Trait: Word Choice

For additional practice focusing on a topic, assign **Your Turn Practice Book** online page 29. Also, see the 5-day Grammar lessons online that connect to this week's writing instruction.

Your Turn Read and discuss the Your Turn writing prompt on page 59 of the **Student Edition**. Have students answer the prompt making sure to include these elements in their writing: Focus on a Topic, Text Structure, and Figurative Language.

COLLABORATE

INQUIRY CHART **EXPAND** the Inquiry Chart. After reading the selection, have partners discuss how natural forces affect us. Have them think about what effects these natural forces have on our world. Add students' ideas to the Inquiry Chart.

Balanced Literacy Guide

Grade 4 • Unit 1 5

exposure to language rather than direct instruction (e.g., Miller & Gildea, 1987; Sternberg, 1987). Further, many reading researchers suggest that reading volume, rather than oral language, explains the individual differences found in vocabulary knowledge (e.g., Frey & Fisher, 2009).

In addition to vocabulary prowess, independent reading provides students:

- the opportunity to apply the skills and strategies that teachers have modeled (Fisher & Frey, 2012).
- increased responsibility for learning by allowing them to try out different approaches and seeing what works with different texts (Sanden, 2012).
- a chance for students to self-select books of interest to them and that they are motivated to read and reread (e.g., Walker, 2013).

Independent Reading in a Balanced Literacy Classroom

The evidence is clear—students need to read a lot. Structuring the classroom so that they can do so is important. Walker (2013) suggested the following considerations for ensuring students read during their independent reading time:

- An accessible, organized, leveled classroom and/or school library
- Appropriate matching of students and texts
- Student- and teacher-led book talks
- Quarterly reading goals set by students
- Consistent time to read independently
- Active teacher instruction, guidance, interaction, and monitoring of students
- Teacher facilitation of regular book conferences with students
- Independent student reading log and response portfolio
- Book response opportunities
- Recognition and feedback for students' independent reading (p. 186)

These guidelines are very useful for ensuring that instructional time devoted to independent reading has the biggest impact possible. Without clear expectations for reading during the independent reading time, students may not maximize their time. As noted in the survey by Ivey and Broaddus (2001), students noted that they read more when they had access to a lot of diverse titles from which to choose. In addition, accountability is an important consideration. Some teachers are recommending rethinking reading logs (e.g., Davis, 2014) in favor things like online book reviews, "Book Buzzes" where students write a weekly reflection about their reading and then share it with others, or "Golden Lines" where students identify the best line that their author wrote and share those with others. Often these alternatives turn into conversations that students have with others and the peers become excited to read the book they've heard about. And these tools allow teachers' to monitor students' progress and instructional needs.

In addition to expectations and accountability, students need time to read. It's not that all students have to read at the same time, but they could. Some teachers have a reading area that serves as a center or station that groups of students visit each day. Other teachers have a dedicated reading time for their class. Either way, time spent reading is an important part of an effective language arts classroom.

Summary

Students need to be taught how to read, and how to read increasingly complex texts. Their teachers can deploy a wide range of instructional strategies useful in teaching reading, ranging from modeling to guided instruction to close reading. To become strong readers, however, students need dedicated time to practice what they have been taught such that reading becomes a habit. Along the way, their vocabulary and background knowledge develop, allowing them to read more and better every year. A simple way to think about this is to consider strength and stamina. Effective reading instruction is a careful balance of both. Students need time to develop their reading stamina with less complex texts and time to develop their reading strengths with more complex texts. Engaging in both stamina and strength results in strong readers who choose to read, which is the goal of every parent and teacher.

References

Davis, S. (2014). Rethinking reading logs. *The Reading Teacher, 68*(1), 45.

Fisher, D., & Frey, N. (2012). Motivating boys to read: Inquiry, modeling, and choice matter. *Journal of Adolescent & Adult Literacy, 55*, 587–596.

Frey, N., & Fisher, D. (2009). *Learning words inside and out: Vocabulary instruction that boosts achievement in all subject areas.* Portsmouth, NH: Heinemann.

Ivey, G., & Broaddus, K. (2001). "Just plain reading": A survey of what makes students want to read in middle school classrooms. *Reading Research Quarterly, 36*, 350–377.

Miller, G. A., & Gildea, P. M. (1987). How children learn words. *Scientific American, 257*(3), 94–99.

Sanden, S. (2012). Independent reading: Perspectives and practices of highly effective teachers. *The Reading Teacher, 66*(3), 222–231.

Stanovich, K. E. (1986). Matthew effects in reading: Some consequences of individual differences in the acquisition of literacy. *Reading Research Quarterly, 21*, 36–407.

Sternberg, R. J. (1987). Most vocabulary is learned from context. In M. G. McKeown & M. E. Curtis (Eds.), *The nature of vocabulary acquisition* (pp. 89–105). Hillsdale, NJ: Erlbaum Associates.

Walker, K. K. (2013). Scaffolded silent reading. *Journal of Adolescent & Adult Literacy, 57*(3), 185-188.

West, R. F., & Stanovich, K. E. (1991). The incidental acquisition of information from reading. *Psychological Science, 2*, 32–330.

Independent Reading

WHAT IS INDEPENDENT READING?

Independent reading is the students' reading of self-selected texts. What students read is based on their personal choice with guidance as needed from the teacher. In some cases, especially in upper elementary grades, students read outside of the classroom. You may, however, want to provide independent reading as an option during center or independent activity time.

Research indicates that independent reading increases students' comprehension and builds their vocabulary. Independent reading of a wide variety of texts also builds students' background knowledge on the topics and concepts that they read about. It provides students with the opportunity to independently apply reading strategies and skills they are taught in class, and helps students make connections with what they are learning. Independent reading can also provide students with consistent opportunities to build reading stamina and fluency. Students are encouraged to read materials that are on their independent reading level, more complex texts about topics that interest them, or reread familiar texts or previously scaffolded texts.

Wonders Balanced Literacy offers a variety of texts from which students can self-select books at their level. Students can choose from the following selections:

- Classroom Library selections
- Leveled Readers
- Literature eBooks online
- Unit Bibliography online

It is important that children read books at their reading level so they are not too frustrated with books that are too hard. You can consult **Leveled Readers At-a-Glance** to view each title's guided reading level and lexile level to help students self-select appropriate texts. See the Text Set Extension charts on pages 132-177 for Classroom Library selections that can complement existing Text Sets and Inquiry Questions. For additional support on helping students select books at their level, see "How to Choose a Good Independent Reading Book" on page 40.

LAUNCHING INDEPENDENT READING

Independent reading is an important part of a reading program. Students are expected to read a high volume of text at their independent reading level. Here are some guiding principles for setting up independent reading time in your classroom:

- Students need to learn how to select and evaluate books at their level.
- Students need to record their independent reading either by using an independent reading journal or a reading log.
- Book clubs can be a fun way to get children excited about reading and help deepen their understanding of a book.
- Provide ideas for how students can respond to their independent reading. See Responding to Independent Reading on pages 42-45 for ideas.

SUGGESTED TIMEFRAMES FOR DAILY INDEPENDENT READING

Grade	Time
Kindergarten	10-15 minutes
Grade 1	10-20 minutes
Grade 2	10-20 minutes
Grades 3-5	30-40 minutes

HOW TO CHOOSE A GOOD INDEPENDENT READING BOOK

The book students choose to read can be easy, at their independent reading level (texts that are "just right") or challenging—but of high interest. Students should be encouraged to choose a book at their independent reading level most of the time.

You can have students use the Five Finger Rule (see page 41) to help them choose an appropriate Independent Reading book. After students choose a text to read, they can open the book to any page and raise a finger for each unfamiliar word. If students have trouble finding any difficult words, that text may be too easy for them. If they raise all five fingers, that text may be too challenging. You can provide the Five Finger Rule handout on page 41 and ask students to keep it in their Independent Reading Journals. To prepare students to choose their own books, model using the Five Finger Rule to self-select a text.

Independent Reading offers students the opportunity to choose a text that is of interest to them, but supervision and guidance is still necessary. Use the Text Extensions on page 132 and **Leveled Readers At-a-Glance** to confirm that students' choices are at their appropriate level. These resources can also act as helpful references should you wish to guide students in selecting books that share a common theme, genre, or author.

Watch the Videos

See Kathy Bumgardner conduct a lesson on **"Independent Reading and Reading Conferences."**

www.connected.mcgraw-hill.com

Five Finger Rule

How to choose a book:

- ✓ Choose a book you want to read.
- ✓ Open the book to any page.
- ✓ Put one finger up for each word you can't figure out.

0 – 1 Fingers

This book will be easy for you. Make sure you don't choose too many books that are too easy for you.

2 – 3 Fingers

This is a great choice!

4 Fingers

Give this book a try.

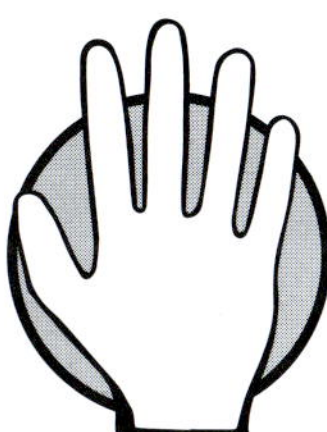

5 Fingers

This is a challenging book. You might want to make another choice.

Responding to Independent Reading

AUTHOR'S INSIGHT

"The evidence is clear—students need to read a lot. Structuring the classroom so that they can do so is important. ... Without clear expectations for reading during the independent reading time, students may not maximize their time."

–Dr. Douglas Fisher, San Diego State University

KEEPING AN INDEPENDENT READING JOURNAL

As students read their self-selected texts, they will be recording what they think about what they read in an Independent Reading Journal. Explain that good readers always ask questions about what they are reading and sometimes find answers to their questions by reading on in the text and sometimes they do not. Readers can also identify words that they do not know and cannot define. They can also note when they encounter confusing or difficult to understand portions of the text.

One way to support and scaffold students to read, think, and reread when needed is to provide K-1 students with simple pre-coded notes they can leave along the way in the books as they read and sticky notes for grades 2-5 students that they can use to leave a "Thinking Code."

USE THINKING CODES

Thinking Codes are letters or symbols, like an asterisk or questions mark, that students can use to mark portions of the text that they find funny, engaging, or confusing. As students read their independent reading books, they can place a sticky note with a Thinking Code at specific place on a page in the text, and then elaborate on their thinking in their Independent Reading Journals. This will help guide students as they think about what the read and respond to it. You can provide students with the chart of Thinking Codes on page 46.

FreeBirdPhotos/Shutterstock.com

TEACHING THE THINKING CODES

It will be important to model for students how to use the Thinking Codes to make entries in an Independent Reading Journal. To start, you may want to model how to respond to a self-selected text by using a Read Aloud you read with the class. After reading a section of the text, model how you would use the Thinking Codes to show how you respond to the text. You may also wish to write model entries to review with students. Point out how to format the entry, and then talk about what makes the entry a good entry. Ask volunteers to provide responses based on one of the Thinking Codes. Then model how to write entries based on their responses. You can provide students with sentence frames for them to use in their journal entries.

As you review the model entries with students, point out that their entries should:

- Show understanding of the text
- Use relevant details
- Use specific text based examples and citations
- Cite text evidence that supports the reader's examples and thinking
- Contain key vocabulary and show understanding of the vocabulary
- Contain clear and relevant reasoning
- Demonstrate sequential response

TRACKING INDEPENDENT READING

At the start of the year, set goals for students' independent reading. You may wish to set a goal of a total number of independent reading entries for the year. You may also wish to identify a minimum number of literature and informational texts that students should read throughout the year. Below are suggestions that should be tailored to your specific class. You can also set up goals by quarter or marking period.

Grade	Number of Texts
Kindergarten	12 texts
Grades 1-2	20 texts
Grades 3-4	30 texts
Grade 5	30-40 texts

Tell students that it will be their responsibility to keep track of their reading each day. Provide students with a daily reading log chart that features columns for the date, title of the text, and genre. You can also include a column for students to mark a positive, negative, or neutral response to the text, and a column for students to note if the text was too difficult, too easy, or just right for their reading level. Model how to fill out the reading log for students. Explain that students should fill in the log daily and identify one day each week that you will check students' logs to ensure they are keeping track of their reading.

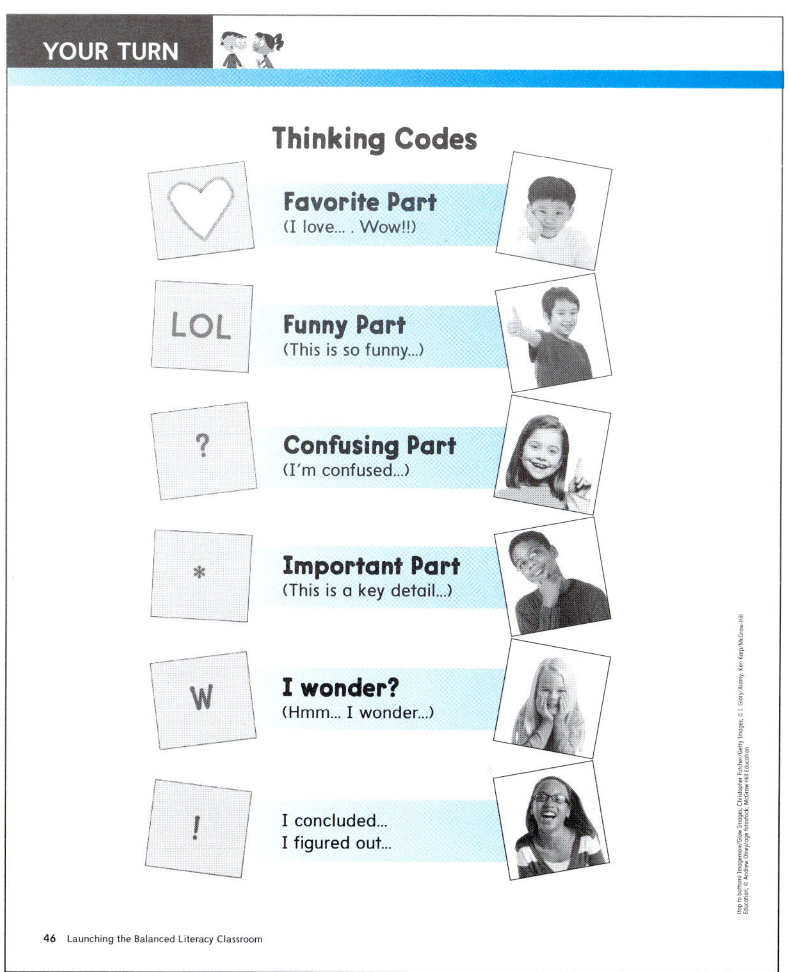

YOUR TURN

Thinking Codes

♡	**Favorite Part** (I love... . Wow!!)
LOL	**Funny Part** (This is so funny...)
?	**Confusing Part** (I'm confused...)
*	**Important Part** (This is a key detail...)
W	**I wonder?** (Hmm... I wonder...)
!	I concluded... I figured out...

46 Launching the Balanced Literacy Classroom

IDEAS FOR RESPONDING TO TEXTS

Independent Reading is a good way to provide opportunities for students to develop more complex thinking about the texts they read. Here are some fun strategies and activities you can use to informally assess your students' independent reading program, while encouraging them to share books with their peers. You can also refer to the Independent Reading Activities in the Small Group: Word Study pages of the Balanced Literacy Guides.

The Perfect Pitch Challenge students to present a 1-2 minute "pitch" about their books. This informal oral presentation should aim to hook the class and entice other students to want to read their book. Students want to reveal enough of the plot to pique interest without giving away the ending.

Design a Movie Poster Have students create a poster for their book with the title, author and a visual that provides a window into the book - characters, conflict, setting and/or themes. Students can design a poster using traditional pen and paper or they can use a digital tool. Have students present their movie posters to the class.

GRADES K-2: AUTHOR STUDY OR CONCEPT STUDY

Have students form an author study group. Guide them to choose an author, such as Tomie DePaola, and provide a number of books by the author that you have preselected to show similarities in the author's ideas, writing style, or use of text structure. Have the group read independently each week and discuss similarities between the books. Questions for students to discuss during their collaborative conversations can include:

- How are these books the same?
- How are they different?

Remind students to use evidence from the text and illustrations to support their opinions and ideas. They decide on how to present their ideas at the end of the study. If they need support, provide them with the following suggestions:

- Write a response comparing the books.
- Write about your favorite book by the author. Tell why.
- Write an article about the author for a newspaper.
- Write a report about the topic.

GRADES 3-5: AUTHOR STUDY

Have students form an independent study group and choose an author to study. Guide them to choose two pieces of work by the author and have them read the selections independently. Students should have collaborative conversations about their reading each week in which they can decide to:

- choose a character and compare their traits
- compare and contrast themes
- compare each author's purpose
- compare the text structures
- compare poetic devices or the use of figurative language and the effect it has on the mood of a text

Remind students to use text evidence to support their opinions and ideas.

GRADES 3-5: BOOK SHARE IDEAS

Have students share their independent reading with their peers with these fun strategies:

Produce and Publish a Movie Trailer Ask students to create a 2-3 minute movie trailer for their books that provides enough plot details to captivate the viewer without spoiling the end. Students can use video editing software applications to create their trailers.

Class Book Share Have students choose an exciting, interesting or descriptive passage to read aloud to the group. The passage should reveal something interesting about a situation in the text and/or provide some insight into a main character.

Book Club Chat Encourage students to form small groups to discuss what they enjoyed or found confusing about a book they all read. Students should create the following roles for their book club:

- A leader to maintain roles and ensure each student gets to ask and answer a question.
- A summarizer to summarize what students read and to retell the most important parts of the characters, setting, and plot events.
- A word finder to look up and define three or four interesting or challenging words from the text.
- An illustrator to draw a picture of his or her favorite part of the story.

Remind students to take turns speaking and listening. When students respond to a peer's comments, they should explain why they agree or disagree. Students can also use their Independent Reading Journals to help them during their book club chats.

GRADES 3-5: CONCEPT STUDY

Have students do a research report on a topic related to their independent reading. Students may choose to study one of the following topics:

- A specific time-period from a text
- A specific concept or idea from a text
- A specific person in history
- The pros and cons of a controversial subject

Have students decide on how to present their ideas at the end of the study. If they need support provide them with the following suggestions:

- Write a research report including an organizational structure that supports the research
- Create an historical timeline of a subject or person
- Write a biographical sketch of a person
- Write a persuasive article for a newspaper
- Create a slideshow presentation for any of the above

Thinking Codes

Favorite Part
(I love... . Wow!!)

LOL

Funny Part
(This is so funny...)

Confusing Part
(I'm confused...)

Important Part
(This is a key detail...)

I wonder?
(Hmm... I wonder...)

I concluded...
I figured out...

(top to bottom) Imagemore/Glow Images; Christopher Futcher/Getty Images; © I. Glory/Alamy; Ken Karp/McGraw-Hill Education; © Andrew Olney/age fotostock; McGraw-Hill Education

Setting Up Classroom Libraries

SETTING UP CLASSROOM LIBRARIES

There is no single way to organize the classroom library. The important thing is that students know how the books are organized so they can easily access books that are a good fit for them. Collections can grow as the year progresses and the teacher is able to add books.

Books can be organized into baskets by author, genre, theme, text type or inquiry topic. Use the Expanding Text Sets charts on pages 132-177, as well as the Unit Bibliographies available online, to help identify additional titles to include in your classroom library.

If needed, you might want to organize a small portion of the classroom library by level (guided reading levels, lexiles, etc.). This might be appropriate for some students who are still in need of additional scaffolding in choosing books that are appropriate for them. Labeling baskets so that students can find books for themselves, and reviewing with students how the books are organized, is critical.

INDIVIDUAL BOOK BOXES

At the lower grades, setting up individual book boxes can help ensure that students are reading each day during the week. Individual book boxes can be housed in anything from ½ gallon zip lock bags to magazine boxes to cereal boxes that are cut to fit students' books and resources. Students can begin to build their own book boxes with two books that they choose from the classroom or school library.

It will be important to set up procedures for how to care for the books and maintain their own boxes and the classroom library. Use minilessons to model

- How to manage book bags or boxes
- Procedures for abandoning books
- Maintaining books and any other materials in book boxes

WORKING WITH THE SCHOOL LIBRARIAN

Have students use the school library as a resource for independent reading and research. Students can check out print or digital media resources to support their independent reading and topics for research, such as the weekly Research Projects or Genre Writing assignments. Prior to taking your students to the library:

1. Share with the librarian the Five Finger Rule (see page 41), or other guidelines you give students about identifying an appropriate book.
2. Share the Inquiry Questions or Research and Inquiry topics with the school librarian ahead of time so he or she can ensure that there are plenty of available resources for students to check out during their visit. This will ensure your time in the library is productive and there are plenty of books for students to check out.
3. You may wish to also share the Web Resources with the librarian so she can help students with their research.
4. Review with children the expectations for behavior in the library, as well as how to determine the relevancy and accuracy of print and digital sources. Remind students that if they need additional information while in the library or have difficulty locating a text, they should consult with the library staff.
5. Encourage them to use their library time wisely, and instruct that if they have additional time after locating their resources, they can begin to read their materials.

Watch the Videos

See Kathy Bumgardner discuss **"Setting Up a Balanced Literacy Classroom."**

www.connected.mcgraw-hill.com

COLLABORATIVE CONVERSATIONS

By Dr. Vicki Gibson

CEO, Gibson, Hasbrouck & Associates
Educational Consultant, What Works With Kids
Owner/Director, Longmire Learning Center

"Students are expected to participate in collaborative discussions that enhance their comprehension and improve their language skills by talking more, sharing more information with their peers, and engaging in collaborative activities."
- *Dr. Vicki Gibson*

Thanks to the ubiquitous wireless devices that we carry around to keep in touch, our communication habits are changing to include less face-to-face conversations and more isolated behind-the-screen communications. Digital natives of the iGeneration engage in informal discourse using abbreviated responses, or text-talk, that often are completed as the participants multitask rather than focus on the topic under discussion (Rosen, 2012). These evolving communication habits are not congruent with the expectations for student performance in state standards.

According to most standards, teachers and students in grades K–3 will participate in collaborative conversations about age-appropriate, grade-level topics and texts after listening attentively to texts read aloud in whole class and small groups. Students are expected to participate and demonstrate understanding as they:

- Continue conversations through multiple exchanges
- Seek help and ask questions to request clarification
- Ask and answer text-dependent questions about key details
- Describe and discuss relevant details by comparing and contrasting, analyzing, and synthesizing information
- Add drawings, visual displays, or audio recordings of stories or poems to clarify ideas, thoughts, and feelings.

In grades 4–5, teachers and students are expected to engage in a range of collaborative discussions whose discourse complexity increases per grade level. The discussions may occur one-to-one, in groups, or during teacher-led conversations about grade-level topics and texts that are read aloud.

Student responsibilities and performance expectations become more challenging as they:

- Come prepared for discussions having read or studied required materials
- Use information and media to explore ideas under discussion
- Build on others' ideas and speak clearly at an understandable pace
- Determine the main ideas and supporting details of text that was read aloud or from information presented in diverse media formats

Nadya Lukic/Shutterstock.com

- Speak in complete sentences using good grammar to report on topics or texts, or tell a story or recount experiences with appropriate facts and details
- Paraphrase portions of a text read aloud and identify reasons and evidence a speaker provides to support particular points
- Summarize written text that was read aloud and identify key details and points, then explain how each claim is supported by reasons and evidence
- Include multimedia components and visual displays in presentations, and
- Differentiate between contexts that call for informal or formal English and adapt their speech to a variety of contexts and tasks using formal English when appropriate to task and situation.

While cooperative learning and collaboration are not new in schools, allowing students to work together and openly share information is not a familiar classroom habit. The adjustments required differ from traditional classroom practice where students worked cooperatively on project-based learning activities (Slavin, 1991a; Slavin, 1991b; Stevens & Slavin, 1995). The new standards approach learning language as a matter of craft, implying that students need explicit instruction and guided practice to learn how to communicate purposefully. Students are expected to participate in collaborative discussions that enhance their comprehension and improve their language skills by talking more, sharing more information with their peers, and engaging in collaborative activities.

The expectation level for students' performance is higher, more sophisticated. According to new standards, students will communicate clearly and persuasively about specific topics or texts under discussion using correct grammar and complete sentences that contain subject-verb agreement. In doing so, students will follow agreed-upon rules for discussions by applying the pragmatics of language and social conversations while engaging in respectful communication. These changes in communication and classroom practice may differ significantly from traditional habits.

Pressmaster/Shutterstock.com

> ...evolving communication habits are not congruent with the expectations for student performance.

Teachers and students will share equal opportunities to participate during explicit instruction, engage in discussions, and complete productive group work either in whole class or small group activities (Archer & Hughes, 2011; Frey, Fisher & Everlove, 2009). Teachers and students will share talking time and follow agreed upon rules for discussions when they:

- Listen actively to determine the speaker's purpose and confirm understanding
- Speak purposefully by organizing information in ways that clearly communicate to a listener
- Wait for a turn to speak and use respectful communication, acceptable word choices, and appropriate voice tones and levels
- Reflect before reacting to others' input
- Share dialogue that follows the topic under discussion and honor a sense of timing to ensure that everyone participates
- Identify expectations for purposeful outcomes and produce a response or product either orally or in a written or digital format.

Clearly the expectations for Speaking and Listening in the new standards represent more formal communication habits than many teachers and students use during classroom discussions. Therefore, implementing the new standards will likely require teachers adjust classroom teaching and practice as they:

- Incorporate more explicit language instruction, particularly focusing on grammar
- Model and use correct grammar that includes subject-verb agreement and complete sentences
- Share the talking time by allowing students to interact more and express ideas and respond orally to text-dependent questions
- Demonstrate how to respond to text-dependent questions using text evidence to support answers and validate opinions in discussions
- Incorporate more small group, differentiated instruction and collaborative practice
- Organize lesson content in ways that follow topics sequentially through thought-provoking progressions
- Select practice activities that support structured and focused collaborative conversations
- Delay written responses until students have received sufficient teaching and practice that includes collaborative discussions to enhance their comprehension.

Implementing current standards will require several shifts in behavioral expectations and traditional classroom practices. Incorporating collaboration will require teachers develop efficient classroom management routines and procedures that help them manage flexible grouping and the freedoms associated with cooperative learning and communications (Gibson & Hasbrouck, 2009; Gibson & Wilson, 2011; Marzano & Pickering, 2001). Establishing consistent classroom management routines across grade levels within schools and teaching students to follow the agreed upon rules for discussions will provide a great jumpstart for successfully implementing the new standards. Teachers can prepare now by following these suggestions:

Implementing current standards will require several shifts in behavioral expectations and traditional classroom practices.

wavebreakmedia/Shutterstock.com

No one-way fix has been established for incorporating collaborative conversations and implementing the new standards....

- Establish routines for managing whole group and small group discussions and participation in cooperative learning activities
- Read text to and with students to facilitate comprehension, then help them organize and use materials to support responses during discussions
- Clearly identify what is acceptable for participating in respectful communication
- Assess students' capabilities for participating in cooperative activities and provide sufficient training to establish habits using multiple practice opportunities
- Practice in whole group by reading and discussing familiar texts, followed by teacher-led discussions and partnering practice
- Model, teach and practice using correct oral grammar that includes complete sentences, subject-verb agreement, and following a topic under discussion
- Select activities that help students connect the reading-speaking-listening link and support collaborative conversations
- Assign practice activities that include more collaborative discussions and less written work until students can perform successfully by speaking, listening and using language to communicate
- Differentiate assessment by not grading collaborative work or every assignment, thereby reducing the competition and encouraging more risk-taking for participation and supportive collaboration
- Assess student performance on independent practice assignments completed after teacher-led instruction and collaborative discussions in small groups.

No one-way fix has been established for incorporating collaborative conversations and implementing the new standards for Speaking and Listening in grades K–5. Certainly the requirements for participation differ from the casual text-talk communications and lecture-format presentations used currently by many teachers and students. Adjusting classroom practices will be necessary to successfully incorporate cooperative learning and increase interactivity in small groups that include collaborative discussions. Making adjustments now in teaching and practice, and embracing collaborative activities, is highly recommended so that students can achieve the expectations for speaking, listening and using language as a craft to communicate collaboratively.

Watch the Videos

See Dr. Vicki Gibson discuss how to **"Encourage Collaboration at Worktables and Workstations."**

www.connected.mcgraw-hill.com

References

Archer, A. & Hughes, C. (2011). *Explicit Instruction: Effective and Efficient Teaching*, The Guilford Press, New York: NY

Common Core State Standards (CCSS). (revised July 2010). Council of Chief State School Officers (CCSS) and U.S. Department of Education, Washington DC

Frey, N., Fisher, D. & Everlove, S. (2009). Productive Group Work: How to Engage Students, Build Teamwork, and Promote Understanding, Alexandria, VA: ASCD

Gibson, V. & Hasbrouck, J. (2009). *Differentiating Instruction: Guidelines for Implementation*, Gibson, Hasbrouck & Associates (GHA), Wellesley: MA

Gibson, V. & Wilson, J. (2011). *Differentiating Teaching and Practice to Support Teaching in Practice in Middle and High Schools*, Gibson, Hasbrouck & Associates (GHA), Wellesley, MA

Marzano, R. & Pickering, D. (2001). *Classroom Strategies That Work*. Alexandria, VA: ASCD Rosen, L. (2012). iDisorder: *Understanding Our Obsession with Technology and Overcoming Its Hold on Us*, Palgrave Macmillan, New York: NY

Slavin, Robert E. (1991a). Synthesis of Research on Cooperative Learning. *Educational Leadership 48* (February 1991): 71-82. EJ 421 354

Slavin, R. (1991b). Student Team Learning: A Practical Guide to Cooperative Learning, Washington, DC: National Education Association. ED 339 518

Stevens, R. & Slavin, R. (1995). The Cooperative Elementary School: Effects on Students' Achievement, Attitudes, and Social Relations. *American Educational Research Journal*, 32, 321-351

Supporting Collaborative Conversations

Establishing collaborative conversation routines will improve language skills and comprehension by allowing students to practice proper grammar and sentence structure, share information with peers, and work together to find text evidence.

INTEGRATED SPEAKING AND LISTENING

Wonders Balanced Literacy provides opportunities for collaborative conversations on inquiry topics and texts with each text set. Opportunities for speaking and listening are integrated into reading, writing, research, and inquiry lessons. Students engage in teacher-led, small-group and one-on-one conversations. Speaking and listening activities vary throughout the text set and include building on each other's ideas, recounting details from a text read, and asking and answering clarifying questions. Use the practices below as you begin your exploration of the text sets.

What are the best practices?

Establish routines for managing discussions in cooperative learning activities.

- Model and monitor how to respond to text-dependent questions using text evidence to support answers and validate opinions.
- In whole group, model reading and discussing texts, followed by partnering practice.
- Model, teach, and practice using correct oral grammar, complete sentences and correct subject-verb agreement.
- Help students stay on topic by organizing their ideas and details from the text as they participate.
- Select activities that link reading, speaking, and listening and support collaborative conversations.

How to Use the Materials

Within each lesson, teachers are provided strategies to effectively model and guide discussions. Students have many opportunities to turn and talk with a partner, thus maximizing their time spent speaking and listening.

Use the videos on Small Group Discussions and How to Give a Presentation (see page 53) to provide models of collaborative conversations. In the videos, watch students begin a discussion of a text and see how teachers help them stay on target in their discussions.

Teachers can also use the Collaborative Conversations handout on page 56 to assist group or partner discussions.

Additionally, each grade offers students Speaking and Listening Checklists found in the **Teacher Resource Book** online. These provide students with reminders of important speaking and listening behaviors for each grade level.

- The Listening Checklist includes reminders to students to listen attentively to the speaker and take turns talking. Students should respect others' ideas; raise their hands when they want to speak; and maintain eye contact.
- The Speaking Checklist highlights skills such as: focusing on speaking purposely and organizing thoughts; staying on topic; and referring to relevant facts and ideas from the readings to support claims, among others.

SPEAKING AND LISTENING CHECKLISTS

Speaking Checklist

Follow these speaking rules when you are sharing ideas with others about your project, presenting your project to the class, or working with a partner, group, or the class.

- ☐ I will wait my turn to speak.
- ☐ I will express my ideas and opinions using accurate information.
- ☐ I will make eye contact with my audience.
- ☐ I will speak in a clear voice and loud enough so others can understand me.
- ☐ I will speak slowly and pronounce my words.
- ☐ I will speak correctly and with expression.
- ☐ I will ask and answer questions thoughtfully and use details about the topic.
- ☐ I will participate in discussions by making related comments or suggestions.
- ☐ I can report on a topic, tell a story, or describe an experience in an organized way, including supporting facts and details.
- ☐ I can make a recording of a story or poem to show my skill at reading aloud.

Speaking Checklist

Listening Checklist

Follow these listening rules when you are talking about project ideas with your class, listening to others presenting, or working with a group.

- ☐ I will listen and look at the person who is speaking.
- ☐ I will listen attentively when others are speaking.
- ☐ I will listen and identify key ideas that are presented.
- ☐ I will ask questions about the topic when I do not understand or to get more information.
- ☐ I will follow group directions.
- ☐ I will listen and repeat directions in order.
- ☐ I will listen and be able to give clear directions to others.
- ☐ I will listen carefully and can state in my own words the main points and reasons a speaker presents.

98 Listening Checklist

TIPS FOR COLLABORATIVE CONVERSATIONS

To support collaborative conversations, explain to students that there are certain guidelines they should follow to make sure they are being respectful and active participants and listeners. Share and discuss the Collaborative Conversations videos online with students, and ask: *What did you notice about how the students in the videos interacted with each other?*

Watch the Videos

Watch students have a book talk in **"Collaborative Conversations: Small Group Discussion."**

www.connected.mcgraw-hill.com

For Kindergarten through Grade 2, when students are organized into partner pairs or small groups, remind them of the following tips for collaborative conversations.

Take Turns Talking Remind students to take turns speaking. They should

- wait for a speaker to finish before they speak. They should not speak over others.
- quietly raise their hands to let others know they would like to speak.
- ask for others' opinions so that all have a chance to share.

Listen Carefully Remind students to listen carefully to speakers. They should

- always look at the person who is speaking.
- respect others by not interrupting them.
- repeat key ideas expressed to check understanding.

Add New Ideas Encourage students to add new ideas to their conversations. They should

- stay on topic.
- connect their own ideas to what their peers have said.
- look for ways to connect their personal experiences or prior knowledge to the conversation.

Provide Details Encourage students to use details to elaborate as they participate. They should

- give details to express their thoughts, feelings, and ideas clearly.
- use details to describe people, places, things, and events.
- give details when asking about something they do not understand.

Have students work in partner and small-group collaborations to discuss the tips from the videos and practice their own conversation skills.

Ask and Answer Questions As students engage in discussions, encourage them to ask and answer questions. They should

- ask questions to clarify ideas or follow up on information.
- wait after asking a question to give others a chance to respond.
- answer questions with complete ideas.

Be Open to All Ideas Remind students to listen to ideas. They should

- understand that all ideas and questions are important.
- respect others' opinions yet not hesitate to offer a different opinion.
- explain their own ideas and insights in light of the discussion.

For Grades 3-5, students' collaborative discussions and presentations should become more thorough and well-prepared. Students should practice researching conversation points and taking turns leading discussions.

Take on Discussion Roles Encourage students to take on roles to help keep the discussion on track. Assigned roles can include

- a questioner who asks questions that keep the discussion moving and makes sure everyone gets a turn.
- a recorder who takes notes and reports to the class.

Before they come to a discussion, students should make sure they are prepared. They should

- read or study the material being discussed before coming.
- use preparation and knowledge about the topic to explore discussion ideas.

As students take part in small-group conversations and presentations, be sure to circulate and monitor their progress. Guide them to stay on topic, use text evidence, and be respectful listeners and speakers.

Watch the Videos

Watch students give presentations in **"Collaborative Conversations: How to Give a Presentation."**

www.connected.mcgraw-hill.com

Reading Conferences

Conducting teacher and peer reading conferences on a regular basis helps provide valuable informal assessment information for both teachers and students.

TEACHER CONFERENCES

A conference is a conversation with a student about his or her reading. During a reading conference, a teacher is studying how a students reads, what areas they need support in and then provides coaching to support those needs. It is important to prepare for a reading conference by following up on something the student was struggling with, looking at their reading journals or notes ahead of time and looking at the data on the student.

To begin, as students are independently reading, you can ask to listen to individual students read aloud to confirm reading level appropriateness. Engage the student in a conversation about what they are reading and why they chose that specific text. Asking additional questions, as appropriate, can provide you with valuable formative assessment information about a student's reading development. These questions may include topics about:

- text's genre
- text features
- referring back to specific "Think Codes" on page 46 that students have left in the text
- general comprehension of text
- more focused questions on how the author presents information in a section of the text the student may have commented on

In addition, you can also make notes about how a student solves problems while reading, what their strengths are and what they need to work on. Listening in for word accuracy, appropriate fluency and comprehension can be done during these independent reading conferences as well.

RECORDING STUDENT PROGRESS

Conferencing individually with students is a great way to keep track of student progress. You can use a notebook with a page for each student, or you may prefer to use preprinted conference pages. To the right is an example of a Reading Conference Sheet you can keep for students. Go online for a printable version that can be found in the **Instructional Routines Handbook**.

After conferencing with a student, it is important to leave the student with a reading goal that he or she should work on. For example, students may need to be encouraged to cite more relevant and explicit text evidence when making statements or giving opinions about what they are reading.

INDEPENDENT READING

READING CONFERENCING CLASS SHEET / NOTES

Student Name: Date: Strengths Noted: Teaching Point:	Student Name: Date: Strengths Noted: Teaching Point:	Student Name: Date: Strengths Noted: Teaching Point:
Student Name: Date: Strengths Noted: Teaching Point:	Student Name: Date: Strengths Noted: Teaching Point:	Student Name: Date: Strengths Noted: Teaching Point:

Track teaching points reviewed with student and note future reading goals.

Note strengths in reading that you observed concerning the text. List areas where a child made an improvement. Check previous notes for weaknesses and growth.

PEER CONFERENCES

Providing students some consistent opportunities to discuss with another student what they are reading can be enriching for students. It allows them to exchange ideas about what they are learning and how they are growing as readers. In addition, it offers a valuable chance to listen in to students sharing their thinking about their reading with others.

The collaborative practice of thinking about and reflecting on what students are reading provides students a chance to solidify their thinking. Pair two (or three) students. You might want to group students who are reading the same text or texts on the same topic or theme. Provide students with specific guidelines to ensure that students will use the time productively. Use the following materials to support students in having effective peer conferences:

- Collaborative Conversations for Peer Conferences, see page 56
- Study Sync Peer Conferencing video online

Students should have opportunities to rehearse what these collaborative conversations should look like and sound like. By using a gradual release of responsibility, the teacher can ensure that students will be focused when they are meeting with a peer to discuss their reading. Be sure to listen in as students conference with their peers to guide students, as necessary.

REFLECT ON WHAT WAS LEARNED

Each conference should be seen as part of a sequence of teaching each student. To be sure you are meeting a students' needs, you may choose to record your audio conference. Afterwards, listen to the conference to determine how it went. Think about next steps for the student. Think about how you can better serve their needs. Did you get the information you need to support their learning? What will you do differently next time?

Often what is learned in a conference can transer to a small group lesson if there are other students with the same needs. Balancing conferences with small group work will help you support more students on a daily and weekly basis.

Watch the Videos

See the **"Study Sync Collaborative Conversations Video: Peer Conferencing"** to see a model of a reading conference.

www.connected.mcgraw-hill.com

Collaborative Conversations

With your partner, share your thoughts and opinions about the book by using the sentence starters below.

I found it interesting that...

Also interesting is...

As I read, I realized that...

Can you point to text evidence that shows...

My opinion is...

I agree or disagree with you because...

Something that confused me was...

I think you are confused because...

Vocabulary

Use the routines in this section to develop vocabulary and fluency skills. For Close Reading Routines, see page 34.

Introduce

Explain to students they will learn about new vocabulary words.

Model

Model the task by introducing and using several new vocabulary words.

Teacher Tips

- Introduce vocabulary words before students read the selection or while reading the text aloud.
- If you read aloud, pause to give a brief explanation for each word you have chosen to teach. Teach the words after reading the story.
- Say the word. Write it. Use the **Syllable Scoop Technique** to pronounce the word and emphasize syllable patterns. For example, draw a small loop under each syllable in *cooperate* as you pronounce it. co op er ate
- Teach the word using the **Define/Example/Ask** routine.
- **Define** the word in simple, student-friendly language.
- Provide an **example** of the word in a meaningful sentence, relevant to students' lives.
- **Ask** a question that requires students to apply the word. They can give an example or explanation, or identify a synonym or antonym.

Guided Practice

Throughout the week, provide daily opportunities for students to use and apply the words. These include sentence starters, exploring different forms of the words, and other vocabulary-building strategies developed by Beck and McKeown. See two examples below.

Connect to Words Read aloud the following sentence prompts, one at a time. Engage students in a discussion. Use the discussion to evaluate each student's depth of word meaning.

1. Would it be harder to adapt to a new teacher or a new way of getting to school? Why?
2. What are the qualities of a good *mentor*?
3. What does it take to *succeed* at a sport?
4. I will *succeed* in school this year because ______ .
5. A *mentor* can help me by ______ .
6. When you *adapt* to a new place, you must ______ .

Example 2: Word Squares Ask students to create Word Squares for each word in their word study notebooks.

- In the first square, students write the word.
- In the second square, students write their own definitions of the word and any related words, such as **synonyms**. Remind students that synonyms are words that mean the same or nearly the same. **Related words** include words with the same base, such as *succeed, success, successful; adapt, adaptation*.
- In the third square, students draw a simple illustration that will help them remember the word. They might also want to write a mnemonic that will help them remember the word. (example: *A mentor helps me learn.*)
- In the fourth square, students write nonexamples, including antonyms for the word. Remind students that **antonyms** are words that mean the opposite. (example: succeed/fail)

Provide Independent Practice

Individual turns allow you an opportunity to assess each student's skill level and provide additional practice for those students who need it.

Near the end of each week, students should write sentences in their word study notebooks using the words.

Olesya Feketa/Shutterstock.com

Fluency: Intonation

Objective Read statements, questions, and exclamations with proper intonation in connected text.

I Do Explain that good readers change their voices to show what sentences mean. Tell students that they should read different types of sentences differently. Write these sentences on the board. *We go to the park. Where is the park? We love the park!* Read them in a flat monotone.

Then model reading each sentence with proper intonation. Explain how you decided to read each sentence differently. Model circling the punctuation in each sentence. Remind students that a sentence that ends with a period is read in a steady way. In a sentence that ends in a question mark, you raise your voice at the end. A sentence that ends with an exclamation point is read with strong feeling or excitement.

We Do Have students turn to the **Student Edition** or **Leveled Reader** for the week and choose a section to read fluently. As a group, circle and name the punctuation mark at the end of each sentence. Have the students tell how each sentence should be read. Provide corrective feedback.

Read aloud the passage and create a summary with the group. Point out how reading different types of sentences with proper expression helps readers understand the passage. Read aloud the passage again.

Model echo reading a few sentences from the passage with a volunteer. Then have students echo read the passage. Have students lead while you respond. Ask students to say how they read each phrase or sentence before you repeat it. Prompt them with this question each time it is your turn: How should I change my voice when I read this sentence?

Have partners practice reading the passage aloud to each other, focusing on reading sentences with correct intonation.

Provide students with one or two comprehension questions about the passage. Have partners discuss questions. Then discuss the questions as a group.

Corrective Feedback Provide corrective feedback for errors in intonation, as well as errors in pronunciation. Point out the student's error and model reading the sentence or word correctly. Then have the student read the sentence or word again.

wavebreakmedia/Shutterstock.com

Fluency: Expression

Objective Understand how to read dialogue with expression.

I Do

Explain to students that a conversation that is written down is called *dialogue*. Say: When dialogue is read aloud, good readers use their voices to sound like the character who is speaking. They express the same feeling as the character. Ask students to listen as you pretend to be helping someone in a store:

"Can I help you? The greeting cards are against the wall. Let me know if you need anything else."

Explain that if the words you just said were written down, they would be called dialogue. Tell students that there are special ways of writing dialogue so readers know who said which part of the conversation and how they sounded when they said those words. Write the sentences below. Model reading each sentence aloud.

"Sarah, did you practice for the game?" John asked.
"Yes, I practiced kicking!" Sarah said.

Circle all the quotation marks. Quotation marks show where someone's exact words begin and end. Reread just the spoken words.

Underline words that aren't enclosed in quotation marks. These words tell who is speaking. They may also tell how the speaker says the words.

Circle the punctuation marks inside the quotation marks. These marks help you know whether to ask a question, make a statement, or show strong feeling. Reread the spoken words, using your voice to indicate sentence changes.

We Do

Have students turn to a **Student Edition** selection or **Leveled Reader** that has dialogue and choose a section to read fluently. Guide students in circling the dialogue. Then have them underline the words that tell who is speaking. Next, have students echo read the passage with you.

You Do

Have students partner-read the passage, reviewing the circled dialogue and underlined words. Remind students to read the dialogue as if they are the characters in the story. Have them alternate reading the other sentences.

Corrective Feedback Provide corrective feedback about reading dialogue with expression. Point out the student's error and model reading the sentence correctly. Have students read the sentence again.

Fluency: Phrasing

Objective Pause at commas and at end punctuation, using appropriate phrasing.

I Do Explain that fluent readers pause after commas and after the punctuation at the end of a sentence as they read aloud. The punctuation marks show them how to use phrasing, or putting in pauses, to make the text more understandable.

Write a **period (.)** on the board: A period tells readers to pause at the end of a sentence. Display these sentences: *The goat kicked the can. Then it began to talk.* Model reading the sentences aloud, pausing at the end of each sentence. Point to each period as you pause.

Write a **question mark (?)** on the board. A question mark tells readers to raise their voice at the end of the question and then pause. Write the sentences as questions. *Did the goat kick the can? Did it begin to talk?* Then model reading each sentence aloud, raising your voice and then pausing. Point to each question mark as you do so.

Write an **exclamation point (!)** on the board. An exclamation point tells readers to read the sentence with strong feeling and then pause. Display these sentences: *The goat kicked the can! Then it began to talk!* Then model reading each sentence aloud, showing strong feeling and then pausing. Point to each exclamation mark.

Write a **comma (,)** on the board. A comma tells readers to pause for a short amount of time. A comma can separate two parts of a sentence; it separates items in a list. It is also used in dialogue. Display: *My cat has a gray coat, but she has white paws. I ate a peach, a pear, and an apple. "Let's go," said Mom.* Circle the comma in each sentence. Model reading the sentences aloud, pausing at the commas and pointing to them.

We Do Have students turn to the **Student Edition** or **Leveled Reader** for the week and choose a section to read fluently. Guide students in circling end punctuation and underlining any commas. Then model reading one sentence at a time as students echo read after you, focusing on phrasing. Repeat lines as needed. Then read the passage chorally with students.

You Do Have students practice partner reading the passage. Have them take turns reading the passage aloud, pausing at commas and at the end of each sentence. Remind them to pause for a short amount of time after commas and a slightly longer time after end punctuation. Remind them to use the appropriate expression and intonation for a period, an exclamation point, or a question mark.

Corrective Feedback Provide corrective feedback for appropriate phrasing by pausing for the appropriate amount of time at commas and at end punctuation. Point out the student's error and model reading the sentence with correct phrasing. Have the students reread the sentence.

Fluency: Rate

Objective Identify and demonstrate when to slow down reading.

I Do Explain to students that good readers slow down their pace of reading when the content is difficult. It is easier to think carefully about what you read when you read more slowly. It is helpful to slow down when reading nonfiction books or articles about science or social studies. When you slow down, you can pay attention to difficult vocabulary and complicated ideas.

Explain that a good reader must decide how and when to slow down reading.

- Is the text nonfiction? Is it about a social studies or science topic?
- Does the text have long words or unfamiliar vocabulary?
- Does the text have new ideas that you want to understand?

Read the following passage aloud. Guide students in recognizing that this is a nonfiction passage with technical words. Read it slowly and clearly. Think aloud as you encounter technical vocabulary by saying: I wonder what that means. I'm going to keep reading to find out.

A shooting star is a meteor. A meteor is a space rock. If the meteor lands on Earth, it is called a meteorite. *The bright streak of a shooting star is hot glowing air. It is made from the heat of a meteor as it speeds through Earth's atmosphere.*

We Do Have students turn to a nonfiction **Student Edition** selection or **Leveled Reader** and choose a section to read fluently. Tell students that this is a nonfiction passage, so they should look for unfamiliar words. Model reading the passage aloud at a slow pace. Help students understand that reading slowly will help them remember facts. Then do a choral reading with students.

You Do Have students partner-read the passage. Ask them to take turns reading the passage aloud. Then provide students a couple of comprehension questions about the text. Have partners discuss the questions. Then discuss the questions as a group.

Corrective Feedback Provide corrective feedback on student's reading rate. Explain that it is important to slow down in order to understand new words and complex text. Point out the student's error and model reading the sentence correctly. Have students repeat reading the sentence.

Fluency: Accuracy

Objective Read words with accuracy and fluency.

Explain to students that when reading aloud, good readers pronounce each word clearly and correctly so their readers will not be confused.

Tell students to listen for a mistake as you say this sentence: *My mother said, "I am making (mumble, mumble).* Say: The way I read this sentence was confusing because you couldn't hear all the words.

Tell students to listen as you read this sentence: *The weether is cold today.* Say: The way I read this sentence was confusing because I didn't pronounce all the words correctly. Point to the word *weather.* I should have pronounced that word /WETHer/, not /WEETHer/. Then you would have understood me.

Write the sentence below and model reading it two or three times, each time with clearer and more correct pronunciation of the words *wind* and *sky*. Then ask students to read the sentence, pronouncing each word clearly and correctly. *The wind blew the kite across the sky.*

Have students turn to a nonfiction **Student Edition** selection or **Leveled Reader** and choose a section to read fluently. Model reading the passage aloud. Point out how you are reading every word clearly and correctly.

Model how to echo read the passage with a volunteer. Then echo read with the class. Read one sentence at a time and have students echo read it. Remind them to pronounce words clearly and correctly.

Have partners echo read the passage aloud to each other. Tell students to let their partners know if they did not understand a word that was read. Give students one or two comprehension questions about the passage. Have partners discuss the questions. Then discuss the questions as a group.

Corrective Feedback Provide corrective feedback for errors in pronunciation or accuracy. Point out the student's error and model reading the sentence correctly. Have students read the sentences again.

Monkey Business Images/Shutterstock.com

IN PRACTICE

Assess Reading to Inform Instruction

Use these Assessment tools to evaluate student progress in reading and help you make decisions about reading levels, small group instruction, and assignments.

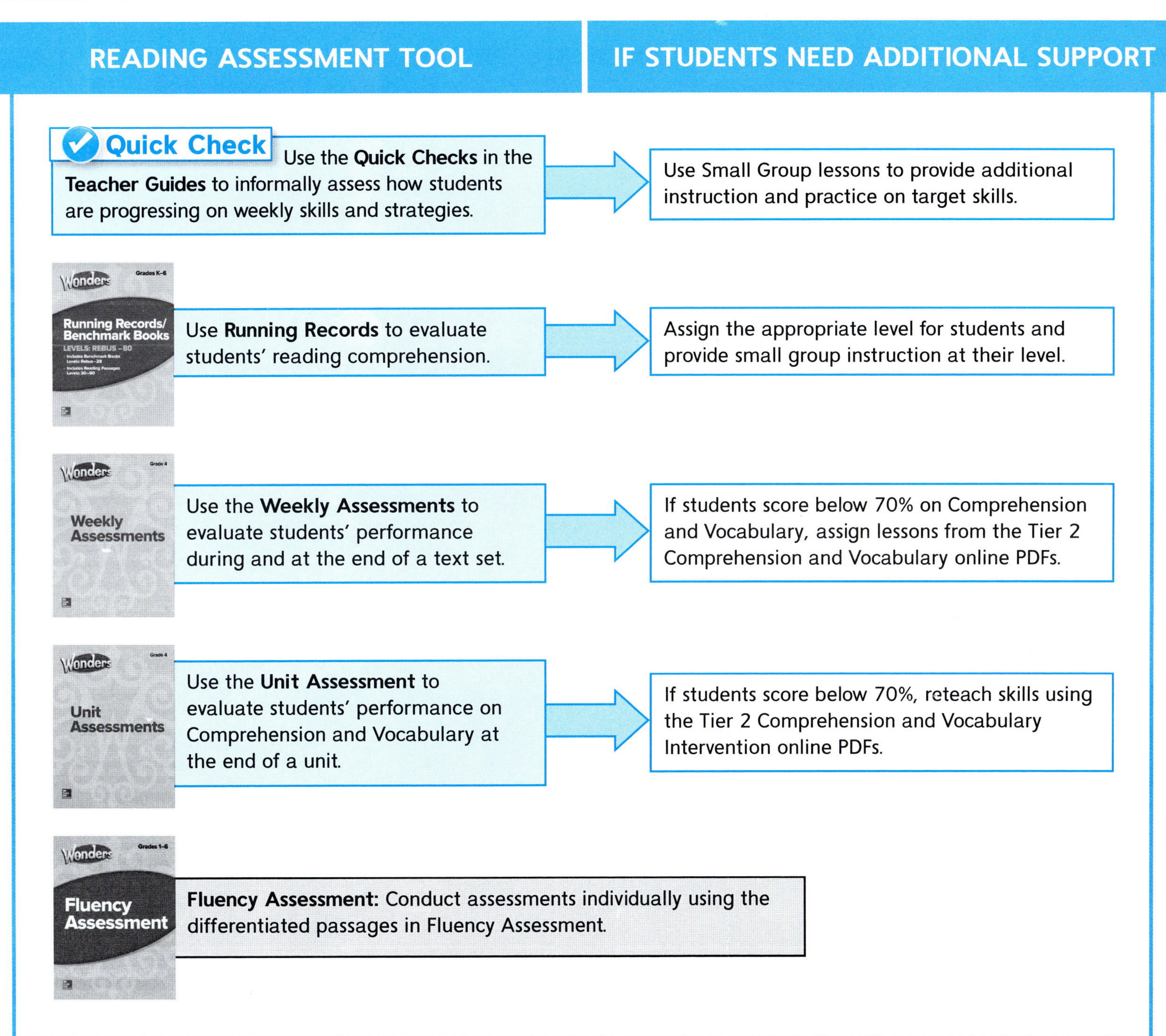

WRITING FROM SOURCES

“To be successful in school and beyond, students must learn to write using the information they have gleaned from the text they have read.”
- *Dr. Douglas Fisher*

By Dr. Douglas Fisher

San Diego State University
Co-Director, Center for the Advancement of Reading, California State University
Author of *Language Arts Workshop: Purposeful Reading and Writing Instruction, Reading for Information in Elementary School;* coauthor of *Close Reading and Writing from Sources, Rigorous Reading: 5 Access Points for Comprehending Complex Text,* and *Text-Dependent Questions, Grades K-5* with N. Frey

Teaching students to write well requires new approaches to instruction. Gone are the days in which teachers can simply assign students a writing prompt and then provide them with feedback based on their responses. Now we have to teach writing, not just assign it. Many educators have always known this, but the new generation of standards demand it. It seems that writing and writing instruction are receiving renewed attention because, as writing professor Leaf Fearn wrote in a personal communication, “Every writer can read, but not every reader can write.”

Graham and Harris (2014, p. 19) note that teaching writing includes four basic writing skills:

1. Learning to write for multiple purposes
2. Producing and publishing well-organized text that is appropriate to the task and purpose by planning, revising, editing, and collaborating with others
3. Using writing to recall, organize, analyze, interpret, and build knowledge about a topic or materials read
4. Applying both extended and shorter writing to facilitate learning of content material

Each of these skills requires instruction and practice. As Shanahan notes (2014, p. 5) “In many ways, the new writing standards aren’t that different from the old ones,” and continues, “That is not to say there are no changes. Perhaps the biggest change in writing goals is that they have been more closely linked to reading.”

There are different ways in which writing is linked to reading. The most direct is when students write about a selection or the topic of a selection. In primary grades, the emphasis on writing about reading is implied, rather than directly required.

Perhaps the biggest change in writing goals is that they have been more closely linked to reading.

michaeljung/Shutterstock.com

In the upper grades, the expectation that students write from the sources they've read is clear. Throughout the grades, students should write their own narrative selections using the texts they read as a model while applying specific genre features from those texts. In these cases, the texts students read serve to mentor them as writers.

To be successful in school and beyond, students must learn to write using the information they have gleaned from text they have read. This requires that students learn to find information, understand that information, and be able to use that information to support the topic of their writing. In other words, writing is more complex than simply teaching students to locate details in the text. They have to learn to strategically use the information they have found.

> In other words, writing is more complex than simply teaching students to locate details in the text.

Instruction That Builds Students' Ability to Locate and Use Evidence

Fisher and Frey (2014) proposed a model for helping students learn to locate and use evidence in their writing. Each of the phases in this model build sequentially, yet are recursive in that earlier components may need to be repeated with new texts. For example, students discussing the evidence from a text may want to go back and read the text more closely. Similarly, when students begin to write from the sources, they may want to revisit their discussions and annotations. For ease in explanation, these steps are presented in a linear fashion, but in practice they can be applied cyclically.

Watch the Videos

See Dr. Douglas Fisher discuss the practice of **"Writing from Sources."**

www.connected.mcgraw-hill.com

Frame the investigation

The process starts with framing the investigation. That may mean that students are exploring a theme or topic and will produce an explanatory piece of text. For example, third graders may be learning about life cycles. Their reading and writing allows them to learn more about this topic. As evidence of their learning, they write explanatory text in response to a writing prompt, but not before engaging in a number of other learning activities.

> Regardless of the source of text, writing begins with the understanding that there is something to learn from the text, which is called the investigation.

Alternatively, framing the investigation may mean that students are exploring an essential question and will be producing original text in which they support their opinion with evidence. For example, a grade 5 class examining the question, "Does equality mean being treated the same?" would read widely on this topic from texts that present divergent views. Students would then choose what view they agreed with and provide evidence for their opinion. Regardless of the source of text, writing begins with the understanding that there is something to learn from the text, which is called the investigation.

Read complex texts closely

Some texts deserve to be read more deeply and carefully (and some do not). Reading closely is a habit that develops over time. Teachers can engage students in close reading lessons that facilitate this habit. Close reading begins with text selection. The text should be appropriately complex. Text complexity is more than the quantitative values. An appropriately complex text also involves the analysis of the qualitative measures within the text, such as density and complexity, levels of meaning, structure and organization, language conventions and clarity, and knowledge demands. Text used for close reading student lessons should also be short. How short has been debated, but the text should be short enough for students to read and reread. That does not mean only stand-alone texts are used, but rather that strategic selections of longer text have been identified.

wavebreakmedia/Shutterstock.com

Monkey Business Images/Shutterstock.com

Close reading also involves rereading. Initial discussions of the text should focus students on the literal level to ensure that they understand the meaning of the text. As students demonstrate this level of understanding, text-dependent questions should be focused on the structure of the text, or how the text works. Over time, the conversation moves to more inferential understanding, with students exploring the meaning of the text.

Complex texts are not easily understood in terms of meaning. Instruction should systematically move students from the literal level, to the structural level, to the inferential level to help them learn from the text, rather than expecting to be told what the text means (Fisher, Frey, Anderson, & Thayre, 2015).

Given that students are expected to use the text later in their discussion and writing, it's helpful for them to annotate the text as they read (Fisher & Frey, 2012). There are any number of annotation systems that can be used to guide students' habit building.

> Initial discussions of the text should focus students on the literal level to ensure that they understand the meaning of the text.

At the elementary level, three foundational annotation skills seem to be most effective:

- *Underline central ideas.* This requires students to identify key information in the text.
- *Circle words or phrases that are confusing or unclear.* This requires that students monitor their understanding of text and allows teachers to notice areas of confusion.
- *Create margin notes.* This requires that students summarize and synthesize their understanding in phrases rather than sentences as they read.

Discuss texts using evidence

Close reading involves student-to-student discussions about the text. Often, their first use of evidence from the text will occur during these collaborative conversations. As others (e.g., Tierney & Shanahan, 1991) have noted, there is a strong relationship between reading and writing. That relationship can be strengthened when students have the opportunity to discuss their ideas from the text before being asked to write about the text. In fact, the speaking and listening standards provide the often-missing link between reading and writing. Students will more easily learn to write from sources when they have opportunities to discuss their ideas.

Teaching students to discuss complex text requires attention and time. Students need to learn the art of argumentation. In this type of conversation, students earn to make a claim, support their claim with evidence, agree and disagree, offer counterclaims, and reach consensus.

Students will more easily learn to write from sources when they have opportunities to discuss their ideas.

Teachers often use sentence frames to guide students' conversations along this sequence. For example, as part of their discussion of a text about the lifecycle of the butterfly, a third grade student said, "The butterfly lifecycle is mainly like the spider's because they both start as eggs." Another student commented, "I agree with you because they both have baby and adult stages." Another said, "I disagree with you because the butterfly comes from a caterpillar and has to change. Spiders grow bigger, but they don't really change." The students in this class are exploring the information they have found and are trying to make sense of it before they write. Their discussions are clarifying in nature and include the elements of good opinion and argument writing. They will be able to take the information they have gathered and combine it with the thinking they have developed.

Write from sources using knowledge gained

Armed with information from excellent sources and an understanding of the task, students are ready to write from the sources they have read. However, this does require the development of a writing prompt. The more detail included in the prompt, the more likely students are to respond correctly. Teachers should provide their own composing processes using evidence from the texts they have read so that students can model the thinking processes used by the teacher to compose text.

A Good Draft

This system should result in students producing reasonably good drafts. And drafts can improve, mainly with feedback from peers and teachers.

It's hard to produce something outstanding if you don't know what constitutes good writing.

As noted in Anchor Standard 5, students should "Develop and strengthen writing as needed by planning, revising, editing, rewriting, or trying a new approach" (NGA Center & CCSSO, 2010, p. 18). This means that students need to write a draft in order to edit and rewrite. It also means that they need clear feedback and examples of what good writing looks like. It's hard to produce something outstanding if you don't know what constitutes good writing. In part, this is addressed as students closely read complex texts. As they do so, they learn about the conventions authors use in different disciplines.

Writing from sources requires that students first read and understand the source. Students should also develop systems for collecting evidence, discussing the evidence, and then using that evidence. As students develop these habits, they will develop a writerly life that allows them to share their thinking with others.

References

Fisher, D., & Frey, N. (2012). Close reading in elementary schools. The Reading Teacher, 66, 179-188.

Fisher, D., & Frey, N. (2014). Close reading and writing from sources. Newark, DE: International Reading Association.

Fisher, D., Frey, N., Anderson, H., & Thayre, M. (2015). Text-dependent questions: Pathways to close and critical reading, grades K-5. Thousand Oaks, CA: Corwin.

Graham, S., & Harris, K.H. (2014). Six recommendations for teaching writing to meet the common core. In K. Ganske (Ed.), Write now! Empowering writers in today's K-6 classroom (pp. 18-33). New York: Guilford.

Shanahan, T. (2014). Writing about reading: Writing instruction in the age of the Common Core State Standards. K. Ganske (Ed.), Write now! Empowering writers in today's K-6 classroom (pp. 3-17). New York: Guilford.

Tierney, R., & Shanahan, T. (1991). Research on the reading-writing relationship: Interactions, transactions, and outcomes. In R. Barr, M.L. Kamil, P. Mosenthal, & P.D. Pearson (Eds.), Handbook of reading research (Vol. 2, pp. 246-280). Mahwah, NJ: Erlbaum.

EFFECTIVE WRITING INSTRUCTION FOR THE BALANCED LITERACY CLASSROOM

By Kathy Rhea Bumgardner, M. Ed.

National Literacy Consultant
North Carolina Educator
Strategies Unlimited, Inc.

Creator of Think Aloud Clouds and Literacy Toolkits for Comprehension; Professional Development Videos for Instructional Best Practices in Literacy

"A balance of whole- and small-group instruction combined with ample independent writing time is key to supporting students in becoming effective and strategic writers."
- Kathy Rhea Bumgardner, M. Ed.

Introduction

To become successful readers, students must read for long stretches of time (Guthrie & Wigfield, 2000). Similarly, writing success is directly correlated to the amount of time spent writing and rewriting (Calkins, Hartman, & White, 2005). In a balanced literacy classroom, students have the opportunity to read and write every day. In a balanced literacy model of writing instruction, the goal is to develop students into lifelong writers who are effective at multiple types of composition.

Balanced literacy teachers must prepare students to meet the rigorous criteria required by the new standards for particular types of writing. Understanding what that looks like in the real world classroom is a daily challenge.

To help clarify how to approach this challenge, this paper will address two major types of writing that students will be asked to produce in a balanced literacy classroom: writing in response to text and writing within a genre. *Wonders Balanced Literacy* provides daily opportunities for both types of writing.

wavebreakmedia/Shutterstock.com

Writing in Response to Texts

When writing in response to text, students respond to a text or texts they have read closely and use text evidence to support their written responses. Reading and writing are closely tied together, and writing instruction is explicitly addressed in the current standards.

At the heart of the instructional shifts for literacy instruction is the requirement that written and oral responses be grounded in text evidence. This requires students to read the text closely to comprehend it on a deeper level and to identify textual evidence to support their ideas and conclusions about the text.

> ...writing success is directly correlated to the amount of time spent writing and rewriting.

When drawing evidence from literary and informational texts, students are required to demonstrate their comprehension skills in relation to the standards. When students are discussing something they have read or written, they must demonstrate their speaking and listening skills.

In *Wonders Balanced Literacy*, writing prompts are included within the reading lessons and are usually labeled "Write to [a selection]" or "Respond and Write". After reading, students are prompted to answer text-dependent questions and to cite evidence in their written responses. Students also have opportunities to share their writing with partners and to discuss how the cited text evidence supports their written ideas.

wavebreakmedia/Shutterstock.com

Genre Writing

The second type of writing is genre writing. Writing within a genre involves identifying a clear purpose and audience and using a style of writing that will successfully communicate key ideas. Students need to be immersed in a genre of writing to understand the structure and craft of each genre. *Wonders Balanced Literacy* provides focused instruction on:

1. Opinion/argument writing

2. Informational/explanatory writing

3. Narrative writing

Writing effectively and thoughtfully on substantive topics in the genres of opinion/argument, informative/explanatory, and narrative are linked directly to college and career readiness (Patterson, 2013).

The Writing Process

During genre writing, students are taught to write using a five-step writing process. Researchers' first attempts to understand what is now called the writing process began in the early 1970s. In 1972, Donald Murray published a brief manifesto titled "Teach Writing as a Process Not Product," an approach that was soon embraced by many writing teachers. Ten years later, in 1982, Maxine Hairston argued that the teaching of writing had undergone a paradigm shift in moving from a focus on written products to writing processes.

The steps in the writing process are:

- Prewrite
- Draft
- Revise
- Edit
- Publish

The Writing Process and Balanced Literacy

Teaching students to follow the writing process works most effectively with a gradual release instructional path that begins with teacher-directed instruction and progresses to independent student practice and application. In a balanced literacy classroom, the progressive stages include the following:

- Modeled writing
- Shared writing
- Guided writing
- Independent writing

Students need to be immersed in a genre of writing to understand the structure and craft of each genre.

As each step of the writing process is taught, teachers can use the gradual release progression to help scaffold the writing steps for students. For example, the Prewrite step may include the teacher sharing several expert writing models of the chosen writing genre. This can be followed by the teacher doing a think-aloud to model for students how to brainstorm a writing topic. The teacher can then scribe for students on a chart during shared writing to create a sample writing outline. Prewriting could continue during small-group guided writing as students create their own outlines and gather text evidence to support their ideas. The Prewrite step might end during independent writing time with one-on-one teacher-student conferencing about each student's writing plan.

Of course, each writing lesson and each group of students may require different levels of instruction. Teachers may or may not go through all four balanced literacy lesson components in every step of the writing process.

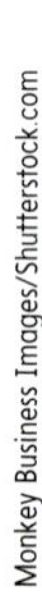
Monkey Business Images/Shutterstock.com

Description of the Writing Process

Prewrite

- Prewriting is the planning step where teachers prepare and guide students to brainstorm and choose their topics, set goals and purpose for writing, gather information, and outline ideas.
- When learning to write within a genre, students need exposure to writing examples of the genre. Exposure to expert and student writing models can begin in the Prewrite step and continue through the subsequent writing steps.
- The teacher must guide the students to consider audience and purpose for writing at this stage, based on the genre of writing to be produced.
- Graphic organizers or diagrams are often used at this stage to help students map out their thoughts.
- If students are writing in the informational or opinion genres, this step will include close reading and gathering of text evidence, which should be taught explicitly in the modeled and shared writing stages.

During the Draft and Revise steps, teachers can use the students' writing as a formative assessment tool to determine where students may need further instruction and scaffolding.

Draft

- Providing modeled and shared writing lessons and referencing expert writing models is critical in the Draft step. Students can then write independently to create their own first draft.
- Students create their initial composition by writing down their ideas in an organized way to convey a particular idea, tell a story, give information, explain a concept or procedure, or present an opinion or argument.
- Teachers will also provide small-group guided writing time for students as appropriate during this step, as well as in the revising and editing steps, to ensure students are moving along proficiently and with understanding.
- The identified audience and purpose for writing need to be carried through in the draft.

Revise

- The goal of the Revise step is to improve the content of the draft. Students should be guided to rearrange, add, and delete content as well as refine word choices and adjust the tone and style as appropriate for the intended purpose and audience.
- As in the Draft step, it is important to provide modeled and shared writing lessons on how to revise.
- Students will tend to be more successful during this step if they are given a clear purpose and focus for their revisions. For example, during narrative writing the teacher may refer back to a mini lesson about dialogue and then have students check the dialogue in their writing to ensure it includes proper punctuation and effectively builds character.
- It is helpful for students to reread their writing and then modify and reorganize their work based on what they hear.
- Small-group guided writing can be most helpful at this step. Through the Revise and Edit steps, students in a balanced literacy classroom can meet in small groups to share their drafts and get feedback (Tompkins, 2013).
- Teacher and peer conferencing is helpful during this step. The teacher will need to provide guided practice for students on how to do peer revisions.
- During the Draft and Revise steps, teachers can use the students' writing as a formative assessment tool to determine where students may need further instruction and scaffolding. The teacher can use this information to create small guided-writing groups and determine the focus of individual writing conferences with students.

Edit

- In the Edit step, writers proofread and correct errors in grammar and mechanics and edit with their eyes to improve style and clarity. They learn to look for and understand the ways in which capitalization, punctuation, and standard usage affect their writing.
- Teacher and peer conferencing is recommended during this step.
- Small-group guided writing that focuses on specific writing conventions can be very helpful to support students at their specific level of need.

Watch the Videos

See Kathy Bumgardner conduct a small group lesson in her video **"Guided and Independent Writing."**

www.connected.mcgraw-hill.com

Publish

- In the Publish step, the final writing is shared with the intended audience.
- Writers receive feedback from peers or the teacher to complete the Publish step to satisfaction.
- Sharing is accomplished through hard copy printing and distributing, blogs, email, webpages, wikis, or other digital publishing forums.

Implementing the Writing Process

The *Wonders Balanced Literacy* Teacher's Guide includes writing lessons for each week of instruction. The online lessons include the specific steps in the writing process that progress through the week and include meaningful links to make the reading-writing connection.

The actual writing that takes place in the classroom may vary from day to day and week to week. Writing processes for some genres may take one week, whereas others may take more or less time. No matter what the specific writing task, the most important criteria is that students write every day.

Not every piece of writing is brought through the complete writing process, but students should be offered multiple opportunities to prewrite, draft, revise, edit, and share writing with others as they develop into proficient readers and writers.

As teachers work with students to implement the writing process, a balance of whole- and small-group instruction combined with ample independent writing time is key to supporting students in becoming effective and strategic writers.

References

Calkins, L., Hartman, A., & White, Z. R. (2005). *One to one: The art of conferring with young writers.* Chicago: Heinemann.

Coleman, D., & Pimentel, S. (2011). *Publishers' criteria for the Common Core State Standards in English Language Arts and Literacy, grades 3–12.* Washington, DC: CCSSO & NASBE.

Gewertz, C. (2012). Common standards drive new reading approaches. *Education Week,* 32(12), S2.

Guthrie, J. T., & Wigfield, A. (2000). Engagement and motivation in reading. In M. L. Kamil, P. B. Mosenthal, P. D. Pearson, & R. Barr (Eds.), *Handbook of reading research: Volume III* (pp. 403–422). New York: Erlbaum.

Hairston, M. (2009). The winds of change: Thomas Kuhn and the revolution in the teaching of writing In Susan Miller (Ed.), *The Norton Book of Composition Studies.* New York: Norton. (Reprinted from *College Composition and Communication* 33(1), pp. 76–88, 1982, Urbana, IL: National Council of Teachers)

Murray, D. M. (2003). Teach writing as a process not product. In Victor Villanueva (Ed.), *Cross-Talk in Comp Theory*, 2nd ed. Urbana, OH: NCTE. (Reprinted from *The Leaflet,* November 1972)

National Governors Association Center for Best Practices & Council of Chief State School Officers. (2010). *Common Core State Standards for English language arts and literacy in history/social studies, science, and technical subjects*. Washington, DC: Authors.

Patterson, J. P. (2013). Preface: *The story of* In Common: *Where the Standards meet the students.* New York: Vermont Writing Collaborative, with Student Achievement Partners and CCSSO. Retrieved from achievethecore.org

Tompkins, G. E. (2010, 2013). *Literacy for the 21st century: A balanced approach* (5th Ed.) Upper Saddle River, NJ: Pearson.

Write to Sources

OVERVIEW OF WRITING

The *Wonders Balanced Literacy* program provides instruction in writing to sources and genre writing throughout grades K-5. Students use the writing process and learn to employ specific writing traits as they develop their writing.

In the Write to Sources lessons, students are expected to write to a prompt that requires them to support a particular opinion with text evidence, provide information about a topic, and make inferences in order to add an event to a narrative. Students must use the details of what is explicitly stated in the text to make valid claims and inferences that support their argument or explanations. Some of the meaningful writing tasks to help students engage more deeply with a text include:

- quick writes to build writing fluency
- taking notes on text evidence
- writing to one or more sources
- comparing and contrasting texts

KINDERGARTEN: WRITING TO SOURCES

In Kindergarten, students participate in Shared, Interactive and Independent writing lessons each week. During Shared Writing, students work together to analyze and respond to a prompt after reading a Literature Big Book. Teachers guide students through the process of responding to the prompt by modeling rereading to identify and record text evidence.

A second prompt offers the opportunity for students to write interactively. After rereading a portion of the Literature Big Book, students learn to form and write complete sentences as they respond to the prompt or question. Teachers share the pen with students, as necessary.

Then students move on to writing independently after a Shared Reading of a short text in the Student Edition. Students analyze a model of student writing to see how specific writing traits are used. Then students are guided to respond to a writing prompt. Students work through each stage of the writing process, engage in a peer review session following the revision of their first draft and a teacher conference after completing a final draft. Students then present, self-evaluate, and publish their written pieces. See page 81 for a detailed description of the writing process.

Students also have the opportunity to write, with guidance, to the Leveled Readers and Classroom Library selections.

GRADE 1: WRITING TO SOURCES

In Grade 1, students participate in Shared, Interactive and Independent writing instruction each week. Grade 1 students learn to:

- Connect sounds to spellings
- Write complete sentences
- Write to sources
- Focus on writing brief narrative, informational, and opinion pieces. (See Genre Writing, page 78 for more information.)

During Shared and Interactive writing students read a short complex text in the Student Edition. Then the teacher models and guides students in identifying text evidence to respond to the prompt. The teacher records students' responses. Then students are given a second prompt to respond to and the teacher works with students to find text evidence to answer it. Students are encourage to now share the pen with the teacher, thus gradually releasing responsibility for writing to students.

Students then independently write to a Your Turn writing prompt in the Student Edition. Before they begin writing, they analyze a student model of writing and learn about the writing traits the student used. Students are encouraged to include these writing traits in their own writing.

In *Wonders Balanced Literacy*, students can also write to the Leveled Readers, Classroom Library selections, or to a text from the Unit Bibliography or Literature eBooks online.

GRADES 2-5: WRITING TO SOURCES

In Grades 2-5, students write to a short read, the Classroom Library selection and to Leveled Readers in each text set. Students learn to:

- Write strong paragraphs and simple multi-paragraph compositions
- Employ writing traits, including Ideas, Organization, Sentence Fluency, Word Choice, and Voice
- Write to sources
- Focus on writing narratives, informative/expository pieces, opinion texts, and research papers. (See page 78 for more information on Genre Writing.)

For each text set, students practice writing fluency by writing to a prompt that relates to the week's short complex text from the Student Edition. When students finish writing, partners collaborate and compare responses. As in Kindergarten and Grade 1, students in Grades 2-5 work together to analyze a grade level appropriate student model that features writing traits that students should strive to use in their own writing. Students then independently write to the Your Turn writing prompt in the Student Edition.

Additional texts for students to write to include the Leveled Readers, Classroom Library selections, and the selections from the Unit Bibliography and Literature eBooks online.

WRITING TRAITS AND SKILLS

To help students develop writing proficiency and create effective writing pieces, *Wonders Balanced Literacy* teaches students how to analyze models of writing for specific traits and skills. These include:

- Organization
- Ideas
- Voice
- Sentence Fluency
- Word Choice

Each week the writing trait and skill is taught and practiced in the context of the genre of the text set. Students write a short response, using the writing trait of the week. Additionally, the writing process genre lessons in each unit requires students to incorporate the writing trait in an extended piece of writing.

Online Support The Writer's Workspace online provide Writing Trait minilessons that connect to a short student model of writing in the Student Edition.

After analyzing the student model, students learn how to apply writing traits to their writing, which they can produce and publish on Writer's Workspace.

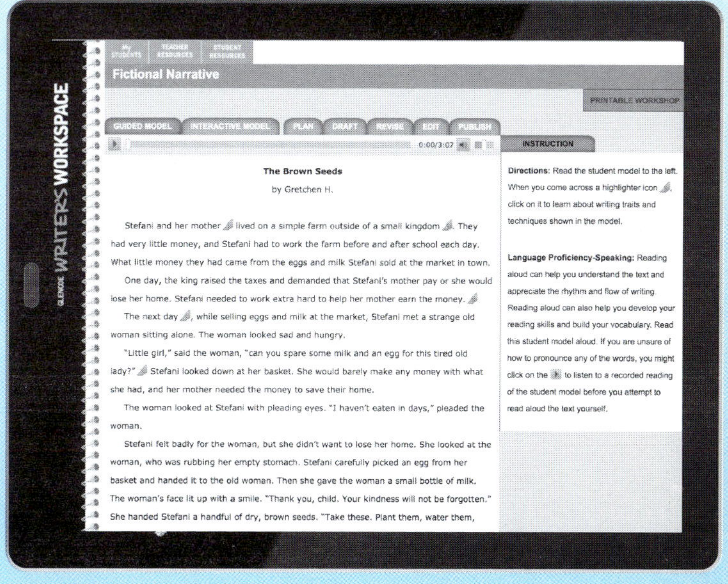

Genre Writing

OVERVIEW

Wonders Balanced Literacy offers focused instruction on writing for different purposes and audiences. Students learn to write in different genres for their intended purposes. The writing forms cover narrative, informational, and opinion writing. After reading and rereading a text, students develop an understanding of genre-specific characteristics and traits in writing. They then use this knowledge as they begin the writing process.

In *Wonders Balanced Literacy,* the writing process is broken down so that students work on one part of the process at a time: prewrite, draft, revise, edit and present/publish. During the writing process, explicit instruction in writing forms, traits and grammar skills is provided to support students' development as writers.

KINDERGARTEN AND GRADE 1

In Kindergarten and Grade 1, genre instruction is woven into the instruction for the text sets. Repeated exposure and instruction in genre characteristics help students develop a common vocabulary for talking about texts. Students gain an appreciation for the variety of different genres and authors and make connections across texts.

During Independent Writing, students write in the genre of the texts in the text sets. Students integrate what they have learned from the texts they have read as they write. Instruction is broken down into steps and students write an extended piece over the course of 3 days. As the year progresses, students encounter increasingly difficult texts within a particular genre and continue to expand their knowledge of writing forms and the corresponding genre characteristics.

GRADES 2-5

In Grades 2 through 5, you can find the extended genre writing lessons online. At the beginning of each lesson, students review the attributes of specific forms of narrative and informational writing, such as fantasy or biography, by examining an Expert Model. Students then begin to plan their writing by choosing a purpose and audience. Minilessons for writing traits and grammar skills are provided to help students sharpen their writing skills. Students then use the writing process to create an extended piece of writing. Graphic organizers are provided to help students organize their thoughts. Minilessons on revising their work as well as teacher and peer conferencing routines are provided to help students revise and strengthen their writing. For the final presentation of their writing, students are provided with print and digital options for publishing their work. Student rubrics and anchor papers are provided to help students evaluate their work.

Peer and Teacher Conferences are also included in the genre writing lessons. Partners can review one another's writing after they have revised their initial drafts. Students can engage in a Teacher Conference upon completion of a final draft.

WRITER'S WORKSPACE ONLINE

The Writer's Workspace online provides a digital pathway for students to produce and publish their writing. Writer's Workspace takes students through each step of the writing process in a digital environment. Instruction, models, rubrics, checklists, grammar and usage references and other important writing support are included to assist students at each stage of the writing process. Students compose their own pieces of extended writing that cover narrative, informational, and opinion genres.

NARRATIVE	INFORMATIVE	OPINION
■ Personal Narrative	■ Research Report	■ Book Review
■ Fictional Narrative	■ Explanatory Essay	■ Opinion Essay
■ Autobiographical Sketch	■ Informational Article	■ Opinion Letter
■ Poetry	■ Summary	
■ Friendly Letter	■ How-to	
	■ Feature Article	
	■ Compare and Contrast	
	■ Invitation with Directions	

TEACHER CONFERENCING

As students work on their writing, it is a good time to walk around the room and confer with them. Conferences should be brief touchpoints where the teacher observes what students are trying to do as writers. Note what the student is doing and if they are make progress on their goals. Decide what you need to teach the student. Then after teaching the student, remind them to use this skill as they write.

To support their extended genre writing assignments, use the following tools to support students.

- Use the Rubric and Anchor Papers provided online in Writer's Workspace as you evaluate student writing. The anchor papers provide samples of papers that score from 1 to 4. These papers reflect the criteria described in the Rubric. Anchor papers offer a standard against which to judge writing.
- Review with individual students the writing goals they have set. Discuss ways to achieve these goals and suggest any further areas of improvement students may need to target.
- As you review students' writing, be sure to talk about the strengths of the writing, focus on how the writer uses text evidence, and offer concrete suggestions for revision.
- When you provide feedback, provide specific direction to help focus young writers.

  Focus on a Sentence: Read the draft and target one sentence for revision.

  Focus on a Section: Underline a section that needs to be revised.

  Focus on a Revision Strategy: Have students use a specific revision strategy, such as replacing.

Anchor Papers • 10

Friendly Letter Score: 4 Points

155 President Street
Brooklyn, NY 11201
February 5, 2014

Dear Brad,

Moving from Florida to Brooklyn, New York, was like moving to another world. First of all, my family arrived with only what we'd crammed into the trunk of our car. The shipping company was three days late delivering our furniture and boxes of personal belongings. We had to sleep on padding on the floor, and eat on paper plates with plastic forks and knives. That was okay. On our first day, my dad got us all to pretend we were camping. My mom let us all have extra dessert too.

Right away, I missed my old house and my friends. My two little sisters complained about being bored, but at least they had each other to play with. On our second day in Brooklyn, Mom announced in a cheerful voice, "It's time to rally the troops!" Then we played an old board game, and Dad told us about all the wonderful things we are going to do and see in New York. Somehow, Dad and Mom made us laugh and laugh.

I was shocked by how cold winter is here. There is snow on the ground and snow that covers the trees. There is snow and ice everywhere.

One day Mom bundled us up and took us to a big park called Prospect Park. It was like we were leaving the city and going to a frozen wilderness. Mom said bears do not live in the park, except maybe in the park's zoo, but my silly sisters pretended that they saw one anyhow. I made Mom promise to take us to that zoo real soon.

Now we have our furniture, and everything else we packed from Florida. I've even started my new school here. There are other boys in my class who moved to Brooklyn not very long ago. These kids say they like it here, even though it is very different from where they used to live. I think I'm going to like it here too.

Your friend,
Jimmy

Writing Rubric • 9

Friendly Letter Rubric	
4 Excellent	• gives a lively, interesting, and detailed description of an event or personal experience • follows letter format • uses sequence words to tell events in a logical, easy-to-follow order • the strong beginning introduces the topic of the letter • uses rich descriptive details • supports ideas with information • has a variety of sentences that flow • is free or almost free of all errors
3 Good	• tells about a personal experience or event with details • has few or no errors in letter format • uses some sequence words and presents events in logical order • the beginning gives some details about the topic • includes a few descriptive details • makes an effort to support ideas with information • has a variety or sentences • has a few errors but is easy to read
2 Fair	• tries to describe a personal experience or topic but lacks details • does not use sequence words and tells some events in confused order • the introduction is weak • provides very few descriptive details • shows little personal involvement • sentences are mostly the same • frequent errors make it hard to understand

PEER CONFERENCING

Peer conferencing is an effective way to help students improve their writing. In Grades K-1, after proofreading their work, students can exchange their drafts and take turns editing them against the weekly skills listed in the Independent Writing assignments. Encourage partners to discuss and fix errors together as they read.

For Grades 2-5, use peer conferencing with the extended genre writing assignments. Use the following materials from the on-ling Genre writing lessons to support writing instruction:

- Have students refer to the Rubric and Anchor Papers while drafting and editing their pieces. Also have them use the Checklist (shown below) to Revise and Edit their work.
- Students can use the Rubric during peer conferences to evaluate classmates' works and provide feedback.
- Review with students the routine for peer review of writing:
  - Listen carefully as the writer reads his or her work aloud.
  - Begin by telling what you liked about the writing.
  - Ask a question that will help the writer think more about the writing.
  - Make a suggestion that will make the writing stronger.

Name ______________________ Date __________

Directions: Use these checklists as you work with peers and work alone to revise and edit your friendly letters.

Revise Checklist

- ☐ Does the letter tell about an important event?
- ☐ Does the letter include a heading with the sender's address and a date?
- ☐ Does the letter include a greeting?
- ☐ Do the opening paragraphs introduce the topic of the letter?
- ☐ Is there friendly and informal tone?
- ☐ Does the letter describe events to a friend or family member?
- ☐ Are sequence words used to help order the events?
- ☐ Are there concrete or sensory details that help explain the writer's ideas?
- ☐ Does the conclusion tell how the writer feels about the experience?
- ☐ Are there a variety of sentences that help make the writing flow?

Edit Checklist

- ☐ Do all sentences begin with a capital letter and end with the correct punctuation mark?
- ☐ Are sentences complete with a subject and predicate?
- ☐ Do verbs agree with their subjects?
- ☐ Are commas used correctly?
- ☐ Are all words spelled correctly?

Unit 1 • Friendly Letter • 8

Watch the Videos

See the **Study Sync Collaborative Conversations Video: Peer Conferencing** to see a model of how students can review their work with one another.

www.connected.mcgraw-hill.com

The Writing Process

Use the writing process below to guide students as they independently write to a source or genre.

STEP 1: PREWRITE

- Writers think about and plan their topic.
- Writers use graphic organizers and other visual devices to help them organize their thinking.
- Writers consider their audience, purpose for writing, and the focus of their topic.
- Writers gather ideas and information, using outside resources as needed. They decide which information to include in their draft.

TIP: Distribute copies of the **Rubric** and **Anchor Papers** for the target genre.

STEP 2: DRAFT

- Writers draft, or put their initial ideas about the topic, into written words.
- Writers use their initial prewriting plans as a guide. They expand or modify these plans as needed.
- The first draft is often in rough form.

TIP: Review the expert model prior to students beginning their drafts.

STEP 3: REVISE

- Writers revisit their drafts to revise for content and structure.
- Writers carefully reread their drafts to make sure all critical information is included, the meaning is clear, and to consider the impact and effectiveness the piece will have on the audience.

TIPS: Use the Anchor Papers as models for students during this stage. Have students refer to the genre rubric as they consider their revisions.

Remind students that revising for conventions of Standard English will improve the effectiveness of their writing.

Model examples for students.

STEP 4: EDIT/PROOFREAD

- Writers revisit their pieces to correct grammar, mechanics, and usage errors.
- Writers understand the importance of creating correct pieces for their audience.

TIPS: Use the **Proofreading Marks Checklist** in the *Teacher's Resource Book.*

Use the **Grammar Handbook** in the **Student Edition** to edit their writing.

STEP 5: PUBLISH

- Writers create a final version of the piece using their best handwriting or a computer software program. This final form reflects their best efforts.

TIP: Use this time as an opportunity to teach or reinforce handwriting and keyboarding skills.

STEP 6: PRESENT AND EVALUATE

- Writers share their pieces with their audience (often classmates) and receive feedback on its content and impact.
- As appropriate, writers incorporate visual displays and other media in their presentations.

TIP: Use the **Speaking and Listening Checklists** in the *Teacher's Resource Book.*

Watch the Videos

See the **Study Sync Collaborative Conversations Video: How to Give a Presentation** to see a model of how to present student work.

www.connected.mcgraw-hill.com

Guidelines for Peer Conferences

TAG
Writing Conference

Tell something you like about the writing.

A

Ask a question about the writing.

Give a suggestion of something to add to the writing.

TAG
Writing Conference

- I really like how you say...
- My favorite part is...
- What I like about your picture is...

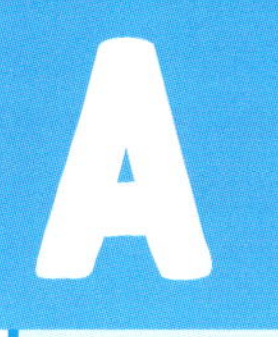

- What does that mean?
- What happened next?
- What else...?

- Can I suggest you add...?
- I think you need another detail...
- Add to your picture...

Assess Writing to Inform Instruction

Use these Assessment tools to evaluate student progress in writing and help you make decisions about small group instruction, conferences and assignments.

WRITING ASSESSMENT TOOL	IF STUDENTS NEED ADDITIONAL SUPPORT
 Use the **Weekly Assessment** Writing Prompts to evaluate students' performance at the end of a text set for Grade 1. For Grades 2-5, use the Weekly Assessment Constructed Response item during and at the end of the text set.	If students score below "3" on the Constructed Response item, assign lessons from the **Tier 2 Comprehension Intervention** PDFs.
 Use the **Unit Assessment** Short Response, Constructed Response and Performance-Based Task on a previously taught genre to evaluate students' performance on Writing at the end of the Unit for Grades 2-5. For the Unit Assessments in mid-Grade 1, students craft a written response to a prompt in a previously-taught genre. In Grade K they are given a prompt on the unit topic to write to.	If students score less than "2" on short response items and "3" on extended constructed response items, then reteach skills using appropriate lessons from the Strategies and Skills and/or Write About Reading sections in the **Tier 2 Comprehension Intervention** online PDFs.
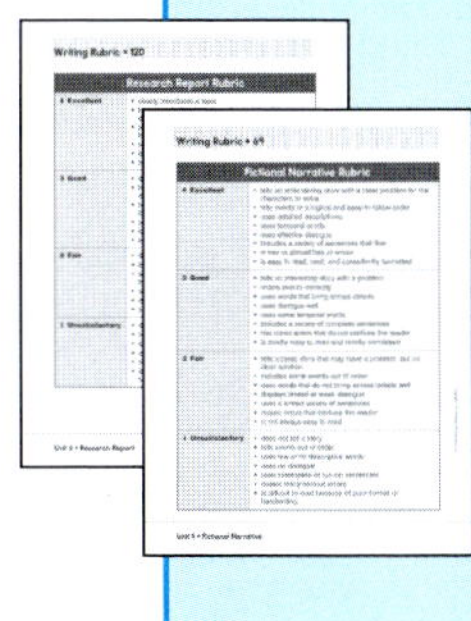 Use the Genre rubrics found in the Genre lessons on Writer's Workspace online to assess Genre Writing for Grades 2-5. For Grades K and 1, assess progress on the weekly Independent Writing by evaluating the student's ability to write in the genre, organize their writing, apply the weekly writing trait and grammar skill.	If students need support, use the Writer's Workspace lessons and the Writing Trait minilessons online for Grades 2-5. For supporting students in Grade K and 1, use the weekly Shared and Interactive Writing lessons in the Teacher's Guides to guide and reinforce writing skills.

ACADEMIC VOCABULARY STUDY: EMBEDDED, DEEP AND GENERATIVE PRACTICES

"Vocabulary standards highlight teaching academic vocabulary as a major instructional shift to improve students' ability to Access Complex Text."
- *Dr. Donald R. Bear*

By Dr. Donald R. Bear

Iowa State University
Professor, Iowa State University
Author of *Words Their Way, Words Their Way with English Learners, Vocabulary Their Way,* and *Words Their Way with Struggling Readers, 4-12*

Introduction

Vocabulary is derived from the Latin word *vox* (*voice in English*). With our vocabularies, we *call out and give voice* to new ideas and concepts that beg to be named. And due to its prominence, new ideas are added to English vocabulary, which just recently surpassed one million words. Vocabulary knowledge is crucial to successful comprehension—current standards recognize this, and take a fresh look at vocabulary learning. In particular, standards now highlight teaching academic vocabulary as a major instructional shift to improve students' ability to ACT (Access Complex Text). Two types of academic vocabulary have been described: general and domain-specific. General academic vocabulary are composed of words and phrases found in all academic texts, such as *analysis, attribute, contrast, discussion, however,* and *in particular*. These general academic words are similar to Tier 2 words. Domain-specific academic vocabulary include specialized vocabulary, and are usually related to a particular field of study like the word *photosynthesis* in biology, *parallelogram* in geometry, and *democratic republic* in social studies or government.

When teachers plan instruction, they examine texts for general and domain-specific vocabulary to explore in more depth; they look for the academic vocabulary that will serve students consistently as tools in their reading and writing. This paper presents principles of academic vocabulary learning and instruction, followed by several practices to help students acquire the ability to learn new ideas and vocabulary, and to name and implement these newly-learned concepts.

General and Domain-Specific Academic Vocabulary

A comparison of two words further illustrates the differences between general and domain-specific vocabulary. This exploration lays the groundwork for the principles and activities for teaching vocabulary.

wavebreakmedia/Shutterstock.com

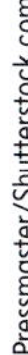
Pressmaster/Shutterstock.com

Procedure – A General Academic Vocabulary Word

The word *procedure* is a *general academic* word because this word can be found in many content areas. Consider words related to procedure: *proceed, procedural, procedurally,* and *procedures*. These are not many words to draw on, but learning can be much deeper when the context of *procedure* is broadened in phrases like the following: *bureaucratic procedure, cataloged procedure, civil procedure, contingency procedure, diagnostic procedure, emergency procedure, operating procedure, parliamentary procedure, standard operating procedure (SOP), standard procedure, standing operating procedure, and surgical procedure* (www.onelook.com).

Tectonic – A Domain-Specific Vocabulary Word

A domain-specific word like *tectonic* has both literal and figurative meanings, but for the most part, the use of the word is found in geology and physics. As you may recall, earthquakes and tsunamis can be caused by tectonic shifts in which two landmasses collide. In a dictionary search, other forms of the word are found: *tectonics, tectonical, tectonically, textonism, tectonite, tectonism, tectono, tectonometer, tectonophysicist, tectonophysics*, and *tectonosphere*. While students benefit just from reading and thinking of the meaning of these variations, most of these forms are simple grammatical shifts.

Consider how much more meaning is brought to the adjective *tectonic* when the search is broadened to phrases: *tectonic-uplift, tectonic activity, tectonic basins and rift valleys, tectonic boundary, tectonic breccia, tectonic change of sea level, tectonic conglomerate, tectonic creep, tectonic earthquake, tectonic environment, tectonic gap, tectonic keratoplasty, tectonic map, tectonic motion, tectonic movement, tectonic plates, tectonic stratigraphy, tectonic theater project, tectonic theory, tectonic window, tectonically active, and tectonics zones of Pakistan* (www. onelook.com). Students' sense of the word tectonic becomes deeper as they consider the meaning of these phrases. All but two of these phrases relate to science, particularly geology. As a classroom activity, students could work with partners to uncover the meaning of a few phrases that they then would share with their classmates either orally or in a classroom vocabulary notebook.

With our vocabularies we call out and give voice to new ideas and concepts that beg to be named.

When *tectonics* is scrutinized morphologically for its root, other related words come into play—words that, again, deepen understanding. *Tectonics* was used in geology for the first time in writing in 1899, and is derived from Latin and Greek terms related to building which can be found in *architect*—literally, the chief (*arch*) builder (*tect*). What a wonderful story this makes, but this may be as far as most students examine the word. You'll find, though, as intermediate grade students become more accustomed to using etymological resources, they become enticed to look more deeply to learn that *tek-* is the Indo-European root for "to make" and is the root of words like *textile* and *texture*. Vocabulary study makes us deeper thinkers. The free etymological resources used in the explorations shared here are presented in the activities to follow.

Five Principles of Academic Vocabulary Instruction

These five principles of vocabulary study can serve as a guide to organize instruction, and they highlight the profound role vocabulary has in expanding students' thinking.

1. Vocabulary learning is intertwined with concept development.

Words describe ideas, and, in discussions of vocabulary, students expand and refine their thinking. The key to vocabulary learning is to uncover the concepts that underlie the vocabulary.

2. Vocabulary is learned in context.

Students learn new vocabulary through extensive reading and writing. It is impossible to teach students all of the vocabulary words they need to know. Rather, the goal is to teach students how to examine and think about words. Teachers show students routines like those that follow to investigate the meanings of new vocabulary as they read for comprehension and write for clarity of expression.

3. Vocabulary is not about teaching just words.

To learn new vocabulary, students need to examine phrases lodged in sentences and paragraphs. The importance of phrases in the discussion of teaching related words can be seen in the examples above. The days of learning a random list of vocabulary words are over; vocabulary must come from the texts students are studying and must be supported by plenty of examples.

4. Vocabulary instruction is deep and generative.

"When students learn one word, they learn ten words," said a good teaching friend, Tamara Baren. As in the examples above, studying related words and phrases widens the context for vocabulary learning. In deep word study, students examine related words and phrases, and this expands their knowledge of the concepts of underlying words.

5. Vocabulary instruction involves the study of morphology, the structure of words.

In vocabulary instruction, students learn the meanings of prefixes and suffixes, and this makes it possible for them to derive the meaning of base words and roots. English grammar is incorporated naturally in vocabulary study as students examine what happens when suffixes are added to bases and roots. For example, they see that *compete*, a verb, turns into a noun when *-tion* is added, or that an adjective is formed from a noun when *-ance* is added to a word (*brilliant/brilliance*). The reading fluency of intermediate readers advances as they learn about words morphologically. In the very beginning of an eye fixation, mature readers peel off the affixes very rapidly (30 milliseconds) to get at the meaning of the roots and base words.

Based on these principles, and with this distinction between types of academic vocabulary in focus, activities to scaffold students' learning of academic vocabulary, both general and domain-specific, can be examined.

Monkey Business Images/Shutterstock.com

Figure 1

Civil War Concept Sort		
Military	**Political**	**Miscellaneous**
South	secession	antebellum
ambush	abolitionist	reconstruction
Appomattox Court House	John Brown	
Fort Sumter	Confederacy	
Ulysses S. Grant	free state	
Union	slavery	
blockade	Confederate States of America	
infantry	Emancipation Proclamation	
John Brown	Dred Scott decision	
Harpers Ferry	border states	
Robert E. Lee	Federal	
conscription	Frederick Douglas	
arsenal	Fugitive Slave Act	
Yankee	sectionalism	
Rebels	Stephen Douglas	
artillery	Gettysburg Address	
Battle of Bull Run / Manassas	Kansas-Nebraska Act	
Battle of Gettysburg	popular sovereignty	
brigade	prejudice	
Clara Barton	Republican Party	
Jefferson Davis	Abraham Lincoln	
ironclads	Lincoln / Douglas debates	
North	Missouri Compromise	
regiment	states rights	
skirmish	Thirteenth Amendment	

Reflection: The first column includes terms about war, its battles and famous soldiers. The second column has a lot of difficult concepts that I need to learn more about. It includes people and terms related to slavery. I do not know what the words in the third column have to do with the Civil War.

Vocabulary Activities

Teachers establish several key vocabulary activities that, once taught, are used throughout the school year. Here are four activities that are a part of many teachers' vocabulary study routines.

Vocabulary Concept Sorts

Vocabulary concept sorts are used at all grade levels with either words or pictures. To create a concept sort, teachers review the text for vocabulary study, including the bolded vocabulary. These words and phrases can be written onto a template with twenty-four boxes in three columns and eight rows. Often with a partner, students cut up the template and then sort the items according to the teachers' instructions. One rule is that students must say the words aloud quietly as they sort. To bypass the use of a sorting template, students can work from a randomized list of the vocabulary. Students then write the words into the appropriate meaning connection columns. Figure 1 presents an example of a written sort for the Civil War. Sorting with partners and sharing the sorts in heterogeneous groups adds the support needed for students reading below level: if they have difficulty reading the words, they learn from their classmates as they read the words. They also learn new ideas when they share their rationales for their sorts.

Students learn new vocabulary through extensive reading and writing.

Sorts can be described as either closed sorts, in which the teacher defines the sorting categories, or as open sorts, in which students create the categories. Usually, teachers will begin with closed sorts to give students a sense of how vocabulary is sorted conceptually. Students usually write these sorts into their vocabulary notebooks. Occasionally, teachers have students generate a written reflection to explain why they sorted each column the way they did. In English and the Language Arts, these concept sorts focus on figurative language in which students sort synonyms and examine nuances in words, or sort words by suffixes and parts of speech.

Concept sorts can be conducted at the beginning, middle, and end of a unit of study, and can be considered formative assessments. At the beginning of a unit, teachers can see if students can read the words accurately, which helps them understand students' conceptual knowledge prior to formal studies. In the middle and end of a unit, teachers can see how easily students sort, as the students are asked to add related terms. Teachers and students alike can see how well they have generalized the ideas and concepts in the unit.

To build independence and ownership, ask students to work with partners and small groups to choose vocabulary in their texts that they think is important to study.

Picture sorts are conducted mainly in the primary grades when students are unable to read the vocabulary they are asked to sort. Furthermore, they are particularly useful for English learners when they do not know the words in English. With partners, students sort the pictures and then give their reasons for sorting the way they did. In bilingual settings, picture sorts are a way for students to share the vocabularies of their primary languages. The picture sorts provide additional experience with vocabulary from read alouds; for example, after a read aloud of Tops and Bottoms (Stevens, 1995), students sort pictures of parts of plants conceptually. In one study, students involved in sorting the pictures from their read alouds heard the words over fifty times, and, in a delayed recall, they knew twice as many words as students who only heard the stories read aloud (Carpenter, 2010).

Vocabulary Self-assessments

After selecting the vocabulary to study for a unit, teachers should ask students to rate their knowledge of the vocabulary. Figure 2 illustrates a student's self-assessment of his knowledge of two terms: abolitionist and Dred Scott Decision. The form has room for students to assess their knowledge at three points over their studies. In this example, it is clear that Antonio could learn more about the Dred Scott Decision. Teachers usually include ten to fifteen items and leave a few rows for students to add other vocabulary they think is important.

Figure 2

Example of a Vocabulary Self-Assessment Chart

Title: Civil War	**Name:** Antonio Estrada		**Codes and Dates** X February 15 ✓ February 23 ¢ March 8	
Knowledge Rating of Vocabulary	**Never heard of it**	**Heard it**	**Have some ideas**	**Know it well**
abolitionist	X			✓ someone who wanted to abolish slavery
Dred Scott Decision	X	✓	¢ decision by Supreme Court, slaves as property	

Vocabulary Notebooks

To build independence and ownership, ask students to work with partners and small groups to choose vocabulary in their texts that they think is important to study. The vocabulary students choose are usually the same as what their teachers would select, and teachers add vocabulary students have overlooked. Vocabulary notebooks are a place for students to record vocabulary they find interesting and which they study deeply. There are six steps to create an entry, as illustrated in Figure 3 (Bear, et al, 2012).

Teachers model vocabulary selections and the deep study of words several times before asking students to work independently or with a partner to create their own entries. Modeling includes showing students how to use dictionaries and etymological references to create their entries. Each week, students study several words in-depth, and then teach their classmates what they learned. They may share their work orally, in an electronic, class vocabulary notebook, or create a chart to post in the room. Students familiar with other languages may include cognates in their entries. With 10,000 to 15,000 cognates between English and Spanish, students may include Spanish vocabulary. Vocabulary notebooks can be divided into separate sections by domain.

Figure 3

abolitionist – someone against slavery		
abolish abolition abolished *Spanish: abolir, abolicionista*	-tion	-ist
abolitio, from abolere to destroy	condition attention	chemist geologist
to get rid of	changes to a noun	changes to a person
"The defeat taught Lincoln that abolitionists and other extreme antislavery men would rather be right...." p. 84		

Vocabulary Notebook Entry Directions

1. ***Collect the word.*** Find an important, interesting, or difficult word. Read around the word and think about its possible meaning.

2. ***Record the word.*** and sentence. Sometimes sentences are too long, so parts of the sentence can be recorded.

3. ***"Take apart."*** Separate word parts - prefixes, suffixes, roots, and bases.

4. ***Think of related words.*** Brainstorm related words by word parts—prefixes, suffixes, roots, and bases.

5. ***Study the word in the dictionary and other resources, and record related words and interesting information.***

6. ***Review and share.*** Prepare an explanation for each word part to share with classmates.

Online Resources

There are numerous dictionaries and etymological websites for students to refer to as they study their vocabulary. At these sites, students can find related words, word histories, explanations of word roots, and examples of the words used in context. Access to these resources may require a request to instructional technology personnel to lower firewalls for students. Experience with these websites teaches students how to use dictionaries and other vocabulary resources.

Below are a few favorite vocabulary websites. While these sites are free, there are advertisements in each.

- ***www.onelook.com*** is a powerful website. Typing in a word sometimes reveals twenty links to various dictionaries. Using their simple codes, students can easily call up a thousand related words. For example, typing syn* presents a thousand words that begin with this prefix, which means together.
- ***www.etymonline.com*** is one of the best websites to provide etymologies. Students learn about word origins as well as short, quaint stories of how the words have been used over time.
- ***www.myEtymology.com*** is an etymological dictionary that lists related words from many other languages. Its first display presents links to the various parts of the word queried, its affixes and root, as well as its cognates in other languages.
- ***www.visuwords.com*** is a graphical dictionary that creates webs with the different meanings of words positioned around the word requested. Each of the branches in the web presents a link to related words, as well as a link to antonyms. In addition, different parts of the web represent various attributes and parts of speech for the word that is being studied.
- ***www.yourdictionary.com,*** like many dictionary sites, provides a brief definition of the word, a pronunciation of the word, and several examples of the word used in sentences.
- ***www.collinsdictionary.com*** is one of the best dictionaries for images. It also provides translations in French, German, and Spanish.

Monkey Business Images/Shutterstock.com

Using these resources to study vocabulary makes it possible for students to study words deeply. By seeing a word or phrase used in a variety of contexts, learning the history of vocabulary, and studying related words makes learning vocabulary interesting. Vocabulary study broadens one's knowledge and divulges the evolution of our thinking. In one of B. F. Skinner's last articles, he wrote that "etymology is the architecture of thought"— for, in the study of words, students learn how language and ideas have evolved as they learn about the subtleties of language and nuances in meaning. This vocabulary knowledge enriches our lives and deepens students' understanding of the world around them.

References

Baumann, J. F., & Graves, M. F. (2010). What is Academic Vocabulary? *Journal of Adolescent & Adult Literacy*, 54(1), 4-12.

Bear, D. R. (2011). Concept Sorts and Vocabulary Learning. Vocabulogic. http://vocablog-plc.blogspot.com/2011/08/concept-sorts-and-vocabularylearning.html.

Bear, D. R., Caserta-Henry, C., Venner, D. (2004). Personal Readers and Literacy Instruction With Emergent and Beginning Readers. Berkeley, CA: Teaching Resource Center.

Bear, D. R., & Helman, L. (2004). Word Study for Vocabulary Development: An Ecological Perspective on Instruction During the Early Stages of Literacy Learning. In J. F. Baumann & E. J. Kame'enui (Eds.), Vocabulary Instruction: Research Practice (pp. 139- 158). New York: Guilford Press.

Bear, D. R., Helman, L., & Woessner, L. (2009). Word Study Assessment and Instruction With English Learners in a Second Grade Classroom: Bending With Students' Growth. In J. Coppola and E. V. Primas (Eds.), One Classroom, Many Learners: Best Literacy Practices for Today's Multilingual Classrooms (pp. 11-40). Newark, DE: International Reading Association.

Bear, D. R., Johnston, F., Invernizzi, M., Templeton, S. (2009). Words Their Way: Letter and Picture Sorts for Emergent Spellers, 2nd edition. Boston: Allyn & Bacon.

Beck, I. L., McKeown, M. G., & Kucan, L. (2008). Creating Robust Vocabulary: Frequently Asked Questions and Extended Examples. New York: Guilford Press.

Bear, D. R., Smith, R. (2009). The Literacy Development of English Learners: What Do We Know About Each Student's Literacy Development? In Helman, L. A. (Ed.) Literacy Development and Instruction of English Learners (pp. 87 - 116). New York: Guilford Press.

Beers, C. S., & Beers, J. W. (1992). Children's Spelling of English Inflectional Morphology. In S. Templeton & D. R. Bear (Eds.), Development of Orthographic Knowledge and the Foundations of Literacy: A Memorial Festschrift for Edmund H. Henderson (pp. 23-251). Hillsdale, NH: Lawrence Erlbaum Associates.

Bowers, P. N., Kirby, J. R., & Deacon, S. H. (2010). The Effects of Morphological Instruction on Literacy Skills: A Systematic Review of the Literature. Review of Educational Research. 80 (2), 144-179.

Carlisle, J. F. (2010). Effects of Instruction in Morphological Awareness on Literacy Achievement: An Integrated Review. Reading Research Quarterly. 45 (4), 464-487.

Carpenter, K. M. (2010). Concept Sorts in the Vocabulary Learning of Kindergarten Children. Doctoral Dissertation, University of Nevada, Reno.

Carpenter, K., Gehsmann, K., Smith, R., Bear, D., Templeton, S. (2009). Learning Together: Putting Word Study Instruction in Practice. The California Reader. 44, 4-18.

Corson, D. (1997). The Learning and Use of Academic English Words. Language Learning. 47, 671-718.

Coxhead, A. (2000). A New Academic Word List. TESOL Quarterly. 34 (2), 213-238.

Fang, Z., Schleppegrell, M. J., & Cox, B. E. (2006). Understanding the Language Demands of Schooling: Nouns in Academic Registers. Journal of Literacy Research. 38 (3), 247-273.

Flanigan, K., Hayes, L., Templeton, S., Bear, D. R., Invernizzi, M., & Johnston, F. (2011). Words Their Way With Struggling Readers: Word Study for Reading, Vocabulary, and Spelling Instruction. Boston: Allyn & Bacon.

Helman, L., Bear, D. R., Invernizzi, M., Templeton, S., Johnston, F. (2011). Words Their Way: Emergent Sorts for Spanish-Speaking English Learners. Boston: Allyn & Bacon.

Helman, L., Bear, D. R., Invernizzi, M., Templeton, S., Johnston, F. (2009). Words Their Way: Letter Namealphabetic Sorts for Spanish-speaking English Learners. Boston: Allyn & Bacon.

Helman, L. A., Bear, D. R., Templeton, S., Invernizzi, M. A., & Johnston, F. (2012). Words Their Way With English Learners: Word Study for Phonics, Vocabulary, and Spelling Instruction, 2nd Edition. Boston: Allyn & Bacon.

Hiebert, E. H., & Lubliner, S. (2008). The Nature, Learning, and Instruction of General Academic Vocabulary. In A. E. Farstrup & S. J. Samuels (Eds.), What Research Has to Say About Vocabulary. Newark, DE: International Reading Association.

Invernizzi, M., Johnston, F., Bear, D. R. (2009). Words Their Way: Word Sorts for Within Word Pattern Spellers, 2nd edition. Boston: Allyn & Bacon.

Johnston, F., Bear, D.R., Invernizzi, M., Templeton, S. (2009). Words Their Way: Word Sorts for Letter Name-alphabetic Spellers. 2nd Edition. Boston: Allyn & Bacon.

Johnston, F., Invernizzi, M., Bear, D. R. (2009). Words Their Way: Word Sorts for Syllables and Affixes Spellers, 2nd edition. Boston: Allyn & Bacon.

Kame'enui, E.J., & Baumann, J.F. (2012). Vocabulary Instruction: Research to Practice, 2nd Edition. New York: Guilford Press.

Lesaux, N., Kieffer, M. J., Faller, S. E., & Kelley, J. G. (2010). The Effectiveness and Ease of Implementation of an Academic Vocabulary Intervention for Linguistically Diverse Students in Urban Middle Schools. Reading Research Quarterly. 45 (2), 196-228.

Nagy, W., & Townsend, D. (2012). Words as Tools: Learning Academic Vocabulary as Language Acquisition. Reading Research Quarterly. 47 (1), 91-108.

National Governors Association Center for Best Practices, Council of Chief State School Officers (2010). Common Core State Standards. Washington, DC: National Governors Association Center for Best Practices, Council of Chief State School Officers.

Schleppegrell, M. J. (2007). The Linguistic Challenges of Mathematics Teaching and Learning: A Research Review. Reading and Writing Quarterly. 23 (2), 139- 159.

Skinner, B. F. (1989). The Origins of Cognitive Thought. American Psychologist. 44, 13-18.

Snow, C., Lawrence, J., & White, C. (2009). Generating Knowledge of Academic Language Among Urban Middle School Students. Journal of Research on Educational Effectiveness. 2 (4), 325-344.

Stevens, J. (1995). Tops and Bottoms. New York: Harcourt Brace & Company.

Templeton, W. S., Bear, D. R. (2011). Phonemic Awareness, Word Recognition, and Spelling. In Rasinski, T. (Ed.), Developing Reading Instruction That Works (pp. 121-146). Bloomington, IN: Solution Tree Press.

Templeton, S., Bear, D. R., Invernizzi, M., & Johnston, F. (2010). Vocabulary Their Way: Word Study With Middle and Secondary Students. Boston, MA: Allyn & Bacon.

Templeton, S., Johnston, F., Bear, D. R., Invernizzi, M. (2009). Words Their Way: Word Sorts for Derivational Relations Spellers. 2nd Edition. Boston: Allyn & Bacon.

Townsend, D., Filippini, A., Collins, P., & Biancarosa, G. (2012). Evidence for the Importance of Academic Word Knowledge for the Academic Achievement of Diverse Middle School Students. Elementary School Journal. 112 (3), 497-518.

Vaughn, S., Martinez, L. R., Linan-Thompson, S., Reutenuch, C. K., Carlson, C. D., & Francis, D. J. (2009). Enhancing Social Studies Vocabulary and Comprehension for Seventh-Grade English Language Learners: Findings From Two Experimental Studies. Journal of Research on Educational Effectiveness. 2 (4), 297-324.

Zwiers, J. (2006). Integrating Academic Language, Thinking, and Content: Learning Scaffolds for Nonnative Speakers in the Middle Grades. Journal of English for Academic Purposes. 5, 317-332.

Zwiers, J. (2008). Building Academic Language: Essential Practices for Content Classrooms. San Francisco, CA: Jossey-Bass.

FOUNDATIONAL SKILLS K–5

By Dr. Jan Hasbrouck, Ph.D.

Senior Research Associate, University of Oregon
Gibson, Hasbrouck & Associates, Austin, TX

"Students who have acquired strong phonics skills are more skillful and confident readers because they can more effectively figure out new or unfamiliar words that they encounter."

-Dr. Jan Hasbrouck, Ph.D.

Introduction

Researchers have made extraordinary progress in understanding what "reading" really is. Numerous complex brain processes involved in the act of reading have been identified, along with many individual component skills that must be learned and used automatically and efficiently by a reader. At this point, compelling evidence from a convergence of reading research indicates that 90% to 95% of all students can achieve literacy levels at or approaching grade level. These statistics include students with dyslexia and other students with learning and cognitive disabilities. Students succeed when intensive, comprehensive, and high-quality prevention and early intervention instruction is provided by well-trained and well-supported teachers. (c.f. Al Otailba, Connor, Foorman, Schatschneider, Greulich, Sidler, 2009; Al Otaiba & Torgesen, 2007; Rashotte, MacPhee, Torgeson, 2001; Shaywitz & Shaywitz, 2006; Torgesen, 2007; Vaughn & Wanzek, 2014; Vellutino & Fletcher, 2007.)

Our Challenge

Given this fact about our students' potential success in reading, many educators, parents, and members of the general community are increasingly frustrated: *If scientists have proven that almost all children can be taught to read at or very close to grade level, why is it that nearly 40% of the fourth-grade students in the United States continue to struggle with reading and understanding grade level material?* This is not a trivial or easily ignored problem. Reading problems negatively affect individual human lives and society in countless ways. Students who struggle with reading typically have lower grades across all their classes, high levels of truancy, and decreased self-esteem and self-efficacy.

...compelling evidence from a convergence of reading research indicates that 90% to 95% of all students can achieve literacy levels at or approaching grade level.

They often exhibit disruptive, challenging, and sometimes violent self-destructive behaviors. Low literacy levels cause unconscionable human suffering outside of school that often extends across multiple generations, including chronic unemployment or underemployment, substance abuse, enduring poverty, and incarceration (Blaunstein & Lyon, 2006). The consequences of illiteracy affect the individuals themselves, their families, and the broader community in which they live.

Foundational Skills

Current standards identify four essential prerequisite foundational skills for reading: Print concepts, phonological awareness, phonics and word recognition, and fluency. These skills have been widely recognized as essential for the "truly extraordinary transformation" (p. 15) of converting print—the written symbols that have no meaning on their own—into a meaningful linguistic code (Shaywitz & Shaywitz, 2006). These four skills presume that beginning readers have acquired a foundation in a spoken language, ideally the same language that they will be learning to read.

Print awareness is the initial stage of literacy in which emergent readers begin to connect the language they understand and are learning to speak to the symbolic representations of letters and words, such as those written on a page in a book, on the screen of a computer or smartphone, or on a sign posted in a restaurant or shop. Print awareness involves an understanding that print has different functions depending on the context in which it appears: a menu lists food choices; a book can tell story; a sign can announce a favorite restaurant or warn of danger; a card or letter can convey thanks or good wishes. Print awareness includes understanding that print is organized in a particular way—for example, knowing that print in English, Spanish, and other languages is read from left to right and top to bottom.

> Reading problems negatively affect individual human lives and society in countless ways.

Print Concept Skills

- Knowing that print represents spoken language.
- Understanding print organization (text reads left to right, top to bottom, and page by page; printed words are strings of letters separated by blank space).
- Recognizing and naming lower- and upper-case letters in the alphabet.
- Recognizing features of a sentence (first word, capitalization, ending punctuation).

Watch the Videos

See Dr. Jan Hasbrouck, Ph.D. discuss the **"Guidelines for Adjusting Instruction."**

www.connected.mcgraw-hill.com

Phonological awareness is the general appreciation of the sounds of speech being distinct from their meaning. The finer-grained ability to notice, identify, and ultimately manipulate the separate sequence of sounds in spoken words is called *phonemic awareness*. These skills involve only auditory processes. Scientific evidence now confirms that having difficulty discriminating the sounds of spoken language is the causal factor of most reading difficulties, including dyslexia. The good news is that this difficulty can often be corrected or significantly improved with intensive and targeted intervention (Snow, Burns, & Griffin, 1998).

Phonological Awareness Skills

- Recognizing rhyming words.
- Counting, pronouncing, segmenting syllables into phonemes (e.g., hunt > /h/ /u/ /n/ /t/); blending individual phonemes, consonant blends, onsets and rimes into words (e.g., /d/ /o/ /g/ > dog; /t/ /r/ /u/ /ck/ > truck; /s/ + /um/ > sum, /g/ + /um/ > gum, /dr/ + /um/ > drum)
- Isolating and pronouncing initial, medial, and final phonemes in spoken single-syllable words; replacing individual phonemes to make new words (e.g., hat > sat; cop > cap; grip > grit)
- Distinguishing long from short vowel sounds in short spoken words

Students who have acquired strong phonics skills are more skillful and confident readers because they can more effectively figure out new or unfamiliar words that they encounter.

Phonics involves knowing which letters symbolize the sounds in a printed word and using that knowledge to sound out or decode words. Phonics is also referred to as the alphabetic principle. Phonics involves a reader using both auditory and visual (or tactile) processes. Students who are blind or visually impaired can also use phonics, but they learn how to associate phonemes with raised dots on a page (Braille) rather than printed letters. Students who have acquired strong phonics skills are more skillful and confident readers because they can more effectively figure out new or unfamiliar words that they encounter. Foundation skills also include the essential ability to instantaneously recognize frequently used but irregularly spelled words, often referred to as sight words or high frequency words. Newer standards are also emphasizing the value of explicitly teaching morphology (root or base words, prefixes and suffixes) in order to expand students' access to word meaning (Bowers, Kirby, & Deacon, 2010). In addition, having students study the spelling of words they are learning to read has been shown to have a powerful and positive effect on reading skill development (Joshi, Treiman, Carreker & Moats, 2008-2009.

SpeedKingz/Shutterstock.com

Phonics and Word Recognition Skills

- Knowing the primary or most common sounds of each consonant, five major long and short vowels, final e, and common consonant digraphs and vowel teams.
- Reading high-frequency, irregularly spelled words by sight (e.g., was, one, have, of, love).
- Being able to distinguish between similarly spelled words and identify inconsistent but common spelling-sound correspondences.
- Decoding regularly spelled words.
- Using knowledge of syllable structure and morphology (roots and affixes) to read words in and out of context.

Reading fluency has been defined as reasonably accurate reading at an appropriate rate with suitable prosody* that leads to accurate and deep comprehension and motivation to read (Hasbrouck & Glaser, 2012). There is a common misconception among educators that fluency is the same as rate or speed, and that having students learn to read as fast as possible will increase their reading proficiency (Rasinski & Hamman, 2010). This is a mistaken notion. Fluency needs to be understood as a complex skill in which accuracy plays a foundational role, along with rate. Students need to learn to use a reading rate that is appropriate to the task at hand, but not to "speed read." Reading too fast can be as detrimental to skillful reading as reading too slowly. Fluency is an important skill because it is necessary (but not sufficient) for students to read and understand what they have read independently, proficiently, and with motivation. Fluent reading is a sign that a reader is reading with automaticity, which is the ability to do a task without having to think about it at a conscious level. When words are read "automatically", the brain isn't occupied with the details of the task itself and can instead attend to the meaning of the text being read (Rasinski, Blachowicz, & Lems, 2012).

Fluency Skills

- Reading with sufficient accuracy and rate to support comprehension.
- Reading on-level text with purpose and understanding.
- Reading on-level text orally with accuracy, appropriate rate, and expression.
- Using context to confirm or self-correct word recognition and understanding.

Watch the Videos

See Dr. Jan Hasbrouck, Ph.D. discuss **"Informal Reading Assessments."**

www.connected.mcgraw-hill.com

(t)Monkey Business Images/Shutterstock.com; (br)McGraw-Hill Education

Introduction and Intervention for Foundation Skills

For many children, especially those who are at risk of academic failure due to the effects of poverty, cognitive challenges, and/or language deficits, learning to read will require a significant amount of carefully designed and systematically delivered instruction (Archer & Hughes, 2011).

Unlike learning to speak, which occurs naturally and organically because human brains are genetically hard-wired for spoken language, learning to read is not "natural." Written language is a relatively new phenomenon in human development and our brains must be taught how to turn the intrinsically meaningless symbols of print into something meaningful—and potentially memorable, useful, and enjoyable. In order for students to master the essential foundational skills for reading, effective instruction must be provided, skillfully differentiated to meet the varied needs of students. Struggling readers will typically need much more explicitly targeted guided practice to master the foundation skills than some of their peers, so care should also be taken by teachers to discern which students need additional, appropriate, and effective intervention, as well as when and how to provide it effectively and efficiently.

References

Al Otailba, S., Connor, C. M., Foorman, B., Schatschneider, C., Greulich, L., & Sidler, J. F. (2009). "Identifying and intervening with Beginning Readers Who Are at-risk for Dyslexia." Perspectives on Language and Literacy, 35(4), 13-19.

Al Otaiba, S., & Fuchs, D. (2006). "Who Are the Young Children for Whom Best Practices in Reading Are Ineffective? An Experimental and Longitudinal Study." Journal of Learning Disabilities, 39(5), 414-431.

Al Otaiba, S., & Torgesen, J. (2007). Effects from Intensive Standardized Kindergarten and First-grade Interventions for the Prevention of Reading Difficulties. In S.R. Jimerson, M.K. Burns, & A.M. VanDerHeyden (Eds.), Handbook of Response to Intervention: The Science and Practice of Assessment and Intervention (pp. 212–222). New York: Springer.

Archer, A. L., & Hughes, C. A. (2011). Explicit Instruction: Effective and Efficient Teaching. NY: Guillford Press.

Blaunstein, P., & Lyon, R. (2006). Why Kids Can't Read: Challenging the Status Quo in Education. Toronto: Rowan and Littlefield. Fielding, L., Kerr, N., & Rosier, P. (2007). Annual Growth for All Students, Catch-Up Growth for Those Who Are Behind. Kennewick: The New Foundation Press.

Bowers, P. N., Kirby, J. R., & Deacon, S. H. (2010). The effects of morphological instruction on literacy skills: A systematic review of the literature. Review of Educational Research, 80, 144–179

Foorman, B.R., Brier, J.I., & Fletcher, J. M. (2003). Interventions Aimed at Improving Reading Success: An Evidence-based Approach. Developmental Neuropsychology, 24(3), 613-639.

Hasbrouck, J., & Glaser, D. R. (2012). Reading Fluency: Teaching and Understanding this Complex Skill. Wellesley, MA: Gibson Hasbrouck & Associates. www.gha-pd.com

Joshi, R., Treiman, R., Carreker, S., & Moats, L.. (2008-2009, Winter). The real magic of spelling: Improving reading and writing. American Educator, 9. http://www.aft.org/sites/default/files/periodicals/joshi.pdf p. 10

Learning First Alliance (June, 1998). Every Child Reading: An Action Plan and Every Child Reading: A Professional Development Guide. Available online from 1001 Connecticut Avenue, N.W. Suite 335 Washington, DC 20036. www.learningfirst.org

Mathes, P., Denton, C. A., Fletcher, J. M., Anthony, J. L., Francis, D. J., & Schatschneider, C. (2005). The Effects of Theoretically Different Instruction and Student Characteristics on the Skills of Struggling Readers. Reading Research Quarterly, 40(2), 148-182.

Moats, L. (Spring, 2011). Knowledge and Practice Standards for Teachers of Reading—A New Initiative by the International Reading Association. Perspectives on Language and Literacy, 51-52.

National Governors' Association Center for Best Practices, Council of Chief State School Officers. (2010). Common Core State Standards. Author: Washington D.C.

NRP (2000). Report of the National Reading Panel NICHD www. nationalreadingpanel.org.

Rashotte, C.A., MacPhee, K., Torgeson, J. K. (2001). The Effectiveness of a Group Reading Instruction Program with Poor Readers in Multiple Grades. Learning Disability Quarterly, 24, 119-134.

Rasinski, T., Blachowicz, C. L. Z, & Lems, K (2012) (Eds.), *Fluency Instruction, Second Edition: Research-Based Best Practices.* New York: Guilford Press.

Rasinski, T. & Hamman, P. (2010). Fluency: Why It Is "Not Hot." Reading Today, 28(1), p. 26. (2012). Curious George and Rosetta Stone: The Role of Texts in Supporting Automaticity in Beginning Reading. In T. Rasinski, C.L.Z. Blachowicz, & K. Lems (Eds.), *Fluency Instruction, Second Edition: Research-Based Best Practices.* (pp.289-309) New York: Guilford Press.

Shaywitz, S. E., & Shaywitz, B. A. (2006). Armed with the Facts: The Science of Reading and its Implications for Teaching. In P. Blaunstein & R. Lyon (Eds.), Why Kids Can't Read: Challenging the Status Quo in Education, pp. 9-29. Toronto: Rowan and Littlefield

Simos, P. G., Fletcher, J. M., Bergman, E., Breier, J. I., Foorman, B. R., Castillo, E. M., et al. (2002). Dyslexia-specific Brain Activation Profile Becomes Normal Following Successful Remedial Training. Neurology, 58, 1203–1213.

Snow, C. E., Burns, S. M., & Griffin, P. (1998). Preventing Reading Difficulties in Young Children. National Research Council. Washington, D.C.: National Academy Press.

Torgesen, J. K. (2000). Individual Differences in Response to Early Interventions in Reading: The Lingering Problem of Treatment Resisters. Learning Disabilities Research & Practice, 15, 55–64.

Vaughn, S., & Wanzek, J. (2014). Intensive interventions in reading for students with reading disabilities: Meaningful impacts. *Learning Disabilities Research & Practice,* 29(2), 46-53.

Vellutino, F. R., & Fletcher, J. M. (2007). Developmental Dyslexia. In M. J. Snowling & C. Hulme, (Eds.) The Science of Reading: A Handbook, pp. 362-278. Malden, MA: Blackwell Publishing.

Wanzek, J., & Vaughn, S. (2009). Students Demonstrating Persistent Low Response to Reading Intervention: Three Case Studies. Learning Disabilities Research & Practice, 24(3), 151-163.

the pitch, tone, volume, emphasis, rhythm of oral reading.

Word Study: Kindergarten and Grade 1

Word study instruction in the Balanced Literacy Guide provides foundational skills practice that can be applied to weekly selections.

1 BEGIN WITH WHOLE GROUP INSTRUCTION

In *Wonders Balanced Literacy,* word study lessons are designed to provide students with opportunities to model, practice, and apply foundational skills. Kindergarten and Grade 1 lessons will help lay the groundwork for skills needed in later grades, so students are prepared to succeed as they move up in grade level.

KINDERGARTEN lessons include weekly songs and poems that introduce children to sounds and sound spellings. Foundational skills lessons provide modeling of skills, and then provide children with guided practice, and individual practice of these skills. Students apply the word study skills they have learned to the weekly Shared Read selections.

IN GRADE 1, the Shared Read lessons focus on foundational skills, high-frequency words, and story words that may be unfamiliar to children. Foundational skills are introduced, modeled, and practiced as a class. These skills are then applied and practiced through the Shared Read from the Student Edition.

2 GUIDE INSTRUCTION IN SMALL GROUP

After whole group modeling, practice, and reading, move on to small group instruction with individual children, as needed. Small group lessons dig deeper into the following skills: phonological awareness, phonemic awareness, phonics, and high-frequency words. Prompts are provided for practice and directly relate to the readings. As students practice activities, such as blending and building words, the lessons make connections between their practice and Shared Read selections of the week.

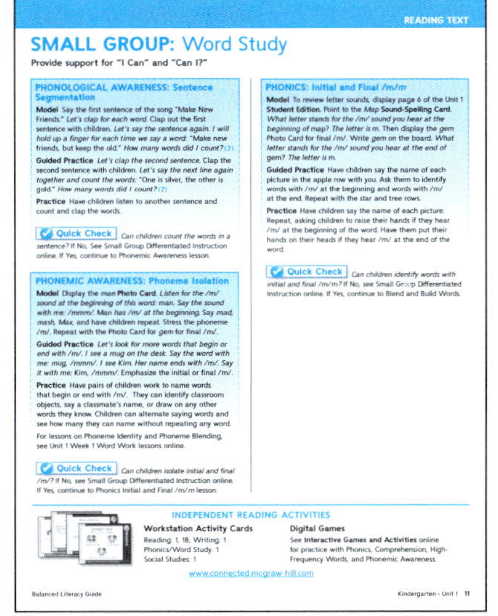
READING TEXT

SMALL GROUP: Word Study

Provide support for "I Can" and "Can I?"

3 DIFFERENTIATED INSTRUCTION

For further instruction, online lessons provide explicit instruction for the following foundational skills at www.connected.mcgraw-hill.com.

- Phonological awareness
- Phonemic awareness
- Phonics
- Structural analysis
- High-frequency words
- Fluency

DIGITAL GAMES AND PRACTICE

Additional student practice materials can be found online by accessing the ConnectEd resources. Digital games, interactive activities, songs, and reproducibles provide practice for specific foundational skills. Some digital games collect data to allow teachers to view student progress and provide support as necessary.

Pre-Decodable and Decodable Readers for Grades K through 2 are provided online and focus on the specific word study skills of the week. These readers give students an opportunity to apply their new skills to readings.

Word Study: Grades 2–5

1 GUIDE INSTRUCTION IN SMALL GROUP

In Grades 2 through 5, small-group word study instruction is provided for teachers to use with students as needed. Lessons focus on phonics and fluency skills as they relate to the instruction of the week. The lessons provide support for students with prompts and activity ideas to explain, model, and guide practice with students. Shared Read selections are utilized in small group lessons to allow for application of skills.

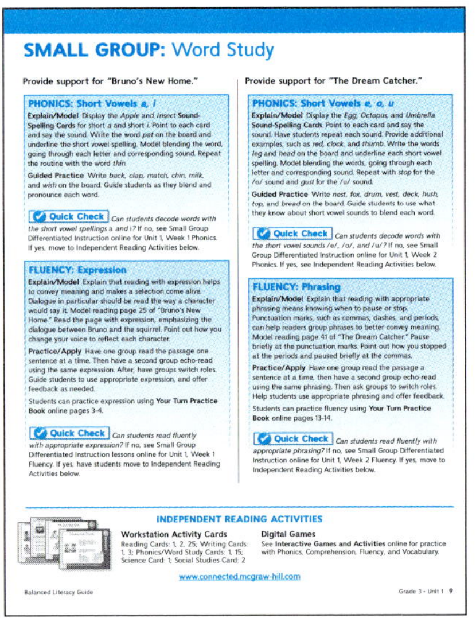

SMALL GROUP: Word Study

Provide support for "Bruno's New Home."

PHONICS: Short Vowels *a, i*

Explain/Model Display the *Apple* and *Insect* **Sound-Spelling Cards** for short *a* and short *i*. Point to each card and say the sound. Write the word *pat* on the board and underline the short vowel spelling. Model blending the word, going through each letter and corresponding sound. Repeat the routine with the word *thin*.

Guided Practice Write *back, clap, match, chin, milk,* and *wish* on the board. Guide students as they blend and pronounce each word.

Quick Check *Can students decode words with the short vowel spellings* a *and* i? If no, see Small Group Differentiated Instruction online for Unit 1, Week 1 Phonics. If yes, move to Independent Reading Activities below.

FLUENCY: Expression

Explain/Model Explain that reading with expression helps to convey meaning and makes a selection come alive. Dialogue in particular should be read the way a character would say it. Model reading page 25 of "Bruno's New Home." Read the page with expression, emphasizing the dialogue between Bruno and the squirrel. Point out how you change your voice to reflect each character.

Practice/Apply Have one group read the passage one sentence at a time. Then have a second group echo-read using the same expression. After, have groups switch roles. Guide students to use appropriate expression, and offer feedback as needed.

Students can practice expression using **Your Turn Practice Book** online pages 3-4.

Quick Check *Can students read fluently with appropriate expression?* If no, see Small Group Differentiated Instruction lessons online for Unit 1, Week 1 Fluency. If yes, have students move to Independent Reading Activities below.

Provide support for "The Dream Catcher."

PHONICS: Short Vowels *e, o, u*

Explain/Model Display the *Egg, Octopus,* and *Umbrella* **Sound-Spelling Cards**. Point to each card and say the sound. Have students repeat each sound. Provide additional examples, such as *red, clock,* and *thumb*. Write the words *leg* and *head* on the board and underline each short vowel spelling. Model blending the words, going through each letter and corresponding sound. Repeat with *stop* for the /o/ sound and *gust* for the /u/ sound.

Guided Practice Write *nest, fox, drum, vest, deck, hush, top,* and *bread* on the board. Guide students to use what they know about short vowel sounds to blend each word.

Quick Check *Can students decode words with the short vowel sounds /e/, /o/, and /u/?* If no, see Small Group Differentiated Instruction online for Unit 1, Week 2 Phonics. If yes, see Independent Reading Activities below.

FLUENCY: Phrasing

Explain/Model Explain that reading with appropriate phrasing means knowing when to pause or stop. Punctuation marks, such as commas, dashes, and periods, can help readers group phrases to better convey meaning. Model reading page 41 of "The Dream Catcher." Pause briefly at the punctuation marks. Point out how you stopped at the periods and paused briefly at the commas.

Practice/Apply Have one group read the passage a sentence at a time, then have a second group echo-read using the same phrasing. Then ask groups to switch roles. Help students use appropriate phrasing and offer feedback.

Students can practice fluency using **Your Turn Practice Book** online pages 13-14.

Quick Check *Can students read fluently with appropriate phrasing?* If no, see Small Group Differentiated Instruction online for Unit 1, Week 2 Fluency. If yes, move to Independent Reading Activities below.

INDEPENDENT READING ACTIVITIES

Workstation Activity Cards
Reading Cards: 1, 2, 25; Writing Cards: 1, 3; Phonics/Word Study Cards: 1, 15; Science Card: 1; Social Studies Card: 2

Digital Games
See **Interactive Games and Activities** online for practice with Phonics, Comprehension, Fluency, and Vocabulary.

www.connected.mcgraw-hill.com

Balanced Literacy Guide — Grade 3 • Unit 1 9

2 DIFFERENTIATED INSTRUCTION

For further instruction, online lessons provide explicit instruction for the following foundational skills:

- Phonics
- Spelling
- Fluency

Lessons provide ideas for class study activities via prompts, games, and student collaborations. The phonics skill of the week is broken down into modeling and guided practice for in-depth instruction. Phonics skills are woven into the readings for the week for reinforcement and context.

The fluency skill of the week is modeled and applied during class collaborations. Fluency is practiced with the weekly reading as students engage in group practice.

Daily spelling instruction and prompts are also provided. Activity and game ideas give teachers further material for student practice with spelling words as a class. Sample sentences are provided to practice words in context.

DIGITAL GAMES AND PRACTICE

Teachers can also find more student practice materials online by accessing the ConnectEd resources for teachers. Grades 2 through 5 online resources provide a variety of games that support the acquisition of phonics and structural analysis skills as well as high-frequency words.

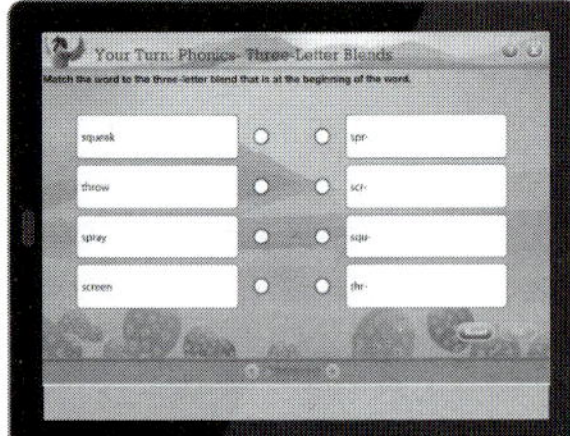

PROFESSIONAL DEVELOPMENT

Online Professional Development videos give further insight, strategies, and teacher support with foundational skills instruction.

Watch some of these professional development videos online:

- Coach Videos: Foundational Skills videos
- Word Automaticity videos
- Balanced Literacy Whole-Group and Small-Group Word Study videos with Kathy Bumgardner

Watch the Videos

Watch Kathy Bumgardner lead **Whole-Group and Small-Group Word Study** instruction online.

www.connected.mcgraw-hill.com

IN PRACTICE

Vocabulary Instruction

PURPOSE OF VOCABULARY INSTRUCTION

In *Wonders Balanced Literacy*, substantial vocabulary growth comes from explicit vocabulary instruction in the contexts of both narrative and informational texts. Vocabulary words appear in multiple contexts so that students receive repeated exposures to each word. Vocabulary instruction includes developing oral vocabulary in the context of read alouds at Kindergarten and Grade 1, which is a necessary foundation for later vocabulary acquisition.

Vocabulary instruction includes the following research-based approach:

- Both academic and domain-specific words are taught.
- Words are pretaught explicitly.
- Words appear in multiple contexts in each text set.
- Instruction activates background knowledge.
- Explicit instruction includes modeling and teaching of critical vocabulary strategies for word learning
- Instruction includes a variety of activities in which student manipulate, sort and categorize words to develop deeper understanding of the words.
- Instruction includes expanding students' word knowledge by learning multiple forms of the chosen words and shades of meaning.
- Additional differentiated instruction is provided online.
- Engaging online games and activities provide reinforcement.

HOW WORDS ARE CHOSEN

Two types of academic word are targeted in this program: general and domain-specific. General academic vocabulary are composed of words and phrases found in all academic texts, such as *analysis, discussion* and *however*. Domain-specific vocabulary are usually related to a particular content area (science, history, social studies, math), such as the word *photosynthesis* in biology and *peninsula* in social studies.

Specific choices were guided by the following resources: *The Living Word Vocabulary* list, *Basic Reading Vocabularies* by Albert Harris and Milton Jacobson, *Words Worth Teaching* by Andrew Biemiller, *High-Incidence Academic Words* by Avril Coxhead, *Building Background Knowledge for Academic Achievement* by Robert Marzano, and *The Educator's Word Frequency Guide* by Susan Zeno et al.

VOCABULARY ROUTINE

Each Visual Vocabulary Card features a Define/Example/Ask routine (see sample below) which provides students with a word's definition, an example of how that word can be used in a sentence and a question that relates to the new vocabulary word. This research-based routine supports students in acquiring new vocabulary each week.

In Kindergarten and Grade 1, the Visual Vocabulary Cards online introduce students to oral vocabulary words before they listen to the week's Interactive Read Aloud. In Grades 2 through 5, the Visual Vocabulary Cards are used to preteach vocabulary words from a short text in the Student Edition.

Using the gradual release of responsibility, students apply what they have learned to an extended text, a Classroom Library selection. Reading the words in a new context reinforces meaning.

The *Wonders Balanced Literacy Guides* provide an overview of the Tier 2 and Tier 3 vocabulary words from the Classroom Library selections, while the Classroom Library lessons feature definitions and instructional support for those words. The ACT (Access Complex Text) features of the Classroom Library lessons also refer to "Specific Vocabulary" to target challenging Tier 3 words that may appear in an extended complex text.

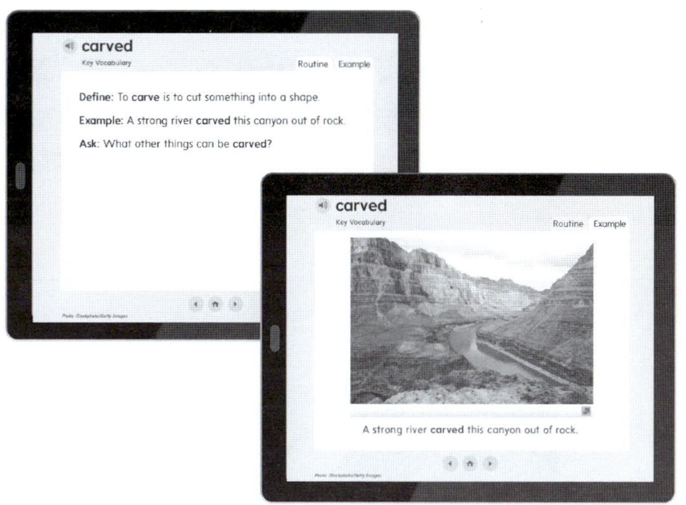

DIFFERENTIATED INSTRUCTION FOR VOCABULARY

The *Wonders Balanced Literacy* Leveled Readers reinforce the weekly vocabulary words to help students deepen their understanding of the words. The same vocabulary words are included across all levels. The EL Leveled Readers include these words as well as additional words or phrases that English learners may be unfamiliar with. For additional information on supporting English Learners' vocabularies, see p. 125.

VOCABULARY STRATEGIES

In Grades 2-5, the small group instruction is provided for support for specific vocabulary strategies. These lessons help build students' knowledge of:

- context clues
- root words
- figurative language
- synonyms and antonyms
- compound words
- prefixes and suffixes
- homographs and homophones
- Greek and Latin roots

After observing a teacher model how to use these strategies to identify the meaning of words in the Shared Read selection from the Student Edition, partners have the opportunity to apply the strategies themselves to define additional words from the Shared Read.

Differentiated Instruction lessons are available online should students require additional practice. These lessons include two sets of **Build Vocabulary** lessons. The first set of lessons follow a five-day sequence that includes:

- **Day 1: Connect to Words** Reinforce students' understanding of the week's vocabulary by providing them with prompts that feature the words in context.
- **Day 2: Expand Vocabulary** Help students generate different forms of the week's vocabulary words by guiding them to add, change, or remove inflectional endings.
- **Day 3: Reinforce the Words** Provide students with sentence stems to help them practice using each of the words from the week in a sentence.
- **Day 4: Connect to Writing** Encourage students to write their own sentences using the week's vocabulary words.
- **Day 5: Word Squares** Ask students to create Word Squares for each of the week's vocabulary words.

The second set of Build Vocabulary lessons online provide more focused instruction on specific topics, including academic vocabulary, idioms, morphology, and shades of meaning. The two sets of Build Vocabulary lessons are not dependent upon once another; they can be taught in combination or independently.

Online interactive lessons, games and practice activities help solidify word meanings and understandings. For students, online vocabulary strategy games provide teachers with data feedback to help teachers target instruction as needed.

Word Study: Overview

Use these Instructional Routines to support Word Study Instruction in *Wonders Balanced Literacy*.

In this section, instructional routines are provided for the following skills. In addition, 5-day explicit instruction for these foundational skills is provided online.

PHONOLOGICAL AWARENESS

- Sentence Segmentation
- Identify/Generate Rhyme
- Alliteration
- Syllable Segmentation
- Syllable Blending
- Blend Onset and Rime
- Segment Onset and Rime
- Syllable Addition
- Syllable Deletion

PHONEMIC AWARENESS

- Phoneme Identity
- Phoneme Isolation
- Phoneme Blending
- Phoneme Segmentation
- Phoneme Categorization
- Phoneme Substitution
- Phoneme Addition
- Phoneme Deletion
- Phoneme Reversal

PHONICS

- Review Sound-Spelling
- Blend Words
- Build Words

STRUCTURAL ANALYSIS

- For all Structural Analysis lessons go online
- For a list of skills see page 115

Word Study: Overview

Use the lessons in this section to give students additional practice on Phonological Awareness, Phonemic Awareness, Phonics, Structural Analysis, and High-Frequency Words.

WHAT IS PHONOLOGICAL AWARENESS?

Phonological Awareness involves the auditory and oral manipulation of sounds. It refers generally to the awareness of words, syllables, or phonemes (individual speech sounds). Phonological awareness tasks include the following:

- detecting rhyme
- clapping syllables
- counting words in sentences
- blending/segmenting onset and rime
- phonemic awareness tasks

Phonemic Awareness is a subset of phonological awareness. It refers specifically to the awareness of individual sounds in words such as /s/ /i/ /t/ in sit. Phonemic awareness tasks include the following:

- phoneme isolation
- phoneme identity
- phoneme categorization
- phoneme blending
- phoneme segmentation
- phoneme addition
- phoneme deletion
- phoneme substitution
- phoneme reversals

WHY IS PHONOLOGICAL AWARENESS IMPORTANT?

An understanding of how to detect, break apart, blend, and manipulate the sounds in spoken language is needed in order for students to understand letter-sound associations. Students must understand that words are made up of speech sounds, or phonemes, in order to read and write. For example, if a student cannot orally blend a word, then sounding out a written word while reading will be difficult. Likewise, if a student cannot orally segment a word sound-by-sound, then spelling a word while writing will be difficult. Research indicates that the most critical phonemic awareness skills are blending and segmenting since they are most closely associated with early reading and writing growth (NICHHD, 2001).

WHAT IS PHONICS?

Phonics is the understanding that there is a relationship between sounds (phonemes) and spellings (graphemes).

WHY IS PHONICS INSTRUCTION IMPORTANT?

Phonics instruction helps beginning readers understand the relationship between letters and sounds. It teaches students to use these relationships to read and write. Research has shown that direct systematic phonics instruction is appropriate and beneficial for advancing students' skills from kindergarten on (NICHD, 2001).

WHAT ARE HIGH FREQUENCY WORDS?

High-Frequency Words are the most common words in the English language. The high-frequency words taught are derived from established word lists, such as the Dolch Basic Sight Vocabulary list of the top 220 words (no nouns), the Fry top 100 words, and the American Heritage Word Frequency Book top 150 words in printed school English. Some of the high-frequency words in English must be taught as sight words because they do not follow regular sound-spelling patterns, such as *said, come,* and *who.*

WHY ARE HIGH-FREQUENCY WORDS IMPORTANT?

Because these words are so common in English school text, mastery of these words is necessary to fluent reading. Many of these words trip up struggling readers (such as words that begin with *th* and *wh*) and can impede comprehension when incorrectly identified during reading.

racorn/Shutterstock.com

Phonological Awareness

SENTENCE SEGMENTATION

I Do Tell children that a sentence is made of words. Explain that you will count words in sentences. Demonstrate how to segment a sentence into words and then count the words. Use the sentence *Spot is a pup.* I am going to say a sentence and clap for each word I say. Clap as you say each word in the following sentence. Listen: *Spot is a pup.* Repeat the sentence as you hold up a finger for each word. The sentence *Spot is a pup* has four words.

We Do Segment sentences with children. Use the sentence *Sam can see Spot.* Say the sentence with me. Now let's clap as we say the words in the sentence. Clap with children as you say each word. *Sam can see Spot.* We clapped four times, because the sentence *Sam can see Spot* has four words.

Write more simple sentences on the board. Say each word. Ask children to clap the words and tell how many words they hear.

Corrective Feedback Model clapping for each word in this sentence and have children repeat. Listen for how many words are in this sentence: *Meg has crayons.* Let's say it together and clap for each word. Repeat the sentence clapping for each word. How many times did we clap? How many words are in the sentence? Yes, there are three words. Repeat this lesson as needed.

IDENTIFY/GENERATE RHYME

I Do Demonstrate how to identify rhyming words. Select words such as *map, cap.* Let's listen for words that rhyme. I will say two words and clap my hands if the words rhyme. Listen: *map, cap. Map* and *cap* rhyme because they both end with /ap/. Listen: /m/ /ap/, *map;* /k/ /ap/, *cap.*

We Do Practice identifying rhyming words. Use words such as *gap* and *hum.* I am going to say two words. If the words rhyme, we will stand up. We will stay seated if the words do not rhyme. Say these words after me: *gap, hum.* Give children time to figure out if the words rhyme. *Gap* and *hum* do not have the same ending sounds. *Gap* and *hum* do not rhyme. Repeat with *dad, had.* Continue activity as needed.

You Do Write more word pairs on the board. Some should rhyme and some should not. Have children tell if the word pairs rhyme and have them identify the ending sounds that are the same. In the later units, you may wish to have children generate an additional rhyming word.

Corrective Feedback Model how to identify rhyming words by isolating the sounds. Let's see if *set* and *met* rhyme. Listen to *set*: /s/ /et/. Listen to *met*: /m/ /et/. Both words end with /et/. *Set* and *met* rhyme. Model how to generate rhyming words by isolating the sounds that must rhyme. Then guide children to add sounds, such as consonants, to generate a rhyming word. Let's name words that rhyme with *set*. Listen: /s/ /et/. *Set* ends with /et/. Listen when I add /b/ to the sounds /et/: /b/ /et/, *bet.* A word that rhymes with *set* is *bet.* Repeat this lesson as needed.

Monkey Business Images/Shutterstock.com

Phonological Awareness

ALLITERATION

I Do Explain to children that they will be listening to words that begin with the same sound. Select words such as *ask, Alex, apple*. Listen to these words: /aaask/, /aaaleks/, /aaapl/. The words *ask, Alex,* and *apple* all begin with the same sound, /a/. Listen for the sound /a/ as we say the words together: *ask, Alex, apple*. These words begin with the sound /a/.

We Do Help children recognize alliteration. Select words such as *silly, seals, sip*. Listen to these words: *silly, seals, sip*. Say the words with me: *silly, seals, sip*. Say the beginning sound in *silly* with me: /s/. Say the beginning sound in *seals* with me: /s/. Now let's say the beginning sound in sip: /s/. The words *silly, seals,* and *sip* begin with the same sound, /s/. Continue with other words with the same beginning sound.

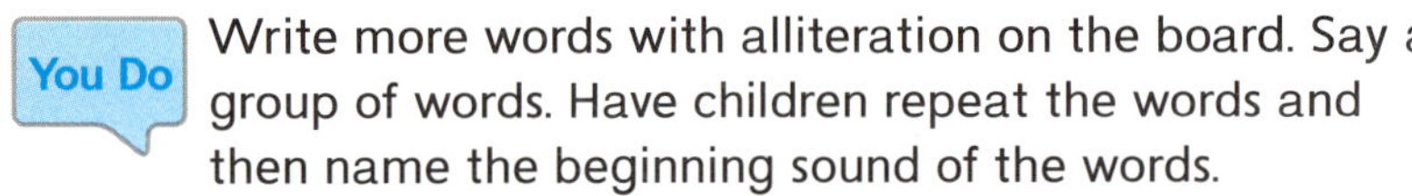

You Do Write more words with alliteration on the board. Say a group of words. Have children repeat the words and then name the beginning sound of the words.

Corrective Feedback Model how to identify alliteration in the following words: *Mike, missed, morning*. Say each word and have children listen for the initial sound. Have them repeat the sound back to you and say the sentence again, emphasizing initial /mmm/. Repeat activity as needed.

SYLLABLE SEGMENTATION

I Do Tell children that they will say the syllables or word parts in words. Select a word such as *rabbit*. Say: I will say and count the syllables, or parts, of a word. I'll clap each word part: /rab/ /it/. Now I will blend the word part to say the word: /rrraaabiiit/, *rabbit*. Explain that every syllable or word part has its own vowel sound. I will say the word parts. Clap as you say each syllable.

We Do Count and blend syllables with children. Collect another word such as *cabin*. Say the word *cabin* with me. Now say and clap the word parts with me: /kab/ /in/. We clapped two times because *cabin* has two syllables. Now let's blend the parts to say the word: /kaaabiiinnn/, *cabin*. Choose other words and continue activity as needed.

You Do Choose more words and write them on the board. Say each word. Ask children to say and clap the syllables and tell how many syllables they hear. Then ask children to blend the sounds together to say the word.

Corrective Feedback Count the syllables in the word children have difficulty with. Then say the syllables in the word children have trouble blending, stretching out the sounds and pausing between syllables. Then model blending the syllables, and guide children to blend independently. Say: Listen as I say the two word parts: /baaasss/ /ket/. Now listen as I blend, or put together, the word parts: /basket/. Say the word parts after me: /baaasss/ /ket/. Now it's your turn to blend the word parts: /basket/. What is the word? Yes, it's *basket*. Repeat this lesson as needed.

Syda Productions/Shutterstock.com

Phonological Awareness

SYLLABLE BLENDING

Say: I am going to say the syllables in a word. Clap as you say each syllable, pausing between the two syllables. /klaaa/ /piiing/. I will blend them together. I'll start by saying each syllable slowly. Then speed up to blend them together. Blend the syllables, clapping slowly at first and then faster as you blend the word. /klaaap/ /piiing/, /klaaapiiing/, the word is *clapping*.

Model using the **Response Board** to help blend syllables. Say to students: Let's practice blending two syllables together. /tāāā/ /bə ə ə lll/. Place markers in two boxes on the Response Board. Start off saying each syllable slowly by itself, and then speed up until they connect together. Move your finger back and forth between the two markers as you say the syllables faster and faster until they are blended together. /tābəl/. *Table.* Continuing modeling with more examples.

Have partners practice blending syllables into words. Distribute **Response Boards** online to students. Say each syllable in the following words slowly and individually, stretching them in length. Then have partners take turns blending the individual syllables into words. Have each partner repeat the blended word after the other. Generate additional words to help students practice.

Corrective Feedback Provide corrective feedback using the word: *basket*.

Say the syllables in the word students have trouble blending, stretching out the sounds and pausing between syllables. Then model blending the syllables, and guide students to blend independently. Say: Listen as I say the two syllables: /baaasss/ /ket/. Now listen as I blend, or put together, the syllables: /basket/. Say the syllables after me: /baaasss/ /keeet/. Now it's your turn to blend the syllables: /basket/. What is the word? Yes, it's basket.

BLEND ONSET AND RIME

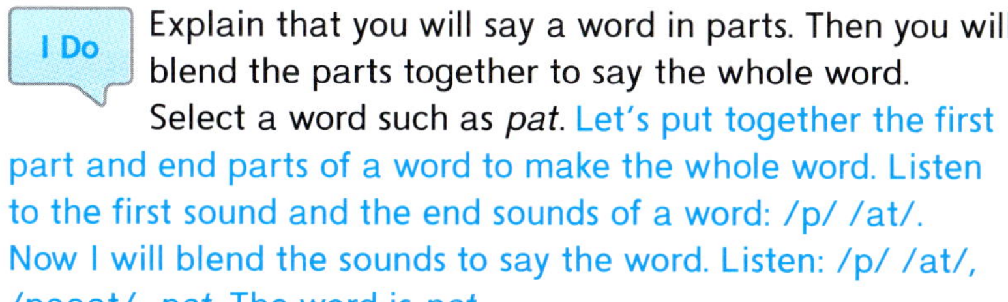

Explain that you will say a word in parts. Then you will blend the parts together to say the whole word. Select a word such as *pat*. Let's put together the first part and end parts of a word to make the whole word. Listen to the first sound and the end sounds of a word: /p/ /at/. Now I will blend the sounds to say the word. Listen: /p/ /at/, /paaat/, *pat*. The word is *pat*.

Help children blend words by onset and rime. Select a word such as *tip*. Listen to the word parts. Repeat the parts and then blend the parts to say the word: /t/ /ip/. Let's blend the sounds together: /tiiip/, *tip*. The word is *tip*. Continue with other words as needed.

Choose more words as examples. Say the onset and rime of each word. Ask children to say each part and then blend the sounds to say the word.

Corrective Feedback Model blending onset and rime in the word, *sat*. Say: The beginning part of the word has the sound /sss/. Have children repeat the sound. The ending part of the word has the sounds /aaat/. Have children repeat the sounds. Now listen as I blend, or put together, the beginning and ending sounds: /s/ /at/, /sssaaat/. Have children blend the sounds. What's the word? Yes, the word is *sat*. Repeat this lesson as needed using different words.

Phonological Awareness

SEGMENT ONSET AND RIME

I Do Remind children that you can break a word into two parts: a beginning sound and the remaining part of the word. Select a word such as *not*. Let's separate the sounds in a word into a beginning part and ending parts. I will say a word. Then I will say the beginning sound and then the end part. Listen: *not*, /n/ /ot/. The first sound in *not* is /n/. The end sounds in *not* are /ot/. Listen: *not*, /nnnooot/, /n/ /ot/.

We Do Help children segment words into onset and rime. Select a word such as *map*. Listen: *map*. Let's say the word together: *map*. Let's say the first sound in the word *map*: /m/. Let's say the ending sounds: /ap/. Listen: *map*, /m/ /ap/. Repeat with other words as needed.

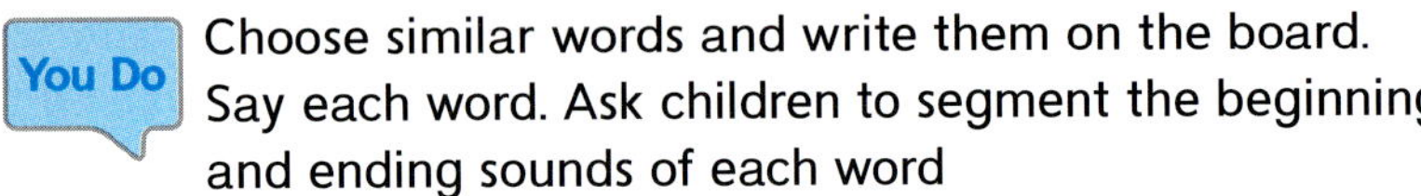

You Do Choose similar words and write them on the board. Say each word. Ask children to segment the beginning and ending sounds of each word

Corrective Feedback Guide children to segment words into parts. Say: Listen as I say the beginning sound and ending sounds in the word *sat*: /sss/ /aaat/. The beginning of *sat* has the sound /sss/. Say the sound after me: /sss/. The ending of *sat* has the sounds: /aaat/. Repeat these sounds after me /aaat/. What is the sound at the beginning? That's right, /s/. What sounds are at the end of the word? That's right, /at/. Repeat this lesson as needed.

SYLLABLE ADDITION

I Do Explain that you will add a word part to make a new word. Select a word such as *buckle*. Listen to this word: *buck*. I will add the word part *le* to the end of *buck* and blend the sounds to make a new word: *buck-le*, *buckle*. The new word is *buckle*.

We Do Help children practice adding syllables to make new words. Select a word such as *cabin*. Say this word after me: *cab*. Let's add the word part *in* to the end of *cab*. Now we'll blend the sounds together: *cab-in*, *cabin*. The new word is *cabin*. Continue with other words as needed.

You Do Choose other two syllable words. Say each word and the syllable to add. Ask children to blend the sounds to say the word.

Corrective Feedback Model syllable addition, and guide children to add the syllables to form the new word. Say: Listen as I say the word pet: /peeet/. *Pet* has one word part. Let's add the word part /kär/ to the beginning of *pet*. Listen as I say each word part: /kär/ /peeet/. Say them with me: /kär/ /peeet/. Listen as I say the word parts together: /kärpet/. Now it's your turn to say the word parts: /kärpet/. What is the new word? Yes, it's *carpet*. Repeat lesson as needed.

Robert Kneschke/Shutterstock.com

Phonological Awareness

SYLLABLE DELETION

I Do Explain that you will take away a word part to make a new word. Select a word such as *almost.* Listen to this word: *almost.* I will take away the word part *al* from the beginning of *almost.* When I take *al* away from *almost,* I get the new word *most.*

We Do Help children practice deleting syllables from words. Select a word such as *because.* Say this word after me: *because.* Let's take away the word part *be* from the beginning of *because* and say the new word: *cause.* Continue with other multisyllabic words.

Choose other multisyllabic words. Say each word and the syllable to delete. Ask children to say the new word. Repeat activity as needed.

Corrective Feedback Segment the syllables in the word *handshake.* Model deleting a syllable, and guide children to identify the new word. Say: Listen as I say each word part in *handshake:* /haaand/ /shāāāk/. Repeat after me: /haaand/ /shāāāk/. If I take away /hand/, I have one part left: /shāāāk/. Say the word part with me: /shāāāk/. This is a new word: *shake.* Repeat lesson as needed using other multisyllabic words.

Tania Kolinko/Shutterstock.com

Phonemic Awareness

PHONEME IDENTITY

I Do Explain that you will identify the same beginning sound in three different words. Select a group of three words from the word list for the unit, such as *man, march,* and *mail.* Listen as I say three words: /mmmaaannn/, /mmmärch/, /mmmaaailll/. I hear the same sound /m/ at the beginning of *man, march,* and *mail.*

We Do Help children practice identifying phonemes. Select words such as *mouse, met, milk.* Listen to these words: *mouse, met, milk.* Let's say the words together: /mmmousssss/, /mmmeeet/ /mmmmiiilllk/. The beginning sound in *mouse, met,* and *milk* is /m/. Say the beginning sound with me: /m/. Continue with other words and lead children to identify the initial, medial, or final sound that is the same.

Write similar word groups on the board. Say the words in a group, and ask children to identify the phoneme that is the same.

Corrective Feedback Say the word, stretching the targeted sound for three seconds: /ssset/. Have children repeat. If the targeted sound is a stop sound, say the sound and then the word: /b/ / bat/. Have children repeat. Model stretching the targeted sound in all three words in a set and identifying the sound that is the same in the words. Repeat this lesson as needed.

PHONEME ISOLATION

I Do Explain to children that you will isolate or separate a sound in a word. Select a word such as *mat.* Today we will listen for and set apart a sound in a word. Then we will say the sound. Listen as I say a word: /mmmaaat/. I hear the sound /m/ at the beginning of *mat,* The first sound in *mat* is /m/.

We Do Help children practice isolating phonemes. Select a word such as *ax.* Listen to this word: /aaaks/, *ax.* Say *ax* with me: /aaaks/. The beginning sound in *ax* is /a/. Say the beginning sound with me: /a/. Repeat with other words as needed.

You Do Select other similar words such as *pat* and write them on the board. Say each word and ask children to isolate the phoneme at the beginning, middle, or end of a word you say.

Corrective Feedback When children make mistakes during phoneme isolation: Say the word, stretching the sound in the targeted position for three seconds: /neeet/. Have children repeat. If the targeted sound is a stop sound, say the sound and then the word: /t/ /tap/. Have children repeat. Then model repeating the sounds in the word and identifying the target sound: I hear /t/ at the beginning of tap. Repeat this lesson as needed.

PHONEME BLENDING

I Do Explain that you will say the sounds in a word. Then you will blend the sounds to say a word. Select a word such as *bad.* Display the **Sound Boxes.** I am going to place one marker in each box as I say each sound in a word. Listen to these three sounds: /b/ /a/ /d/. Place the markers. Now I will blend the sounds to say the word: /baaad/, *bad.* I blended the word *bad.*

We Do Guide children to blend sounds to say words. Provide children with markers and **Response Boards online.** Select a word such as *fan.* Say these sounds after me: /f/ /a/ /n/. Let's say the sounds again. As you say each sound, put one marker in a box. Now let's blend the sounds together: /fffaaann/, *fan.* The word is *fan.* Continue with other words from the word lists that follow.

You Do Choose more words as examples. Say the sounds in each word. Ask children to blend the sounds to say the whole word. Children may use markers and **Response Boards** online as needed.

Corrective Feedback When children make mistakes during blending: Model how to place a marker in a Response Board sound box for each sound in the word. Move your finger from left to right as you stretch the sounds. Blend the sounds to say the word. Then repeat the routine using the same sound set, asking children to respond with you. Repeat this lesson as needed.

wavebreakmedia/Shutterstock.com

Phonemic Awareness

PHONEME SEGMENTATION

Explain that you will be taking apart the sounds in a word. Select a word from the word list for the unit and week, such as *sat*. Display the **Sound Boxes.** I am going to say a word. Then I will say it sound by sound. As I say each sound, I will place one counter in each box. Listen: *sat*. I will stretch the sounds in *sat:* /sssaaat/. Now I will say the sounds in *sat,* one at a time: /s/ /a/ /t/. The first sound is /s/. The middle sound is /a/. The last sound is /t/. Watch as I place a marker in a box for each sound I hear: /sss/ /aaa/ /t/. The word *sat* has three sounds, /s/ /a/ /t/. I have placed three markers.

Work with children to segment phonemes in words. Provide children with markers and **Response Boards** online. Select a word from the list, such as *map*. Say this word after me: *map*. First, we'll stretch the sounds in the word: /mmmaaap/. Now we'll say the sounds one at a time: /m/ /a/ /p/. Put one marker in a box for each sound you hear. The word *map* has three sounds, /m/ /a/ /p/. Continue with other words as needed.

Choose more words and write them on the board. Say a word. Ask children to say each sound in the word and tell how many sounds they hear. Children may use markers and **Response Boards** online as needed.

Corrective Feedback When children make mistakes during segmenting: Say the word, stretching the sounds. Have children repeat. Say the word again, stretching the sounds as you place a marker on the Response Board sound boxes for each sound. Say the sound as you touch each marker. Then repeat the routine using the same word, asking children to respond without you. Use the same routine with any words missed before proceeding with additional examples. Repeat this lesson as needed.

PHONEME CATEGORIZATION

Tell children that you will say three words. Explain that two of the words begin with the same sound and one word begins with a different sound. Select words such as *sail, sand, talk*. Listen to the first sound of each word I say: *sail, sand, talk*. Two of these words begin with the same sound; one does not. *Sail* and *sand* begin with the sound /s/. The word *talk* begins with the sound /t/. The word *talk* does not belong.

Lead children to repeat each word you say and listen for the beginning sound. Select words such as *ticket, tomato, pour*. Two of these words begin with the same sound. One does not. Which word does not belong? Yes, the word *pour* does not belong. *Ticket* and *tomato* begin with the sound /t/. *Pour* does not. *Pour* begins with the /p/ sound. It does not belong. Continue with other words as needed.

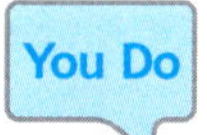

Choose two words with the same beginning sound and one with a different beginning sound. Ask children to say each word and listen for the beginning sounds. Have them identify the word with a different sound in each group.

Corrective Feedback When children make mistakes during categorization: Say the word, stretching the sound in the targeted position for three seconds: /pennn/. Have children repeat. If the targeted sound is a stop sound, say the sound and then the word: /t/, /bat/. Have children repeat. Model stretching the sound in the targeted position for the three words in the set and identifying which two words have the same target sound (for initial, medial, or final sound). Emphasize how the word that doesn't belong contains a different sound in the target position. Repeat this lesson as needed.

Phonemic Awareness

PHONEME SUBSTITUTION

I Do Tell children that you will change one sound in a word to make a new word. Select a word such as *box*. Listen as I say a word: /b/ /o/ /ks/, /boooks/, *box*. The first sound is /b/. I will change the /b/ to /f/ and make a new word. Listen: /f/ /o/ /ks/, /fffoooks/, *fox*. The new word is *fox*. Repeat by changing the middle sound in *cab* from /a/ to /o/ to get *cob* and by changing the final sound in *him* from /m/ to /d/ to get *hid*.

We Do Help children practice substituting phonemes. Select a word such as *dog*. Say this word after me: *dog*. The first sound is /d/. Let's change the /d/ to /f/. Say the sounds: /f/ /o/ /g/, *fog*. The new word is *fog*. Repeat by changing the middle sound in *map* from /a/ to /o/ to get *mop* and by changing the final sound in *lock* from /k/ to /g/ to get *log*. Continue with other similar words.

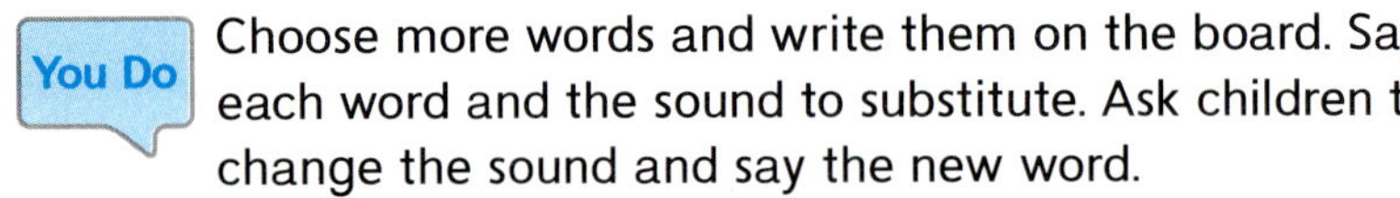

You Do Choose more words and write them on the board. Say each word and the sound to substitute. Ask children to change the sound and say the new word.

Corrective Feedback Say the word, stretching the sounds. Have students repeat. Say the word again, stretching the sounds as you place a marker in the **Sound Boxes** for each sound. Move your finger from left to right as you stretch the sounds. Blend the sounds to say the word. Then point to the box for the targeted sound, remove its marker, and replace it with a new marker as you say the new sound. Have students chorally blend the new word formed. Have students repeat the routine with their own **Response Boards** and markers. Repeat lesson as needed.

PHONEME ADDITION

I Do Tell children you will add a sound to the beginning of a word to make a new word. Select a word such as *ape*. Listen to this word: *ape*. Now I will say the word again and add the sound /k/ to the beginning. When I add /k/ to the beginning of *cape*, I make a new word: /k/ /ape/, *cape*. The new word is *cape*. Repeat by adding the sound /d/ to the end of the word *bran* to make the new word *brand*.

We Do Work with children to add phonemes to words. Select a word such as *chat*. Say this word after me: *at*. Now let's add the sound /ch/ to the beginning of *at* to make a new word: /ch/ /at/, *chat*. The new word is *chat*. Repeat by adding the sound /t/ to the end of the word *day* to make the new word *date*. Continue with other words that can have letters added to make new words.

You Do Choose similar words and write them on the board. Say the word and the sound to be added. Ask children to add the sound and say the new word.

Corrective Feedback When children make mistakes during phoneme addition: Say the word, stretching the sounds. Have children repeat. Say the word again, stretching the sounds as you place a marker in the **Sound Boxes** for each sound. Model how to add the new sound and place the markers in the correct positions. Have children chorally blend the new word formed. Have children repeat the routine with their own **Response Boards** and markers.

wavebreakmedia/Shutterstock.com

Phonemic Awareness

PHONEME DELETION

Tell children you will take away the beginning sound of a word to make a new word. Select a word from the word list for the unit and week, such as *bad.* Listen as I say this word: /b/ /a/ /d/, *bad.* I will take away the first sound: /b/. Listen: /a/ /d/, *add.* The new word is *add. Bad* without /b/ is *add* .

Work with children to delete phonemes from words. Select a word from the list, such as *block.* Say this word after me: *block.* Now let's take away the first sound: /b/. We will say the sounds that are left: /l/ /o/ /k/, *lock.* The new word is *lock. Block* without /b/ is *lock.* Continue using similar words that allow phoneme deletion.

Choose from the word lists that follow. Say the word and the sound to be deleted. Ask children to say the new word.

Corrective Feedback Say the word, stretching the sounds. Have children repeat. Say the word again, stretching the sounds as you place a marker in **Sound Boxes** for each sound. Then point to the box for the targeted sound and remove its marker. Say the new word formed. Have children repeat the routine with their own **Response Boards** and markers. Repeat lesson as needed.

PHONEME REVERSAL

Explain that you will reverse sounds to make new words. Select a word such as *boot.* Listen as I blend these sounds: /b/ /ü/ /t/, /büüüt/, *boot.* Now I will say the sounds backward and blend them to make a new word. Listen: /t/ /ü/ /b/, /tüüüb/, *tube.* The new word is *tube.*

Help children practice reversing sounds in words. Select a word such as *caught.* Let's say these sounds together and blend them: /k/ /ô/ /t/, /kôôôt/, *caught.* Now let's say the sounds backward and blend them to make a new word: /t/ /ô/ /k/, /tôôôk/, *talk.* Repeat with more such as *loot, mood, tune, zoo, gum, lane,* and *nap.*

Choose words such as *back, net, pool, peek, sub, taught,* and *tops* and write them on the board. Say the sounds in a word. Have children blend the sounds to make a word. Then have them say the sounds backward and blend them to make another word.

Corrective Feedback Say the word, stretching the sounds. Have students repeat. Say the word again, stretching the sounds as you place a marker in the **Sound Boxes** for each sound. Then model reversing the sounds and blending the new word. Sweep your fingers under the sound boxes in the reverse direction as you blend the sounds. Have students repeat with their own **Response Boards** and markers. Repeat lesson as needed.

Syda Productions/Shutterstock.com

Phonics

REVIEW SOUND SPELLING

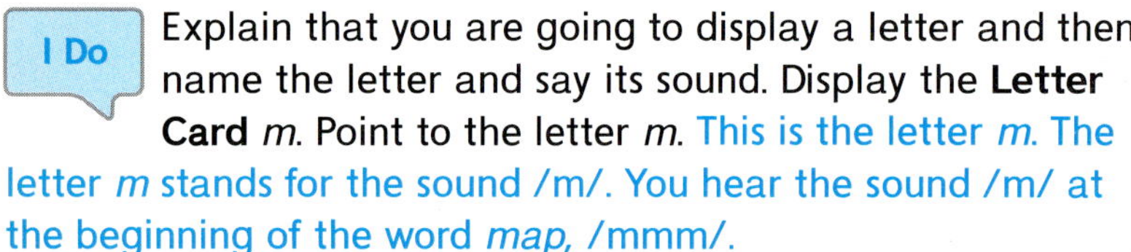

Explain that you are going to display a letter and then name the letter and say its sound. Display the **Letter Card** *m*. Point to the letter *m*. This is the letter *m*. The letter *m* stands for the sound /m/. You hear the sound /m/ at the beginning of the word *map*, /mmm/.

Repeat with the words *mad, man, mat,* and *am, ram,* and *Sam* stretching the /m/ sound to identify the beginning or final letter *m* and the sound /m/.

Distribute **Response Boards**. Help children practice identifying letters and sounds. Select a word from the list, such as *map*, and lead children to identify the beginning sound /m/. Let's write the letter *m* on our Response Boards because *map* begins with /m/. The letter *m* stands for /m/. Let's say it together, /mmm/. Now let's write *m* on our Response Boards because /mmm/ is the sound the letter *m* stands for. Repeat with the words *mail, mend,* and *mix* to identify the beginning letter *m* and the sound /m/ and the words *ham, jam,* and *ram* to identify and isolate final *m*. Repeat with other words to identify the targeted initial, medial, or final sounds.

Corrective Feedback Choose more similar words. Have children identify the initial, medial, or final target letter and the sound it stands for.

Sound-Spelling Errors: When children make mistakes with Sound-Spelling correspondences:

If a child missed the /a/ sound spelled *a*, display the *Apple* **Sound-Spelling Card** and say: The letter *a* stands for the /a/ sound as in *apple*. What is the sound? What letter stands for that sound? Have children repeat that sound. Display the word *am*. Point to the letter *a* as you stretch the /a/ sound for three seconds: /aaam/, *am*. Have children repeat as they stretch the /a/ sound and say the word. Repeat this lesson as needed.

BLEND WORDS

Explain that you are going to practice blending sounds to make words. I will model how to blend sounds to make a word. Write the letter *a* on the board or display it in a pocket chart. When I tap under the letter *a*, I will say its sound. Point to the letter *a*, tap under it and say: /aaa/. The letter a stands for the /a/ sound. Listen: /aaa/. Repeat for the letter *m*, then say: Now I will blend the sounds these letters make to form a word. Sweep your hand under the letters *a* and *m*, and say: /aaammm/, *am*. I blended the sounds /a/ and /m/ to form the word these letters stand for: /aaammm/, *am*.

Help children practice blending sounds to make words. Help children say the sound each letter stands for when you point to the letter. Guide them to blend the sounds when you sweep your hand under the letters. This is the letter *a*. It stands for the /aaa/ sound. This is the letter *m*. It stands for the /mmm/ sound. Run your finger below each letter as you extend the sounds. Let's blend these sounds together: /aaammm/, /aaammm/, *am*. The word is *am*. Say it with me: /aaammm/, *am*.

Choose words from the lists in the next column. Be sure children have been taught all the individual sound-spellings prior to blending them. Have children practice the blending routine until they become comfortable reading the words more quickly.

Corrective Feedback: Display a word that children had difficulty blending, such as *mat*. Model blending the sounds in the word *mat* by sweeping your finger under the letters of the word. Say: Listen to me as I blend the word: /m/ /a/ /t/, /mmmaaat/, *mat*. Then lead children in chorally blending the sounds. Now blend the sounds in the word with me. Monitor each blending step, offering feedback as necessary. Repeat this lesson as needed with other words children are having difficulty with.

wavebreakmedia/Shutterstock.com

Phonics

BUILD WORDS

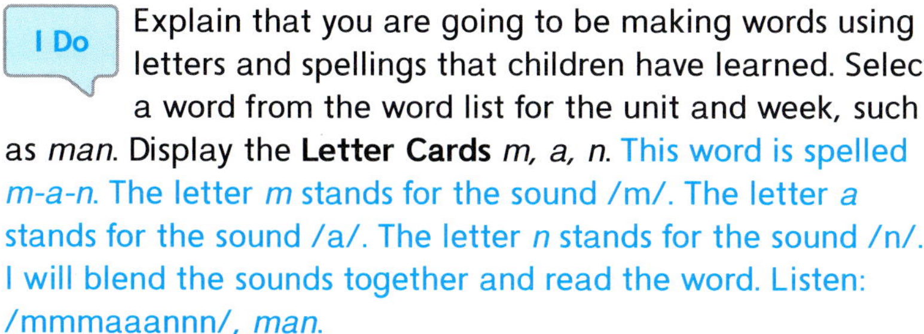

I Do Explain that you are going to be making words using letters and spellings that children have learned. Select a word from the word list for the unit and week, such as *man*. Display the **Letter Cards** *m, a, n*. This word is spelled *m-a-n*. The letter *m* stands for the sound /m/. The letter *a* stands for the sound /a/. The letter *n* stands for the sound /n/. I will blend the sounds together and read the word. Listen: /mmmaaannn/, *man*.

We Do Help children build and blend more words. Select a word that has just one letter different than in *man*, such as *can*. Replace the **Letter Card** *m* with the **Letter Card** *c*. Let's change *m* to *c*. What is the new word we made? The letter *c* stands for the sound /k/. The letter *a* stands for the sound /a/. The letter *n* stands for the sound /n/. Let's blend the sounds together and read the word: kaaannn/, *can*. The new word is can. Say it with me: /kaaannn/, *can*. Now we will build another word. Replace the **Letter Card** *n* with the **Letter Card** *p*. Let's change *n* to *p*. What is the new word we made? The letter *c* stands for the sound /k/. The letter *a* stands for the sound /a/. The letter *p* stands for the sound /p/. Let's blend the sounds together and read the word: /kaaap/, *cap*. The new word is *cap*. Continue changing one letter at a time as needed.

You Do Choose from the word lists that follow. Have children use **Letter Cards** or their **Response Boards** to build and blend a word. Then have them change one or more letters to build and blend a set of words.

Corrective Feedback Display a word that children had difficulty building, such as *sad*. Model blending the sounds in the word: Listen to me as I blend a word: /s/ /a/ /d/, /sssaaad/, *sad*. Then model replacing the *s* in *sad* with *h*: The letter *h* makes the /h/ sound. Let's blend the sounds: /h/ /a/ /d/, /haaad/, *had*. The new word is had. Guide children to repeat the exercise with similar words. Repeat lesson as needed using similar words.

Robert Kneschke/Shutterstock.com

High Frequency Words

READ/SPELL/WRITE

High-frequency words are the most common words in the English language. The words taught are derived from established word lists, such as the *Dolch Basic Sight Vocabulary* list of the top 220 words (no nouns), the Fry top 100 words, and the *American Heritage Word Frequency Book* top 150 words in printed school English. Because these words are so common in English school text, mastery of these words is necessary to fluent reading. Many of these words trip up struggling readers and can impede comprehension when incorrectly identified during reading.

When introducing high-frequency words to students, use the **Read/Spell/Write** Routine that follows.

STEP 1: Read Tell students that throughout the year you will be introducing them to high-frequency words that will appear in many texts they read. Display the High-Frequency Word Card for *said*. Say: This is the word *said*. What is the word? Have students chorally repeat.

look

said

again

of

around

STEP 2: Spell Spell aloud the word *said*. Have students repeat. Say: The word said is spelled s-a-i-d. Spell it with me: s-a-i-d.

When appropriate, point out any spelling patterns students have learned to help them distinguish the word. Say: What's the first sound you hear in *said*? (/s/) What letter have we learned for the /s/ sound? (s) What letter do you see at the beginning of the word *said*? (s). Repeat with the ending sound and letter.

STEP 3: Write Have students write the word multiple times as they spell it aloud. Say: Watch as I write the word *said*. I will say each letter as I write the word. s-a-i-d. Model writing the word on the board. Now it is your turn. Write the word *said* five times. Spell it aloud as you write it. Provide practice by guiding children to complete sentence frames by writing the high-frequency word.

Structural Analysis

OVERVIEW OF LESSONS

Wonders Balanced Literacy provides a comprehensive selection of Structural Analysis lessons for students. The following is a list of lessons you can find at **www.connected.mcgraw-hill.com.**

STRUCTURAL ANALYSIS

For lessons on Structural Analysis related to the following skills go online:

- Plural Nouns *-s*
- Inflectional Ending *-s* (no spelling change)
- Plural Nouns *-es*
- Inflectional Ending *-es* (no spelling change)
- Closed Syllable
- Inflectional Ending *-ed* (no spelling change)
- Inflectional Ending *-ing* (no spelling change)
- Possessives (singular)
- Inflectional Endings *-ed, -ing* (drop final e)
- Inflectional Endings *-ed, -ing* (double final consonant)
- CVC*e* Syllables
- Prefixes *re-, un-, dis-*
- Suffixes *-ful, -less*
- Compound Words
- Contractions with *'s, 're, 'll, 've*
- Contractions with not
- Inflectional Endings and Plurals (change *y* to *i*)
- Comparative Inflectional Endings *-er, -est* (no spelling changes)
- Irregular Plurals
- Abbreviations
- *r*-Controlled Syllables
- Consonant +*le* Syllables (+*el*, +*al*, extend with +*il*)
- Vowel Team Syllables
- Comparative Inflectional Endings *-er, -est* (with spelling changes)
- Three or More Syllable Words
- Plural Possessives
- Prefixes *pre-, non-, mis-*
- Suffixes *-y, -ly* (includes part of speech and spelling change *y* to *i*)
- Suffixes *-ness, -able, -ment, -ous*
- Corrective Feedback
- Additional Words List
- Decodable Reader Correlation

IN PRACTICE

Assess Word Study to Inform Instruction

Use these Assessment tools to evaluate student progress in word study and help you make decisions about reading levels, small group instruction, and assignments.

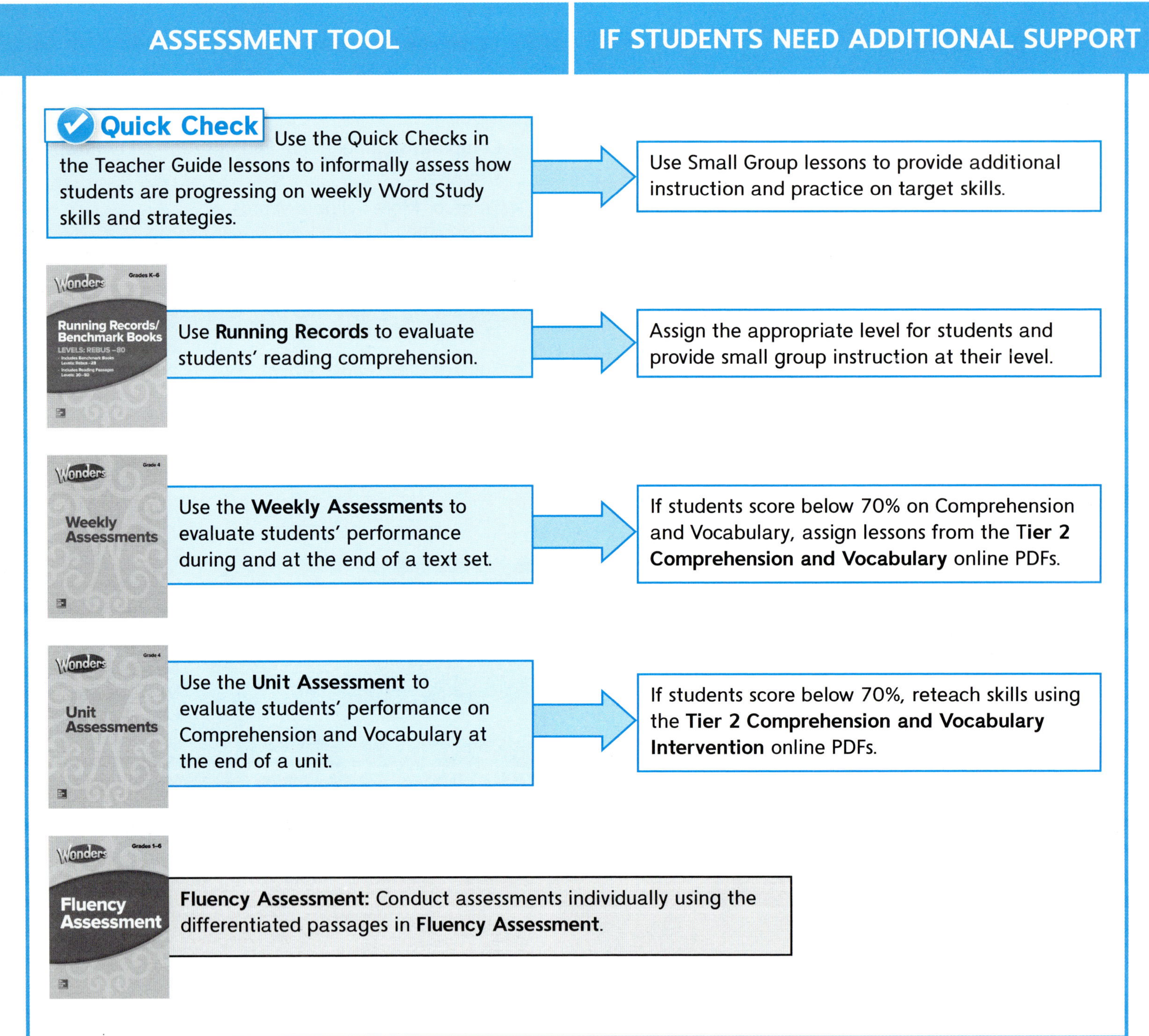

IMPROVING LITERACY FOR ENGLISH LEARNERS: WHAT TEACHERS NEED TO KNOW

By Dr. Jana Echevarria

Professor Emerita and founding researcher and developer of the SIOP Model
Co-author of 14 books in the SIOP Model series, including *Developing Academic Language with the SIOP Model* and *Making Content Comprehensible for English Learners: The SIOP Model*

"English learners benefit from exposure to grade-level texts and discussions to build their language and literacy skills. However, focused, explicit teaching of the skills they need will help them become more effective and efficient readers and writers."

-Dr. Jana Echevarria

wavebreakmedia/Shutterstock.com

The future of the United States will be impacted by the quality of instruction offered to English learners. If that statement sounds like hyperbole, consider that the number of English learners in our schools has reached nearly 5.5 million, comprising about 10% of the U.S. school population. Between 1998 and 2009, the number of English learners increased by more than 50%, far exceeding the growth of the overall school population (National Clearinghouse for English Language Acquisition 2011). Although many English learners are immigrants, 76% of elementary-age English learners were born in America, providing the opportunity for teachers to have a positive influence on their learning from the outset of their school careers.

Amid increased academic rigor and high standards for all K–12 students, teachers are challenged to prepare their students to be college and career ready. They are concerned for English learners in particular since these students must make academic progress in English language development and academic content and literacy simultaneously. The large, and growing, number of English learner students underscores the necessity for the kind of literacy instruction and language development that supports their learning.

The future of the United States will be impacted by the quality of instruction offered to English learners.

The status of English learners in schools has prompted an increased number of studies that have investigated effective instruction for these students.

Research-based Practice

Best practices for English learners include a number of strategies and techniques that make content comprehensible while developing their academic English (August and Shanahan 2010; Echevarria, Vogt, and Short 2013; Genesee, Lindholm-Leary, Saunders, and Christian 2006). Although English learners learn in many of the same ways that English speakers do, their unique linguistic needs require that additional supports be provided. Some of the common instructional techniques that are effective with all students include having clear goals and objectives that direct the lesson and give it a specific focus. The objectives are reviewed at the beginning of the lesson so that students are aware of the lesson's expectations and are better able to participate. Also, linking new learning to previous learning makes important connections for students and reinforces previously taught skills and concepts. Effective teachers model new skills and procedures as part of the learning process (e.g., "I do," "You do," "We do"). Once students see how to accomplish a task, they move more quickly to working independently and completing the task. Finally, active engagement and participation by students enhance learning. Students cannot be expected to learn unless they concentrate, work, and invest themselves in mastering the tasks of lessons.

Additional Supports for English Learners

English learners require additional supports beyond what we know are effective practices for all students. Some of these supports are intended to build English learners' language proficiency in English, and others are designed to provide access to academic content. English proficiency is the greatest predictor of academic success for English learners, more than all other factors combined (Suarez-Orozco, Suarez-Orozco, and Todorova 2008). The language required for school tasks—reading, writing, speaking, and listening in English to learn and demonstrate understanding of lesson concepts—is called academic English. Academic language differs from conversational English in that it is more complex and not typically encountered in everyday settings. Thus, it is the type of language that, to a large extent, must be explicitly taught (e.g., key vocabulary terms or functional use of language, such as how to confirm information, describe, and disagree). Academic language use is particularly challenging for English learners who are acquiring English at the same time that school tasks require a high level of English usage.

> Although English learners learn in many of the same ways that English speakers do, their unique linguistic needs require that additional supports be provided.

English learners also need instruction adjusted so they can access academic content. Imagine trying to learn a new, difficult concept when the person explaining it is speaking a language you are unfamiliar with. That is the situation English learners face in class every day. Effective teachers of English learners use teaching techniques that make the spoken message and written text more comprehensible for them (Echevarria, Vogt, and Short, 2013).

The kinds of supports that facilitate access to content and develop English language proficiency include:

Using multiple media

Words and concepts are brought to life for English learners through the use of a variety of supports. Through retelling cards, students have multiple exposures to the story's sequence and ideas or the information read. Video clips are especially useful for introducing the concept of the week and for showing vocabulary words visually (e.g., *armadillo, hibernate,* and *lightning*). Technology offers myriad options for creating a context, illustrating a word or concept, and organizing information into chunks that are more easily learned and remembered.

Providing additional practice and repetition

Learning new information, words, and concepts in a new language is quite challenging. English learners need multiple exposures to new material and benefit from opportunities to practice interacting with it in authentic ways.

Building background knowledge

The experiences and knowledge that English learners bring to a lesson are important resources on which to build. Teachers explicitly link the lesson's concepts to students' background to improve comprehension and make lessons relevant.

English learners need multiple exposures to new material and benefit from opportunities to practice interacting with it in authentic ways.

Providing explicit instruction of literacy skills

English learners benefit from exposure to grade-level texts and discussions to build their language and literacy skills. However, focused, explicit teaching of the skills they need will help them become more effective and efficient readers and writers. The result will be greater participation in lessons and overall achievement.

Highlighting and teaching vocabulary

English learners need enhanced, explicit vocabulary development. Direct instruction of high-frequency words and abstract words is critical for supporting comprehension. Since these students need to acquire thousands of English words to be proficient, vocabulary learning can be expedited through explicit teaching of word-learning strategies such as understanding word parts (e.g., roots and affixes). Also, Spanish speakers benefit from learning cognates so that they see the relationship between Spanish and English (e.g., *artículo*/article and *ejemplo/example*).

wavebreakmedia/Shutterstock.com

Ensuring opportunities for oral discourse

Specific time allotted for speaking practice is essential for developing language and literacy skills. Collaborative conversations, including those around productive group work, provide these opportunities. However, lessons need to include explicit instruction on how to carry on collaborative conversations. Further, interactive teaching is important where teachers structure engaging interactions with students according to their language proficiency levels. Academic language development is hindered by a lack of planned speaking practice. The more exposure students have and the more time students spend using academic language, the faster they will develop language proficiency (Saunders and Goldenberg 2010).

Capitalizing on students' native language

Although literacy in English can be developed without proficiency in the native language, academic literacy in the native language facilitates the development of academic literacy in English. Students' native language is a rich resource that can be used as a foundation for learning.

The Importance of Fidelity

Research evidence confirms the importance of using the best practices discussed in this paper for helping English learners perform well academically. Since we know these practices provide the support English learners need for accessing content and developing English proficiency, they should become part of every teacher's instructional repertoire. When teachers use these practices only occasionally or selectively, their students do not achieve as much as those students whose teachers use them consistently

The more exposure students have and the more time students spend using academic language, the faster they will develop language proficiency.

to a high degree (Echevarria, Richards-Tutor, Chinn, and Ratleff 2011). To improve literacy and language development for English learners—and to help them be college and career ready—research-based practices need to be part of each and every lesson.

Watch the Videos

See Dr. Jana Echevarria discuss the **"Best Practices for Teaching English Learners."**

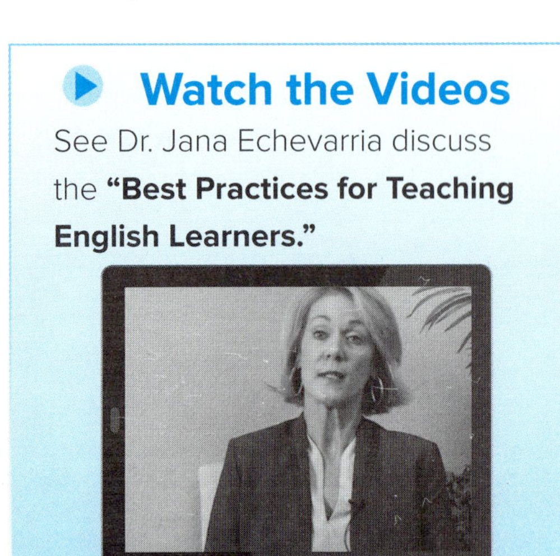

www.connected.mcgraw-hill.com

References

August, D., and D. Shanahan. 2010. "Effective English Literacy Instruction for English Learners." In *Improving Education for English Learners: Research-Based Approaches*. Sacramento, CA: California Department of Education, pp. 209–249.

Echevarria, J., C. Richards-Tutor, V. Chinn, and P. Ratleff. 2011. "Did They Get It? The Role of Fidelity in Teaching English Learners." *Journal of Adolescent and Adult Literacy*. 54(6), 425–434.

Echevarria, J., M.E. Vogt, and D. Short. 2013. *Making Content Comprehensible for English Learners: The SIOP® Model*, Fourth Edition. Boston: Allyn & Bacon.

Genesee, F., K. Lindholm-Leary, W. Saunders, and D. Christian. 2006. *Educating English Language Learners: A Synthesis of Research Evidence*. New York: Cambridge University Press.

National Clearinghouse for English Language Acquisition. 2011. "The Growing Numbers of English Learner Students." Retrieved from www.ncela.gwu.edu/files/uploads. Saunders, W.M. and C. Goldenberg. 2010. "Research to Guide English Language Development Instruction." *Improving Education for English Learners: Research-Based Approaches* (pp. 21–81). Sacramento: California Department of Education.

Suarez-Orozco, C., M. Suarez-Orozco, and I. Todorova. 2008. *Learning a New Land: Immigrant Students in American Society*. Boston: Harvard University Press.

IN PRACTICE

English Learner Profiles

OVERVIEW

The English learners in your classroom have a variety of backgrounds. An increasing portion of English learners are born in the United States. Some of these students are just starting school in the primary grades; others are long-term English learners with underdeveloped academic skills. These students have more exposure to English than other English learners. Some students come from their native countries with a strong educational foundation. The academic skills of these newly arrived students are well developed and are parallel to skills of native English-speaking peers. Other English learners immigrate to the United States with little academic experience.

These English learners are not "blank slates." Their oral language proficiency and literacy in their first languages can be used to facilitate literacy development in English. Systematic, explicit, and appropriately scaffolded instruction and sufficient time help English learners attain English proficiency and meet high standards in core academic subjects.

PROFICIENCY LEVEL DESCRIPTORS

Proficiency Level Descriptors (PLDs) for English learners reflect a spectrum in language education. The three levels—Emerging, Expanding, and Bridging—represent the different stages of a student's development of listening, speaking, reading, and writing in the English language. The PLDs are useful tools in gauging a student's progress as they learn the intricacies of the English language.

EMERGING

This level of language proficiency is often referred to as the "silent" stage, in which students' receptive skills are engaged and typically more advanced than their speaking skills. It is important for teachers and peers to respect an English learner's initial silence or allow the student to respond in his or her native language. It is also important to realize that these beginning students have a wide range of abilities in their first language. They are able to transfer knowledge and skills from their first language as they develop English and learn grade-level content. Emerging students include those with limited formal schooling, though other students have had schooling in their native language and are academically parallel to native English-speaking peers.

The **Emerging** student . . .

- recognizes English phonemes that correspond to phonemes produced in primary language;
- is able to apply transferable grammar concepts and skills from the primary language;
- initially demonstrates more receptive than productive English skills;
- produces English vocabulary words and phrases to communicate basic needs in social and academic settings;
- may respond with gestures or short phrases or sentences;
- begins to demonstrate an internalization of English grammar and usage by recognizing and correcting some errors when speaking and reading aloud.

wavebreakmedia/Shutterstock.com

EXPANDING

Students at this proficiency level begin to tailor their English language skills to meet communication and learning demands with increasing accuracy. They possess vocabulary and knowledge of grammatical structures that allow them to more fully participate in classroom activities and discussions. They are generally more comfortable producing both spoken and written language.

The **Expanding** student . . .

- produces most English phonemes correctly while reading aloud;
- can identify more details of information that has been presented orally or in writing;
- uses more complex vocabulary and sentences to communicate needs and express ideas;
- uses specific vocabulary learned, including academic language;
- participates more fully in discussions with peers and adults;
- reads and comprehends a wider range of reading materials;
- writes brief narratives and expository texts;
- demonstrates a deeper internalization of English grammar and usage by recognizing and correcting errors when speaking and reading aloud.

BRIDGING

Students at this language proficiency level possess vocabulary and grammar structures that approach those of an English-proficient speaker, and they can communicate effectively with peers and adults in both social and academic situations. Students can understand grade-level text but still need some English language development support, such as preteaching concepts and skills. While the English language proficiency of these students is advanced, some linguistic support for accessing content is still necessary.

The **Bridging** student . . .

- applies knowledge of common English morphemes in oral and silent reading;
- understand increasingly more nonliteral social and academic language;
- responds using extensive vocabulary;
- participates in and initiates more extended social conversations with peers and adults;
- communicates orally and in writing with fewer grammatical errors;
- reads with good comprehension a wide range of narrative and expository texts;
- writes using more standard forms of English on various content-area topics;
- becomes more creative and analytical when writing.

wavebreakmedia/Shutterstock.com

Oral Language

Providing multiple opportunities to speak in the classroom and welcoming all levels of participation will motivate English learners to take part in class discussions and build oral proficiency.

STRATEGIES FOR ENGLISH LEARNERS These teaching strategies will encourage whole class and small group discussions for all language proficiency levels of English learners.

Wait/Different Responses

- Give students enough time to answer the question. They may need more time to process their ideas.
- Students can respond in different ways. They can:
  - answer in their native language; then you can rephrase in English
  - ask a more proficient EL speaker to translate
  - answer with nonverbal cues

Teacher: How would you describe Charlotte?

EL Response: Very nice. (Emerging)

She is nice. (Expanding)

She is very nice to Wilbur. (Bridging)

Repeat

- Give positive confirmation to the answers that each English learner offers. If the response is correct, repeat what the student has said in a clear voice and at a slower pace. This validation will motivate other English learners to participate.

Teacher: How would you describe the faces of the bobcats?

EL Response: They look scared. (Emerging)

They look scared of the lions. (Expanding)

They look scared of the lions waiting behind the bush. (Bridging)

Teacher: That's right, Silvia. They are scared. Everyone show me your scared face.

Revise for Form

- Repeating an answer allows you to model a proper response. Correct any grammar or punctuation errors.

Teacher: Who are the main characters in the story *Zathura*?

EL Response: Danny and Walter is. (Emerging)

Danny and Walter is the characters. (Expanding)

Danny and Walter are main characters. (Bridging)

Teacher: Yes. Danny and Walter are the main characters. Remember to use the verb are when you are telling about more than one person. Let's repeat the sentence.

Revise for Meaning

- Repeating an answer offers an opportunity to clarify the meaning of a response.

Teacher: Where did the golden feather come from?

EL Response: The bird. (Emerging)

It came from the bird. (Expanding)

The golden feather came from the bird in the sky. (Bridging)

Teacher: That's right. The golden feather came from the Firebird.

Elaborate

- If students give a one-word answer or nonverbal cue, elaborate on the answer to model fluent speaking.
- Provide more examples or repeat the answer using proper academic language.

Teacher: Why does the girls' mother have her arms crossed?

EL Response: She is mad. (Emerging)

She is mad at the girls. (Expanding)

She is mad at her two daughters. (Bridging)

Teacher: Can you tell me more? Why is she mad?

EL Response: Because the girls are late. (Emerging)

She's mad because the girls are late. (Expanding)

She's mad because her daughters got home late. (Bridging)

Elicit

- Prompt students to give more comprehensive responses by asking questions or guiding them to answer.

Teacher: Listen as I read the caption under the photograph. What information does the caption tell us?

EL Response: Butterfly. (Emerging)

It tells about the butterfly. (Expanding)

It tells about the butterfly in the meadow. (Bridging)

Teacher: What did you find out about the butterfly?

EL Response: It has nectar. (Emerging)

It drinks a lot of nectar. (Expanding)

It drinks nectar from every flower. (Bridging)

Teacher: Yes. The butterfly drinks nectar from the flower.

COLLABORATIVE CONVERSATIONS FOR ENGLISH LEARNERS

Throughout each unit, students engage in class, small group, and partner discussions. The chart below provides prompt frames and response frames that will help students at different language proficiency levels interact with each other in meaningful ways.

You may want to post these frames in the class for student reference. Also remind students to follow turn-taking rules during all discussions.

CORE SKILLS	PROMPT FRAMES	RESPONSE FRAMES
Elaborate and Ask Questions to Request Clarification	Can you tell me more about? Can you give some details on...? Can you be more specific? What do you mean by...? How/Why is that important?	I think it means that... In other words... It's important because... It's similar to when...
Support Ideas with Text Evidence	Can you give any examples from the text? What are some examples from other texts? What evidence do you see for that? How can you justify that idea? Can you show me where the text says that?	The text says that... An example from another text is... According to... Some evidence that supports that is...
Build on and/or Challenge Partner's Ideas	What do you think of the idea that...? Can we add to this idea? Do you agree? What are other ideas/points of view? What else do we need to think about? How does that connect to the idea...?	I would add that... I want to follow up on your idea... Another way to look at it is... What you said made me think of...
Paraphrase	What do we know so far? To recap, I think that... I'm not sure that was clear. How can we relate what I said to the topic/question?	So, you are saying that... Let me see if I understand you... Do you mean that...? In other words... It sounds like you are saying that...
Determine the Main Idea and Supporting Details	What have we discussed so far? How can we summarize what we talked about? What can we agree upon? What are the main points or ideas we can share? What relevant details support the main points or ideas? What key ideas can we take away?	We can say that... The main idea seems to be... As a result of this conversation, we think that we should... The evidence suggests that...

VOCABULARY DEVELOPMENT FOR ENGLISH LEARNERS

Define/Example/Ask Routine for English Learners

An effective method of helping students learn English vocabulary is the Define/Example/Ask routine. When introducing a new vocabulary word, first provide the word's definition, both in English and in Spanish. Also refer to the word's cognate, if applicable. Then model using the vocabulary word in a sentence. To reinforce students' understanding of the word, ask them a question that relates to the vocabulary word. Students may find it helpful to hear an example in both languages as well. See below for an example of the Define/Example/Ask routine.

One word in the selection is *team*. Say it with me: *team*.

1. **Define:** A team is a group of people who work together in a sport or other activity.
2. **Example:** The girls play on a team.
3. **Ask:** What are some teams you know about?

Leveled Readers for English Learners

Wonders Balanced Literacy offers vocabulary support for English learners in the Leveled Readers. While all Leveled Readers note important vocabulary words, EL Leveled Readers provide additional words that English learners may be unfamiliar with. Taking care to review these words with English learners can help to strengthen their understanding of content vocabulary.

These words are listed on the inside cover of the EL Leveled Readers. They can be taught using the provided Digital Visual Vocabulary Cards online. See "Visual Support for English Learners," at right, for more information on how these cards are structured and presented.

VISUAL SUPPORT FOR ENGLISH LEARNERS

Purpose and Use

The English Learner Digital Visual Vocabulary Cards are photo-word cards that visually introduce specific vocabulary from the program. The photos are intended to preteach vocabulary to English learners and offer additional, meaningful language and concept support. The English Learner Vocabulary is selected from the weekly Shared Reads as well as the EL Leveled Readers. These words are central to the content of the Shared Reads and Leveled Readers and support comprehension of the fiction or nonfiction texts.

Structure of the Cards

Each English Learner Digital Visual Vocabulary Card focuses on one of the English Learner Vocabulary words from the Shared Read or Leveled Reader. This word is written at the top of the card beside a speaker icon that can be clicked to play an audio recording of the word being spoken aloud. Each card also features two tabs labeled "Example" and "Routine." The Example tab features a large photo for visual reference. Below the photo is a sample sentence to reinforce how the vocabulary word is used in English. The Routine tab features the Define/Example/Ask routine.

Additional Routines

English learners can engage in activities that provide strategies to get them talking and using new language in a collaborative setting. Students can:

- chorally pronounce vocabulary words to focus on articulation.
- engage in conversations with a peer using structured sentence frames to use new words in oral speech.
- role-play to make vocabulary words come to life and to use the words in everyday situations.
- engage in movement activities to experience a new word's meaning.

These techniques make instruction engaging and memorable for English learners. These low-risk ways to practice speaking help students make connections, collaborate, and develop understanding as they acquire vocabulary.

IN PRACTICE

Language Development

SOUND AND PHONICS TRANSFERS

To read and speak fluently in English, English learners need to master a wide range of phonemic awareness, phonics, and word study skills. The Sound and Phonics Transfer Charts on pages 6-13 of the **Language Transfers Handbook** online are designed to help you anticipate and understand possible student errors in pronouncing or perceiving English sounds.

- **Highlight Transferrable Skills** If the phonics skill transfers from a particular native language to English and that language group is the only one being taught, state that during the lesson. In most lessons an English learner feature will indicate which sounds do and do not transfer in specific languages.
- **Preteach Non-Transferrable Skills** Prior to teaching a phonics lesson, check the chart to determine if the sound and/or spelling transfers from a student's native language into English. If it does not, preteach the sound and spelling during Small Group time.
- **Provide Additional Practice and Time** If the skill does not transfer from the student's native language into English, the student will require more time and practice mastering the sound and spellings. Continue to review the phonics skill during Small Group time in upcoming weeks until the student has mastered it.

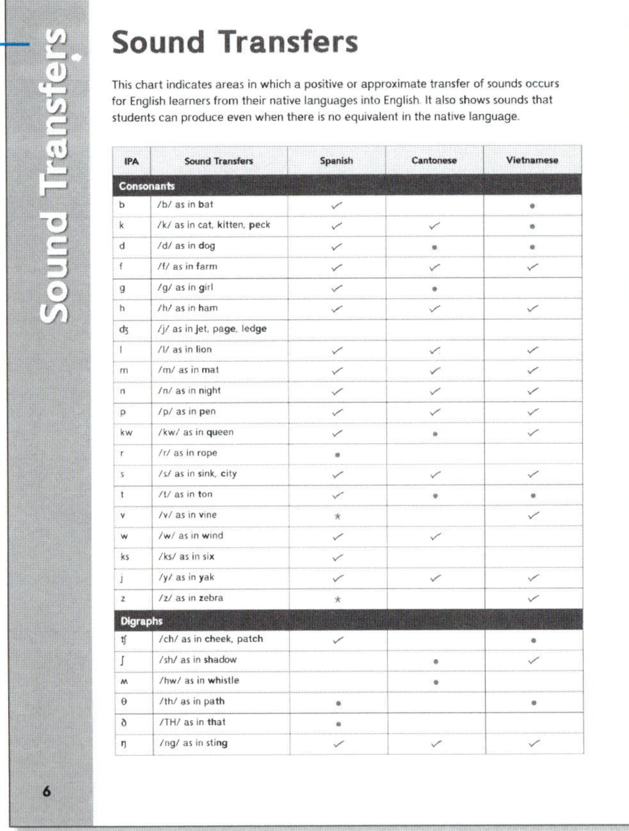

Sound Transfers

Sound Transfers

This chart indicates areas in which a positive or approximate transfer of sounds occurs for English learners from their native languages into English. It also shows sounds that students can produce even when there is no equivalent in the native language.

IPA	Sound Transfers	Spanish	Cantonese	Vietnamese
Consonants				
b	/b/ as in bat	✓		•
k	/k/ as in cat, kitten, peck	✓	✓	•
d	/d/ as in dog	✓	•	•
f	/f/ as in farm	✓	✓	✓
g	/g/ as in girl	✓	•	
h	/h/ as in ham	✓	✓	✓
ʤ	/j/ as in jet, page, ledge			
l	/l/ as in lion	✓	✓	✓
m	/m/ as in mat	✓	✓	✓
n	/n/ as in night	✓	✓	✓
p	/p/ as in pen	✓	✓	✓
kw	/kw/ as in queen	✓	•	✓
r	/r/ as in rope	•		
s	/s/ as in sink, city	✓	✓	✓
t	/t/ as in ton	✓	•	•
v	/v/ as in vine	*		✓
w	/w/ as in wind	✓	✓	
ks	/ks/ as in six	✓		
j	/y/ as in yak	✓	✓	✓
z	/z/ as in zebra	*		✓
Digraphs				
ʧ	/ch/ as in cheek, patch	✓		•
ʃ	/sh/ as in shadow		•	✓
ʍ	/hw/ as in whistle		•	
θ	/th/ as in path	•		•
ð	/TH/ as in that	•		
ŋ	/ng/ as in sting	✓	✓	✓

6

Use the Sound Transfers chart to review positive or approximate sound transfers that occur from English to native languages of English learners.

Phonics Transfers

Phonics Transfers: Sound-Symbol Match

Sound-Symbol Match	Spanish	Cantonese	Vietnamese
Consonants			
/b/ as in bat	✓		✓
/k/ as in cat	✓		✓
/k/ as in kitten	✓		✓
/k/ as in peck			
/d/ as in dog	✓		✓
/f/ as in farm	✓		
/g/ as in girl	✓		✓
/h/ as in ham			✓
/j/ as in jet, page, ledge			
/l/ as in lion	✓		✓
/m/ as in mat	✓		✓
/n/ as in night	✓		✓
/p/ as in pen	✓		✓
/kw/ as in queen			✓
/r/ as in rope			
/s/ as in sink, city	✓		✓
/t/ as in ton	✓		✓
/v/ as in vine	✓		✓
/w/ as in wind	✓		
/ks/ as in six	✓		
/y/ as in yak	✓		
/z/ as in zebra			
Digraphs			
/ch/ as in cheek, patch	✓		
/sh/ as in shadow			
/hw/ as in whistle			
/th/ as in path			✓
/TH/ as in that			
/ng/ as in sting	✓		✓
Short Vowels			
/a/ as in cat			✓
/e/ as in net	✓		✓
/i/ as in kid			
/o/ as in spot			✓
/u/ as in cup			

10

Use the Phonics Transfers chart to review sound-symbol matches between English and native languages of English learners.

GRAMMAR TRANSFER

English language grammar differs widely from that of many other languages. For example, a student's primary language may use a different word order than English does, may not use parts of speech in the same way, or may use different verb tenses. The Grammar Transfers Charts on pages 16-19 of the Language Transfers Handbook are designed to help you anticipate possible transfer errors in speaking and writing in Standard English.

- **Highlight Transferrable Skills** If the grammar skill transfers from the student's native language to English and that language group is the only one being taught, state that it transfers during the first few sessions. In many lessons, an English learner feature will indicate which skills do and do not transfer.
- **Preteach Non-Transferrable Skills** Prior to teaching a grammar lesson, check the chart to determine if the skill transfers from the student's native language into English. If it does not, preteach the skill during Small Group time. Provide sentence frames and ample structured and unstructured opportunities to use the skill in spoken English.

Grammar Transfers

Grammatical Form	Transfer Mistakes in English	Native Language	Cause of Difficulty
Pronouns			
Gender-Specific Pronouns	**Uses pronouns with the inappropriate gender** *He is my sister.*	Cantonese, Hmong, Korean, Spanish, Tagalog, Vietnamese	The third person pronoun in the native language is gender free, or the personal pronoun is omitted.
	Uses inappropriate gender, particularly with neutral nouns *The day is sunny. She is beautiful.*	Spanish, Vietnamese, Hmong	Nouns have feminine or masculine gender in the native language, and the gender may be carried over into English.
Object Pronouns	**Confuses subject and object pronouns** *Her talks to me.*	Cantonese, Hmong	The same pronoun form is used for subject and object in the native language.
	Omits object pronouns *That girl is very rude, so nobody likes.*	Korean, Vietnamese	The native language does not use direct objects.
Pronoun and Number Agreement	**Uses the wrong number for pronouns** *I saw many red birds. It was pretty.*	Cantonese, Korean, Arabic	The native language does not require number agreement.
Subject Pronouns	**Omits subject pronouns** *Mom isn't home. Is at work.*	Korean, Spanish, Vietnamese	Subject pronouns may be dropped because in the native language the verb ending gives information about the number and/or gender.
Pronouns in Clauses	**Omits pronouns in clauses** *If don't do homework, they will not learn.*	Cantonese, Vietnamese, Tagalog	The native language does not need a subject in the subordinate clause.
Pronouns and Nouns	**Overuses pronouns with nouns** *This school, it is very good.*	Vietnamese	This is popular in speech in some languages. The speaker mentions a topic, then makes a comment about it.
	Avoids pronouns and repeats nouns *Carla visits her sister every Sunday, and Carla makes a meal.*	Korean, Vietnamese	In the native language, the speaker repeats nouns and does not use pronouns.
Pronoun *one*	**Omits the pronoun *one*** *I saw two dogs, and I like the small.*	Spanish, Vietnamese	Adjectives can stand alone in the native language, but English requires a noun or *one*.
Possessive Forms	**Confuses possessive forms** *The book is my.*	Cantonese, Hmong, Vietnamese	Cantonese and Hmong speakers tend to omit the final *n* sound, which may create confusion between *my* and *mine*.

17

Use the Grammar Transfers chart to address common mistakes that some English learners make when they transfer grammatical forms from their native languages into English.

- **Provide Additional Practice and Time** If the skill does NOT transfer from the student's native language into English, the student will require more time and practice mastering it. Continue to review the skill during Small Group time.
- **Use Contrastive Analysis** When you are teaching a single language group, tell students when a skill does not transfer and include contrastive analysis work to make the students aware of how to correct their speaking and writing for standard English.
- **Increase Writing and Speaking Opportunities** Increase the amount of structured writing and speaking opportunities for students needing work on specific grammatical forms. Sentence starters and paragraph frames such as those found in the lessons, are ideal for both written and oral exercises. Plays, memorizing short poems, focused conversations, and song lyrics are other ways of doing this.
- **Focus on Meaning** Always focus on the meaning of sentences in all exercises. As students improve and fine-tune their English speaking and writing skills, work with students on basic comprehension of spoken and written English.

COGNATES

Cognates are words that have similar spellings, meanings, and sometimes similar pronunciations across two languages. They make up one third to one half of the words in languages that share cognates with English, for example, Spanish, French, and Portuguese. Cognates are often useful in promoting comprehension for students whose native language has a Latin base. For example, using "*calculate the mass/volume ratio*" may be easier for some students to understand than "*figure out the mass/volume ratio*" as "*calcular*" is a Spanish cognate.

Studies indicate that—under some circumstances—English learners whose first language shares cognates with English are able to draw on first language knowledge to figure out the meanings of cognates in their second language. See the strategies for cognate instruction below for information on how to teach cognates to English Learners.

COGNATES STRATEGY INSTRUCTION

Help students whose first language shares cognates with English draw on their first language knowledge by teaching how to use cognate knowledge:

- Explain what cognates are: cognates are words that look similar, sound similar, and share meanings across some languages.
- Explain that many words have multiple meanings and sometimes cognates share one meaning but not others.
- Explain that sometimes words look and/or sound alike but are not cognates. *Pie* is an example. It means "foot" in Spanish but "a type of pastry" in English.
- Model differences and similarities, in sounds and letters, for example *mysterious* and *misterioso*.
- Ask students whose first language shares cognate status with English to pronounce the pairs and note similarities and differences in sounds.
- Asks students to find letters in the pairs that are similar.
- Give students the opportunity to find cognates in authentic text.
- Ask students to check to see if the meaning of the word in their first language makes sense in the English sentence.
- Check a dictionary to confirm.

SAMPLE LESSON

See the following sample teacher lesson for ideas about how to teach students to use cognates.

- Show cognate word pairs and images on an interactive whiteboard or screen (*liberty/libertad*).
- Explain that these words are cognates. They are in two different languages, but they look similar, they sound similar, and they mean approximately the same thing.
- Model differences and similarities for *liberty* and *libertad*:
  - They have many of the same letters, but some letters are different.
- Ask a native Spanish speaker to say *liberty* and compare the sounds in *libertad*. The consonants are similar, but some of the vowels and the ending sound different.
- Partner-talk: *Look at the words* liberty/libertad *and* disagreeable/desagradble. *Which letters are the same? Do the words sound similar enough that you would recognize they may be related?*
- Explain to students that when they encounter a word they don't know, but it has lots of the same letters and sounds the same, it may be a cognate, and they should check to see if the meaning of the word in their native language makes sense in the English sentence that includes the cognate. It is always important to then check a dictionary.
- Explain to students that words can have multiple meanings. Not all meanings of a cognate will be the same in both languages. Explain to students that they also need to watch out for false cognates, which are words that sound the same and/or are spelled the same, but have different meanings such as (*pie/pie*).
- Give students an opportunity to practice.
- Have students use the table in the student chart to practice checking words for cognate status.
- For each word pair, have students rate whether the words *look* the same and/or *sound* the same on a scale of 1-3 (3 is perfect or near perfect correspondence).
- Students should use a dictionary or the sample sentence to test the meaning of each English word and indicate whether the words in the pair share the same *meaning*.
- Students should indicate whether the pair is a cognate pair based on their ratings.

Progress Monitoring

STUDENT RUBRICS

English Learners can benefit from self-evaluation of their proficiency in reading, writing, and speaking and listening. Rubrics that assess the following skills are available online:

- Speaking
- Opinion Writing
- Informative Writing
- Narrative Writing
- Listening in Collaborative Conversations
- Speaking in Collaborative Conversations
- Listening to Presentations
- Speaking during Presentations

The student rubrics use the Emerging, Expanding, and Bridging proficiency levels described on pages 121-122. They function as a useful framework for students to gauge the development of their academic skills. The Writing Rubrics will draw students' attention to the range of their vocabulary; use of descriptive language; understanding of grammatical constructs; knowledge of verb tenses, adverbials, and noun phrases; and understanding of coherent organization. The Collaborative Conversation and Presentation Rubrics will help students focus on asking questions and follow-up questions; understand and use of academic language; comprehend compound and complex sentences; contribute to class, group, and partner discussions; express reasoned opinions; adjust tone in response to audience; and use modal expressions.

Below is an example of the Opinion Writing Rubric for Grade 3.

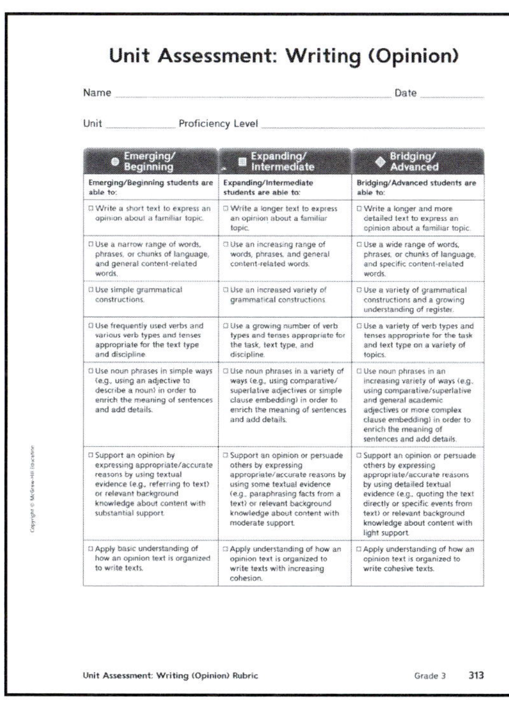

Unit Assessment: Writing (Opinion)

Name ______________________ Date __________

Unit __________ Proficiency Level ______________________

Emerging/ Beginning	Expanding/ Intermediate	Bridging/ Advanced
Emerging/Beginning students are able to:	**Expanding/Intermediate students are able to:**	**Bridging/Advanced students are able to:**
☐ Write a short text to express an opinion about a familiar topic.	☐ Write a longer text to express an opinion about a familiar topic.	☐ Write a longer and more detailed text to express an opinion about a familiar topic.
☐ Use a narrow range of words, phrases, or chunks of language, and general content-related words.	☐ Use an increasing range of words, phrases, and general content-related words.	☐ Use a wide range of words, phrases, or chunks of language, and specific content-related words.
☐ Use simple grammatical constructions.	☐ Use an increased variety of grammatical constructions.	☐ Use a variety of grammatical constructions and a growing understanding of register.
☐ Use frequently used verbs and various verb types and tenses appropriate for the text type and discipline.	☐ Use a growing number of verb types and tenses appropriate for the task, text type, and discipline.	☐ Use a variety of verb types and tenses appropriate for the task and text type on a variety of topics.
☐ Use noun phrases in simple ways (e.g., using an adjective to describe a noun) in order to enrich the meaning of sentences and add details.	☐ Use noun phrases in a variety of ways (e.g., using comparative/superlative adjectives or simple clause embedding) in order to enrich the meaning of sentences and add details.	☐ Use noun phrases in an increasing variety of ways (e.g., using comparative/superlative and general academic adjectives or more complex clause embedding) in order to enrich the meaning of sentences and add details.
☐ Support an opinion by expressing appropriate/accurate reasons by using textual evidence (e.g., referring to text) or relevant background knowledge about content with substantial support.	☐ Support an opinion or persuade others by expressing appropriate/accurate reasons by using some textual evidence (e.g., paraphrasing facts from a text) or relevant background knowledge about content with moderate support.	☐ Support an opinion or persuade others by expressing appropriate/accurate reasons by using detailed textual evidence (e.g., quoting the text directly or specific events from text) or relevant background knowledge about content with light support.
☐ Apply basic understanding of how an opinion text is organized to write texts.	☐ Apply understanding of how an opinion text is organized to write texts with increasing cohesion.	☐ Apply understanding of how an opinion text is organized to write cohesive texts.

Unit Assessment: Writing (Opinion) Rubric Grade 3 313

TEACHER RUBRICS

Also available online are Teacher Rubrics to help you monitor the progress of your English Learners. These rubrics can guide your Level Up decisions as you assess your students' proficiencies in reading, writing, speaking and listening.

The rubrics use the Emerging, Expanding, and Bridging proficiency levels. If students consistently fall within the Bridging category, they can likely level up to On Level texts. The Level Up rubrics will help you focus on students' ability to:

- participate in collaborative conversations
- identify details in text and illustrations
- use context clues to define unfamiliar words and interpret idioms
- compare and contrast two ideas or concepts
- summarize texts
- comprehend appropriate lexical, syntactic, phonological, and discourse features when addressing new or unfamiliar topics

Below is a sample Level Up rubric for Grade 2.

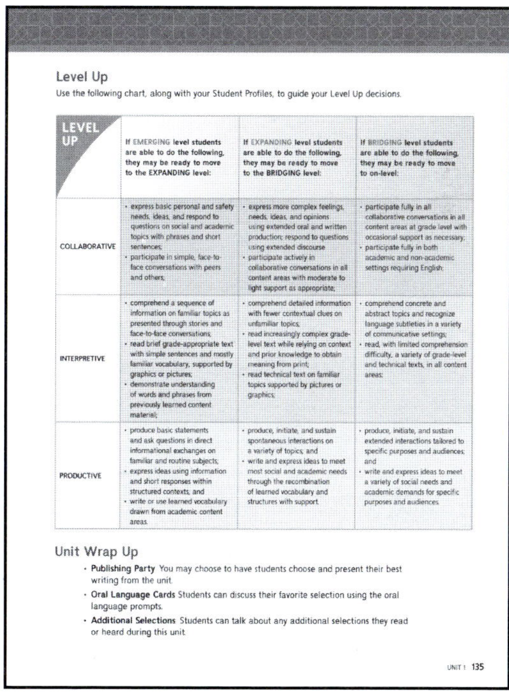

Level Up

Use the following chart, along with your Student Profiles, to guide your Level Up decisions.

LEVEL UP	If EMERGING level students are able to do the following, they may be ready to move to the EXPANDING level:	If EXPANDING level students are able to do the following, they may be ready to move to the BRIDGING level:	If BRIDGING level students are able to do the following, they may be ready to move to on-level:
COLLABORATIVE	• express basic personal and safety needs, ideas, and respond to questions on social and academic topics with phrases and short sentences; • participate in simple, face-to-face conversations with peers and others;	• express more complex feelings, needs, ideas, and opinions using extended oral and written production; respond to questions using extended discourse • participate actively in collaborative conversations in all content areas with moderate to light support as appropriate;	• participate fully in all collaborative conversations in all content areas at grade level with occasional support as necessary; • participate fully in both academic and non-academic settings requiring English;
INTERPRETIVE	• comprehend a sequence of information on familiar topics as presented through stories and face-to-face conversations; • read brief grade-appropriate text with simple sentences and mostly familiar vocabulary, supported by graphics or pictures; • demonstrate understanding of words and phrases from previously learned content material;	• comprehend detailed information with fewer contextual clues on unfamiliar topics; • read increasingly complex grade-level text while relying on context and prior knowledge to obtain meaning from print; • read technical text on familiar topics supported by pictures or graphics;	• comprehend concrete and abstract topics and recognize language subtleties in a variety of communicative settings; • read, with limited comprehension difficulty, a variety of grade-level and technical texts, in all content areas;
PRODUCTIVE	• produce basic statements and ask questions in direct informational exchanges on familiar and routine subjects; • express ideas using information and short responses within structured contexts; and • write or use learned vocabulary drawn from academic content areas.	• produce, initiate, and sustain spontaneous interactions on a variety of topics; and • write and express ideas to meet most social and academic needs through the recombination of learned vocabulary and structures with support.	• produce, initiate, and sustain extended interactions tailored to specific purposes and audiences; and • write and express ideas to meet a variety of social needs and academic demands for specific purposes and audiences.

Unit Wrap Up

- **Publishing Party** You may choose to have students choose and present their best writing from the unit.
- **Oral Language Cards** Students can discuss their favorite selection using the oral language prompts.
- **Additional Selections** Students can talk about any additional selections they read or heard during this unit.

UNIT 1 135

Expanding Text Sets

The text sets in *Wonders Balanced Literacy* can be expanded or modified to meet the needs of your students. The resources below allow you to expand or modify the text sets. Selections below cover a wide range of genres, Lexiles, and Guided Reading levels.

Text Extension Charts

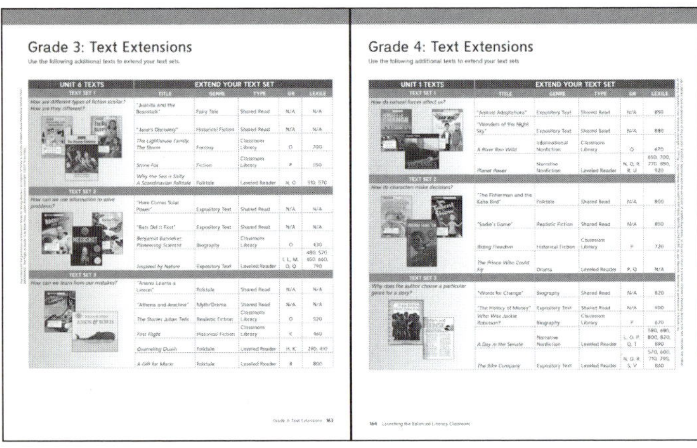
Grade 3: Text Extensions

Grade 4: Text Extensions

The Text Extension Databases on pages 132-177 can be used to extend the text sets. The Kindergarten and Grade 1 Charts include recommendations for adding Literature Big Books, Interactive Read Alouds and Classroom Library selections. For Grades 2-5, the recommended texts are culled from the Student Edition, Classroom Library and Leveled Readers selections.

Leveled Reader Online Database

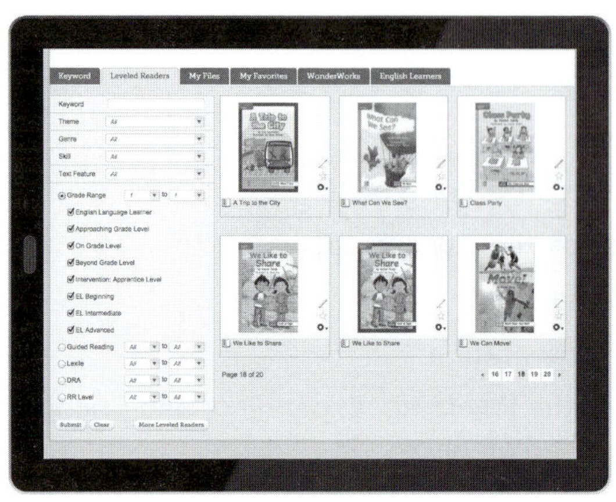

Use the **Leveled Reader Online Database** to locate additional Leveled Readers to go with your text sets. You can sort Leveled Readers by Theme, Genre, Skill, and Text Features. The database also provides lexile and guided reading levels to help you choose the books that are just right for your students.

Literature eBooks

Choose from the **Literature eBooks** online for a wide variety of genres and authors of award-winning selections to extend your text sets. The eBooks provide interactive features such as audio, interactive graphic organizers, multilingual audio summaries, and access to the student binder tool where students can record notes and answer questions about the selections.

Time for Kids Online Selections

Time For Kids Online Articles cover current topics and are related to grade-level social studies and science content. Each grade has six unique articles that include interactive features, such as maps, videos and photos that allow students to explore the topics in depth. Additionally, some of the articles provide students with follow-up activities to deepen their understanding of the content.

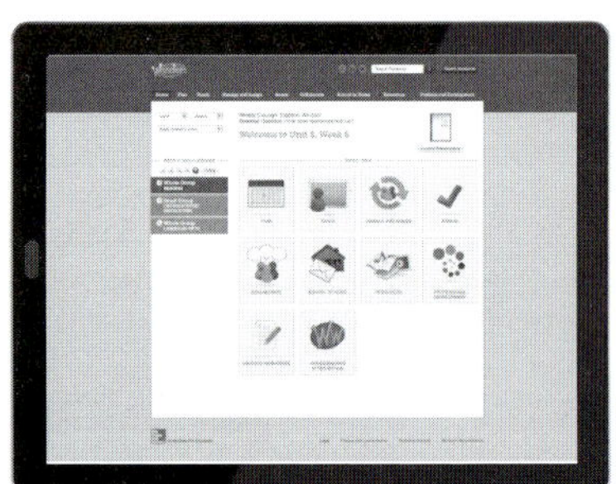

Go Digital!

Reader's Theater Online

Reader's Theater Plays online provide extra opportunities to study drama and practice choral reading. Plays can be used to expand text sets on related inquiry topics.

Unit Bibliography Online

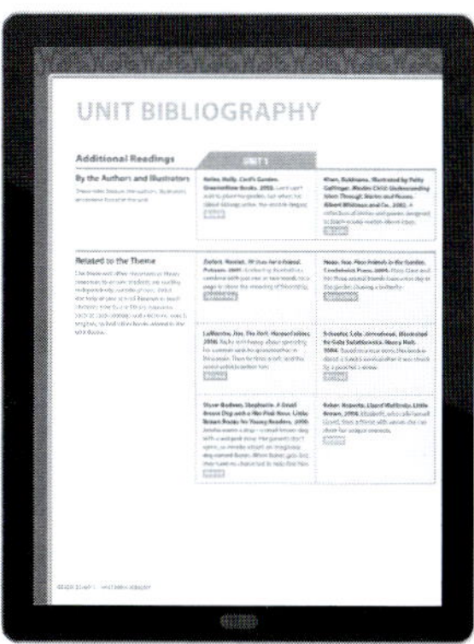

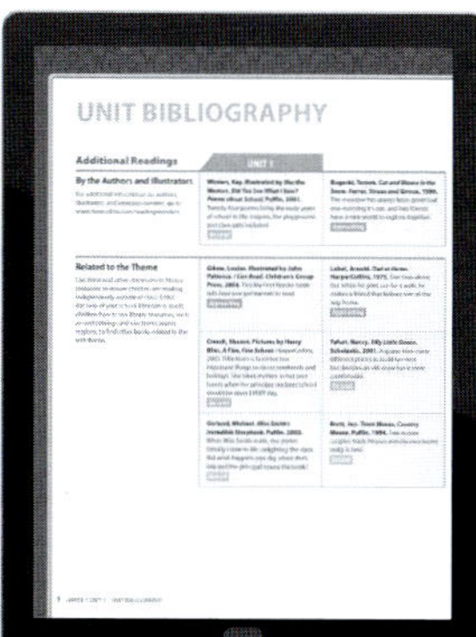

The Unit Bibliography online is organized to help teachers find additional readings related to the text sets and inquiry topics. Selections are labeled as Approaching, On Level, or Beyond to ensure each student is reading at the appropriate level.

BUILD YOUR OWN TEXT SET

Purpose of Text Sets

A text set is a collection of rich, complex grade-level texts that are organized around a topic. The texts are related and connect in a meaningful way to each other to help deepen students' understanding of the topic. While reading the texts in the set, students build a body of knowledge around the topic.

How to Build a Text Set

Wonders Balanced Literacy offers flexible resources that can be modified and adapted to meet the needs of your students. You may use the categories below to build your own text set. In building a text set, students should be able to easily discern the connection between the texts. Be sure to include books that support Reading Aloud, Close Reading, Guided Reading and Independent Reading in your text set. (See Table of Contents for more information on the instructional purposes of each form of reading.)

- Genre
- Theme
- Inquiry Topic
- Content Area

Grade K: Text Extensions

Use the following additional read-aloud texts to extend your text sets. Note that reading levels are not applicable.

UNIT 1 TEXTS	EXTEND YOUR TEXT SET				
TEXT SET 1	**TITLE**	**GENRE**	**TYPE**	**GR**	**LEXILE**
How can we get along with new friends?	*Little Bear*	Fantasy	Classroom Library	N/A	N/A
	Bear Snores On	Fantasy	Literature Big Book	N/A	N/A
	"The Bundle of Sticks"	Fiction	Interactive Read Aloud	N/A	N/A
	Just a Little Bit	Fiction	Classroom Library	N/A	N/A
TEXT SET 2					
How do we move?	*Put Me In the Zoo*	Fantasy	Classroom Library	N/A	N/A
	The Relatives Came	Fiction	Classroom Library	N/A	N/A
	When Daddy's Truck Picks Me Up	Fiction	Literature Big Book	N/A	N/A
TEXT SET 3					
How can your senses help you learn?	*The Handiest Things in the World*	Nonfiction	Literature Big Book	N/A	N/A
	"A Tour of the Seasons"	Nonfiction	Interactive Read Aloud	N/A	N/A
	"Field Trips"	Nonfiction	Interactive Read Aloud	N/A	N/A
	I Read Signs	Nonfiction	Classroom Library	N/A	N/A

Grade K: Text Extensions

Use the following additional read-aloud texts to extend your text sets. Note that reading levels are not applicable.

UNIT 2 TEXTS	EXTEND YOUR TEXT SET				
TEXT SET 1	**TITLE**	**GENRE**	**TYPE**	**GR**	**LEXILE**
How do tools help us? 	*Roadwork*	Nonfiction	Literature Big Book	N/A	N/A
	"Helping Out at Home"	Nonfiction	Interactive Read Aloud	N/A	N/A
	"Farms Around the World"	Nonfiction	Interactive Read Aloud	N/A	N/A
	Whose Shoes? A Shoe for Every Job	Informational Text	Literature Big Book	N/A	N/A
TEXT SET 2					
What shapes do you see around you? 	*An Orange in January*	Nonfiction	Literature Big Book	N/A	N/A
	I Read Signs	Nonfiction	Classroom Library	N/A	N/A
	"Field Trips"	Nonfiction	Interactive Read Aloud	N/A	N/A
	Senses at the Seashore	Informational Text	Literature Big Book	N/A	N/A
	The Handiest Things in the World	Nonfiction	Literature Big Book	N/A	N/A
TEXT SET 3					
What can you find out when you explore? 	"The King of the Winds"	Fiction	Interactive Read Aloud	N/A	N/A
	In the Small, Small Pond	Fiction	Classroom Library	N/A	N/A
	"Timimoto"	Fiction	Interactive Read Aloud	N/A	N/A
	Please Take Me for a Walk	Fiction	Literature Big Book	N/A	N/A
	We're Going on a Bear Hunt	Fiction	Classroom Library	N/A	N/A

Grade K: Text Extensions

Use the following additional read-aloud texts to extend your text sets. Note that reading levels are not applicable.

UNIT 3 TEXTS	EXTEND YOUR TEXT SET				
TEXT SET 1	**TITLE**	**GENRE**	**TYPE**	**GR**	**LEXILE**
What can you learn by going to different places?	*When Daddy's Truck Picks Me Up*	Fiction	Literature Big Book	N/A	N/A
	We're Going on a Bear Hunt	Fiction	Classroom Library	N/A	N/A
	What's the Big Idea, Molly?	Fantasy	Literature Big Book	N/A	N/A
TEXT SET 2					
What are the different sounds we hear?	*Library Lion*	Fiction	Classroom Library	N/A	N/A
	Green Eggs and Ham	Fiction	Classroom Library	N/A	N/A
	What Can You Do with a Paleta?	Fiction	Literature Big Book	N/A	N/A
	"Timimoto"	Fiction	Interactive Read Aloud	N/A	N/A
TEXT SET 3					
What can you see when you go places?	*Truck*	Informational Text	Classroom Library	N/A	N/A
	Senses at the Seashore	Informational Text	Literature Big Book	N/A	N/A
	"Kites in Flight"	Informational Text	Interactive Read Aloud	N/A	N/A
	"Cultural Festivals"	Nonfiction	Interactive Read Aloud	N/A	N/A
	Ana Goes to Washington, D.C.	Informational Text	Literature Big Book	N/A	N/A
	"The Best of the West"	Informational Text	Interactive Read Aloud	N/A	N/A

Grade K: Text Extensions

Use the following additional read-aloud texts to extend your text sets. Note that reading levels are not applicable.

UNIT 4 TEXTS	EXTEND YOUR TEXT SET				
TEXT SET 1	**TITLE**	**GENRE**	**TYPE**	**GR**	**LEXILE**
What jobs do people do?	*How a House is Built*	Nonfiction	Classroom Library	N/A	N/A
	"Field Trips"	Nonfiction	Interactive Read Aloud	N/A	N/A
	Roadwork	Nonfiction	Literature Big Book	N/A	N/A
	"Farms Around the World"	Informational Text	Interactive Read Aloud	N/A	N/A
TEXT SET 2					
What can you learn from your neighbors?	"The Bundle of Sticks"	Fiction	Interactive Read Aloud	N/A	N/A
	"The Elves and the Shoemakers"	Tale	Interactive Read Aloud	N/A	N/A
	Please Take Me for a Walk	Fiction	Literature Big Book	N/A	N/A
	Green Eggs and Ham	Fiction	Classroom Library	N/A	N/A
TEXT SET 3					
How can people work to make their community better?	*How a House is Built*	Nonfiction	Classroom Library	N/A	N/A
	"Field Trips"	Nonfiction	Interactive Read Aloud	N/A	N/A
	Whose Shoes? A Shoe for Every Job	Informational Text	Literature Big Book	N/A	N/A
	"Cultural Festivals"	Nonfiction	Interactive Read Aloud	N/A	N/A
	Follow the Water from Brook to Ocean	Nonfiction	Classroom Library	N/A	N/A

Grade K: Text Extensions

Use the following additional read-aloud texts to extend your text sets. Note that reading levels are not applicable.

UNIT 7 TEXTS	EXTEND YOUR TEXT SET				
TEXT SET 1	**TITLE**	**GENRE**	**TYPE**	**GR**	**LEXILE**
How are some animals alike and how are they different? 	"The Family Pet"	Informational Text	Interactive Read Aloud	N/A	N/A
	Panda Kindergarten	Informational Text	Literature Big Book	N/A	N/A
	The Year at Maple Hill Farm	Nonfiction	Classroom Library	N/A	N/A
TEXT SET 2					
How do different animals move? 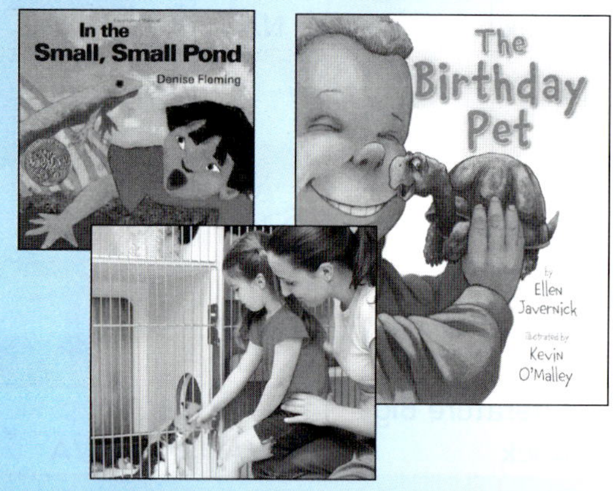	*Pouch!*	Fiction	Literature Big Book	N/A	N/A
	"The Tortoise and the Hare"	Fiction	Interactive Read Aloud	N/A	N/A
	I Love Bugs!	Fiction	Literature Big Book	N/A	N/A
	Please Take Me for a Walk	Fiction	Literature Big Book	N/A	N/A
TEXT SET 3					
Where do animals live? 	*Pouch!*	Fiction	Literature Big Book	N/A	N/A
	I Love Bugs!	Fiction	Literature Big Book	N/A	N/A
	"The Turtle and the Flute"	Fiction	Interactive Read Aloud	N/A	N/A
	Please Take Me for a Walk	Fiction	Literature Big Book	N/A	N/A

Grade K: Text Extensions

Use the following additional read-aloud texts to extend your text sets. Note that reading levels are not applicable.

UNIT 8 TEXTS	EXTEND YOUR TEXT SET				
TEXT SET 1	**TITLE**	**GENRE**	**TYPE**	**GR**	**LEXILE**
What can help you go from here to there?	*The Relatives Came*	Fiction	Classroom Library	N/A	N/A
	Green Eggs and Ham	Fiction	Classroom Library	N/A	N/A
	Please Take Me for a Walk	Fiction	Literature Big Book	N/A	N/A
	"Timimoto"	Fiction	Interactive Read Aloud	N/A	N/A
TEXT SET 2					
What do you know about our country?	*Senses at the Seashore*	Informational Text	Literature Big Book	N/A	N/A
	"Kites in Flight"	Informational Text	Interactive Read Aloud	N/A	N/A
	"Cultural Festivals"	Nonfiction	Interactive Read Aloud	N/A	N/A
	"A View from the Moon"	Informational Text	Interactive Read Aloud	N/A	N/A
TEXT SET 3					
What do you see in the sky?	"The King of the Winds"	Tale	Interactive Read Aloud	N/A	N/A
	I Love Bugs!	Fiction	Literature Big Book	N/A	N/A
	Clang! Clang! Beep! Beep! Listen to the City	Fiction	Literature Big Book	N/A	N/A
	Mama, Is It Summer Yet?	Fiction	Literature Big Book	N/A	N/A
	Rain	Fiction	Literature Big Book	N/A	N/A

Grade K: Text Extensions

Use the following additional read-aloud texts to extend your text sets. Note that reading levels are not applicable.

UNIT 9 TEXTS	EXTEND YOUR TEXT SET				
TEXT SET 1	**TITLE**	**GENRE**	**TYPE**	**GR**	**LEXILE**
What do we learn as we grow?	*Pouch!*	Fiction	Literature Big Book	N/A	N/A
	"Spider Woman Teaches the Navajo"	Tale	Interactive Read Aloud	N/A	N/A
	Little Bear	Fiction	Classroom Library	N/A	N/A
	"The Boy Who Cried Wolf"	Fiction	Interactive Read Aloud	N/A	N/A
TEXT SET 2					
What do good citizens do?	"The Boy Who Cried Wolf"	Fiction	Interactive Read Aloud	N/A	N/A
	How Do Dinosaurs Go to School?	Fantasy	Literature Big Book	N/A	N/A
	"The Bundle of Sticks"	Fiction	Interactive Read Aloud	N/A	N/A
TEXT SET 3					
How can things in nature be used to make new things?	"Kites in Flight"	Informational Text	Interactive Read Aloud	N/A	N/A
	"Farms Around the World"	Informational Text	Interactive Read Aloud	N/A	N/A
	How a House is Built	Nonfiction	Classroom Library	N/A	N/A
	Roadwork	Nonfiction	Literature Big Book	N/A	N/A

Grade K: Text Extensions

Use the following additional read-aloud texts to extend your text sets. Note that reading levels are not applicable.

UNIT 10 TEXTS	EXTEND YOUR TEXT SET				
TEXT SET 1	TITLE	GENRE	TYPE	GR	LEXILE
What can happen when we work together?	"The Lion and the Mouse"	Fiction	Interactive Read Aloud	N/A	N/A
	"The Bundle of Sticks"	Fiction	Interactive Read Aloud	N/A	N/A
	"The Boy Who Cried Wolf"	Fiction	Interactive Read Aloud	N/A	N/A
	"The Frog and the Locust"	Folktale	Interactive Read Aloud	N/A	N/A
TEXT SET 2					
In what ways are things alike? How are they different?	"The Lion and the Mouse"	Fiction	Interactive Read Aloud	N/A	N/A
	"The Tortoise and the Hare"	Fiction	Interactive Read Aloud	N/A	N/A
	Mama, Is It Summer Yet?	Fiction	Literature Big Book	N/A	N/A
	The Birthday Pet	Fiction	Literature Big Book	N/A	N/A
TEXT SET 3					
How can you learn new things?	"Field Trips"	Nonfiction	Interactive Read Aloud	N/A	N/A
	"Cultural Festivals"	Nonfiction	Interactive Read Aloud	N/A	N/A
	Senses at the Seashore	Informational Text	Literature Big Book	N/A	N/A
	The Handiest Things in the World	Nonfiction	Literature Big Book	N/A	N/A
	Ana Goes to Washington, D.C.	Informational Text	Literature Big Book	N/A	N/A

Grade 1: Text Extensions

Use the following additional read-aloud texts to extend your text sets. Note that reading levels are not applicable.

UNIT 1 TEXTS	EXTEND YOUR TEXT SET				
TEXT SET 1	**TITLE**	**GENRE**	**TYPE**	**GR**	**LEXILE**
How do your friends help you?	*The Cow that Went OINK*	Fiction	Classroom Library	N/A	N/A
	Seven Blind Mice	Fiction	Classroom Library	N/A	N/A
	Super Fly Guy	Fiction	Classroom Library	N/A	N/A
	"The Elephant's Child"	Folktale	Interactive Read Aloud	N/A	N/A
	"Why the Sun and Moon are in the Sky"	Folktale	Interactive Read Aloud	N/A	N/A
	"The Sheep, the Pig, and the Goose Who Set up House"	Fantasy	Interactive Read Aloud	N/A	N/A
TEXT SET 2					
How do families like to spend their time?	*Mystery Vine*	Fiction	Literature Big Book	N/A	N/A
	Little House in the Big Woods	Fiction	Classroom Library	N/A	N/A
	"The Great Big, Gigantic Turnip"	Fiction	Interactive Read Aloud	N/A	N/A
	Interrupting Chicken	Fiction	Literature Big Book	N/A	N/A
	Ling and Ting: Not Exactly the Same!	Fiction	Classroom Library	N/A	N/A
TEXT SET 3					
What makes a pet special?	*Little House in the Big Woods*	Fiction	Classroom Library	N/A	N/A
	Super Fly Guy	Fiction	Classroom Library	N/A	N/A
	"Ming's Teacher"	Fiction	Interactive Read Aloud	N/A	N/A

UNIT 1 TEXTS	EXTEND YOUR TEXT SET				
TEXT SET 4	**TITLE**	**GENRE**	**TYPE**	**GR**	**LEXILE**
What do friends do together?	"Luis's Library"	Nonfiction	Interactive Read Aloud	N/A	N/A
	"Let's Dance!"	Nonfiction	Interactive Read Aloud	N/A	N/A
	Family Pictures	Nonfiction	Classroom Library	N/A	N/A
TEXT SET 5					
How does your body move?	*Go Go Go!: Kids on the Move*	Nonfiction	Classroom Library	N/A	N/A
	What Do You Do With a Tail Like this?	Nonfiction	Classroom Library	N/A	N/A
	Friends All Around	Nonfiction	Literature Big Book	N/A	N/A

Grade 1: Text Extensions

Use the following additional read-aloud texts to extend your text sets. Note that reading levels are not applicable.

UNIT 2 TEXTS	EXTEND YOUR TEXT SET				
TEXT SET 1	**TITLE**	**GENRE**	**TYPE**	**GR**	**LEXILE**
What jobs do people do in our families and communities? How do they help us?	*The Top Job*	Fiction	Classroom Library	N/A	N/A
	"Ming's Teacher"	Fiction	Interactive Read Aloud	N/A	N/A
	Super Fly Guy	Fiction	Classroom Library	N/A	N/A
TEXT SET 2					
Why are homes important?	"Goldilocks"	Fiction	Interactive Read Aloud	N/A	N/A
	Owl At Home	Fiction	Classroom Library	N/A	N/A
	"The Sheep, the Pig, and the Goose Who Set up House"	Fantasy	Interactive Read Aloud	N/A	N/A
TEXT SET 3					
How do different animals live in nature?	*Cactus Hotel*	Nonfiction	Classroom LIbrary	N/A	N/A
	Starfish	Nonfiction	Classroom Library	N/A	N/A
	"Animals Working Together"	Nonfiction	Interactive Read Aloud	N/A	N/A
	"Animals in Winter"	Nonfiction	Interactive Read Aloud	N/A	N/A

UNIT 2 TEXTS	EXTEND YOUR TEXT SET				
TEXT SET 4	**TITLE**	**GENRE**	**TYPE**	**GR**	**LEXILE**
How do people help out in the community?	*Raising Dragons*	Fiction	Classroom Library	N/A	N/A
	"Anansi's Sons"	Fiction	Interactive Read Aloud	N/A	N/A
	Millie Waits for the Mail	Fiction	Literature Big Book	N/A	N/A
TEXT SET 5					
How can you find your way around?	"Pioneers"	Nonfiction	Interactive Read Aloud	N/A	N/A
	How People Learned to Fly	Nonfiction	Classroom Library	N/A	N/A
	"Great Inventions"	Nonfiction	Interactive Read Aloud	N/A	N/A

Grade 1: Text Extensions

Use the following additional read-aloud texts to extend your text sets. Note that reading levels are not applicable.

UNIT 3 TEXTS	EXTEND YOUR TEXT SET				
TEXT SET 1	**TITLE**	**GENRE**	**TYPE**	**GR**	**LEXILE**
How can characters in a story change over time?	*Little House in the Big Woods*	Fiction	Classroom Library	N/A	N/A
	The Cow that Went OINK	Fiction	Classroom Library	N/A	N/A
	"Paul Bunyan and the Popcorn Blizzard"	Tall Tale	Interactive Read Aloud	N/A	N/A
	"Ming's Teacher"	Fiction	Interactive Read Aloud	N/A	N/A
	Millie Waits for the Mail	Fiction	Literature Big Book	N/A	N/A
TEXT SET 2					
How do things change over time?	*The Last Train*	Fiction	Literature Big Book	N/A	N/A
	Little House in the Big Woods	Fiction	Classroom Library	N/A	N/A
	Raising Dragons	Fiction	Classroom LIbrary	N/A	N/A
TEXT SET 3					
What can folktales teach us?	"The City Mouse and the Country Mouse"	Fiction	Interactive Read Aloud	N/A	N/A
	"Rabbit and Coyote Race"	Fiction	Interactive Read Aloud	N/A	N/A
	"The Little Red Hen"	Fiction	Interactive Read Aloud	N/A	N/A
	"The Elephant's Child"	Fiction	Interactive Read Aloud	N/A	N/A
	"Why the Sun and Moon are in the Sky"	Fiction	Interactive Read Aloud	N/A	N/A
	"Anansi's Sons"	Fiction	Interactive Read Aloud	N/A	N/A

UNIT 3 TEXTS	EXTEND YOUR TEXT SET				
TEXT SET 4	TITLE	GENRE	TYPE	GR	LEXILE
How do authors show us how things are the same and different?	*A Picture Book of George Washington*	Nonfiction	Classroom Library	N/A	N/A
	How People Learned to Fly	Nonfiction	Classroom Library	N/A	N/A
	"Great Inventions"	Nonfiction	Interactive Read Aloud	N/A	N/A
	Snowflake Bentley	Nonfiction	Classroom Library	N/A	N/A
	A Weed is a Flower	Nonfiction	Classroom Library	N/A	N/A
TEXT SET 5					
How do we get our food?	"Pioneers"	Nonfiction	Interactive Read Aloud	N/A	N/A
	A Weed is a Flower	Nonfiction	Classroom Library	N/A	N/A

Grade 1: Text Extensions

Use the following additional read-aloud texts to extend your text sets. Note that reading levels are not applicable.

UNIT 4 TEXTS	EXTEND YOUR TEXT SET				
TEXT SET 1	**TITLE**	**GENRE**	**TYPE**	**GR**	**LEXILE**
What can we learn about animals and their features?	*Lon Po Po*	Fiction	Classroom Library	N/A	N/A
	Seven Blind Mice	Fiction	Classroom Library	N/A	N/A
	The Cow that Went OINK	Fiction	Classroom Library	N/A	N/A
	The Three Little Dassies	Fiction	Literature Big Book	N/A	N/A
	"Rabbit and Coyote Race"	Fiction	Interactive Read Aloud	N/A	N/A
TEXT SET 2					
How can animals use their features to help themselves and each other?	*Move!*	Nonfiction	Literature Big Book	N/A	N/A
	Meet the Meerkat	Nonfiction	Classroom Library	N/A	N/A
	"Animals in the Desert"	Nonfiction	Interactive Read Aloud	N/A	N/A
	Cactus Hotel	Nonfiction	Classroom Library	N/A	N/A
	Starfish	Nonfiction	Classroom Library	N/A	N/A
TEXT SET 3					
How do animals survive in nature?	"Animals in the Desert"	Nonfiction	Interactive Read Aloud	N/A	N/A
	Babies in the Bayou	Nonfiction	Literature Big Book	N/A	N/A
	Meet the Meerkat	Nonfiction	Classroom Library	N/A	N/A
	Cactus Hotel	Nonfiction	Classroom Library	N/A	N/A
	"Animals Working Together"	Nonfiction	Interactive Read Aloud	N/A	N/A
	"Insect Hide and Seek"	Nonfiction	Interactive Read Aloud	N/A	N/A

UNIT 4 TEXTS	EXTEND YOUR TEXT SET				
TEXT SET 4	**TITLE**	**GENRE**	**TYPE**	**GR**	**LEXILE**
What insects do you know about? How are they alike and different?	"Anansi's Sons"	Fiction	Interactive Read Aloud	N/A	N/A
	"Meet the Insects"	Nonfiction	Literature Anthology eBook	N/A	N/A
	"Glowing Bugs Fly By"	Nonfiction	Decodable Reader eBook	N/A	N/A
TEXT SET 5					
What can different animals do?	"Our Pets"	Nonfiction	Interactive Read Aloud	N/A	N/A
	"Insect Hide and Seek"	Nonfiction	Interactive Read Aloud	N/A	N/A
	"Animals Working Together"	Nonfiction	Interactive Read Aloud	N/A	N/A
	"Animals in Winter"	Nonfiction	Interactive Read Aloud	N/A	N/A
	"Animals in the Desert"	Nonfiction	Interactive Read Aloud	N/A	N/A
	Move!	Nonfiction	Literature Big Book	N/A	N/A

Grade 1: Text Extensions

Use the following additional read-aloud texts to extend your text sets. Note that reading levels are not applicable.

UNIT 5 TEXTS	EXTEND YOUR TEXT SET				
TEXT SET 1	**TITLE**	**GENRE**	**TYPE**	**GR**	**LEXILE**
How can we categorize the things see around us?	"The City Mouse and the Country Mouse"	Fiction	Interactive Read Aloud	N/A	N/A
	The Three Little Dassies	Fiction	Literature Big Book	N/A	N/A
	"The Three Little Pigs"	Fiction	Interactive Read Aloud	N/A	N/A
	The Cow that Went OINK	Fiction	Classroom Library	N/A	N/A
TEXT SET 2					
What can you see in the sky?	*A Second is a Hiccup*	Fiction	Literature Big Book	N/A	N/A
	The Top Job	Fiction	Classroom Library	N/A	N/A
TEXT SET 3					
What can we invent?	*A Weed is a Flower*	Nonfiction	Classroom Library	N/A	N/A
	How People Learned to Fly	Nonfiction	Classroom Library	N/A	N/A

UNIT 5 TEXTS	EXTEND YOUR TEXT SET				
TEXT SET 4	TITLE	GENRE	TYPE	GR	LEXILE
What are the sights and sounds that surround you?	"The Cat's Bell"	Fiction	Interactive Read Aloud	N/A	N/A
	Raising Dragons	Fiction	Classroom Library	N/A	N/A
	Alicia's Happy Day	Fiction	Literature Big Book	N/A	N/A
	The Cow that Went OINK	Fiction	Classroom Library	N/A	N/A
	"Paul Bunyan and the Popcorn Blizzard"	Fiction	Interactive Read Aloud	N/A	N/A
TEXT SET 5					
How are things created?	*Snowflake Bentley*	Nonfiction	Classroom Library	N/A	N/A
	"Great Inventions"	Nonfiction	Interactive Read Aloud	N/A	N/A
	How People Learned to Fly	Nonfiction	Classroom Library	N/A	N/A

Grade 1: Text Extensions

Use the following additional read-aloud texts to extend your text sets. Note that reading levels are not applicable.

UNIT 6 TEXTS	EXTEND YOUR TEXT SET				
TEXT SET 1	**TITLE**	**GENRE**	**TYPE**	**GR**	**LEXILE**
What is the theme in a story?	*Little House in the Big Woods*	Fiction	Classroom Library	N/A	N/A
	Ling and Ting: Not Exactly the Same!	Fiction	Classroom Library	N/A	N/A
	Interrupting Chicken	Fiction	Literature Big Book	N/A	N/A
TEXT SET 2					
How can we help the world around us?	*A Picture Book of George Washington*	Nonfiction	Classroom Library	N/A	N/A
	A Weed is a Flower	Nonfiction	Classroom Library	N/A	N/A
	The Story of Martin Luther King Jr.	Historical Fiction	Literature Big Book	N/A	N/A
	"Luis's Library"	Nonfiction	Interactive Read Aloud	N/A	N/A
TEXT SET 3					
What can we learn from our families?	*Little House in the Big Woods*	Fiction	Classroom Library	N/A	N/A
	"Anansi's Sons"	Fiction	Interactive Read Aloud	N/A	N/A
	The Top Job	Fiction	Classroom Library	N/A	N/A

UNIT 6 TEXTS	EXTEND YOUR TEXT SET				
TEXT SET 4	**TITLE**	**GENRE**	**TYPE**	**GR**	**LEXILE**
How are families the same and different?	"The City Mouse and the Country Mouse"	Fiction	Interactive Read Aloud	N/A	N/A
	Little House in the Big Woods	Fiction	Classroom Library	N/A	N/A
	The Story of Martin Luther King Jr.	Historical Fiction	Literature Big Book	N/A	N/A
TEXT SET 5					
What holidays do we celebrate in our country? Why do we celebrate them?	*Family Pictures*	Nonfiction	Classroom Library	N/A	N/A
	"Let's Dance!"	Nonfiction	Interactive Read Aloud	N/A	N/A
	"Measuring Time"	Nonfiction	Interactive Read Aloud	N/A	N/A

Grade 2: Text Extensions

Use the following additional texts to extend your text sets.

UNIT 1 TEXTS	EXTEND YOUR TEXT SET				
TEXT SET 1	**TITLE**	**GENRE**	**TYPE**	**GR**	**LEXILE**
What can you learn from a character's actions?	"A Visit to the Desert"	Realistic Fiction	Shared Read	N/A	N/A
	"The Boy Who Cried Wolf"	Folktale	Shared Read	N/A	N/A
	Cowgirl Kate and Cocoa	Fiction	Classroom Library	K	400
	The Treasure	Fiction	Classroom Library	K	490
	Fox and His Friends	Fantasy	Classroom Library	J	200
	Cam Jansen Case #10: The Mystery at the Monkey House	Fiction	Classroom Library	L	530
TEXT SET 2					
What can our families and pets teach us?	"César Chávez"	Biography	Shared Read	N/A	N/A
	Pets at the White House	Nonfiction	Classroom Library	I	470
	City Communities	Nonfiction	Leveled Reader	G, J, K, O	290, 400, 470, 620
TEXT SET 3					
How do characters make decisions?	"Maria Celebrates Brazil"	Realistic Fiction	Shared Read	N/A	N/A
	"The Boy Who Cried Wolf"	Fable	Shared Read	N/A	N/A
	"Starry Night"	Fiction	Shared Read	N/A	N/A
	The Raft	Realistic Fiction	Classroom Library	O	540
	The Fire Cat	Fantasy	Classroom Library	J	400
	Where Are They Going?	Realistic Fiction	Leveled Reader	J, K	380, 440

Grade 2: Text Extensions

Use the following additional texts to extend your text sets.

UNIT 2 TEXTS	EXTEND YOUR TEXT SET				
TEXT SET 1	**TITLE**	**GENRE**	**TYPE**	**GR**	**LEXILE**
What can we learn from animals in stories?	"Finding Cal"	Fiction	Shared Read	N/A	N/A
	The Raft	Realistic Fiction	Classroom Library	O	540
	Henry and Mudge: The First Book	Fiction	Classroom Library	J	460
	Cowgirl Kate and Cocoa	Fantasy	Classroom Library	K	400
	Cat and Dog	Fiction	Leveled Reader	C, E	70, 230
TEXT SET 2					
How do animals survive?	"Alaska: A Special Place"	Nonfiction	Shared Read	N/A	N/A
	Life in an Ocean	Nonfiction	Classroom Library	G	290
	Where Do Polar Bears Live?	Nonfiction	Classroom Library	N/A	690
	People Helping Whales	Nonfiction	Leveled Reader	E, I, J, M	240, 360, 550, 610
TEXT SET 3					
What do we love about animals?	"In the Sky"	Poetry	Shared Read	N/A	N/A
	"A Visit to the Desert"	Realistic Fiction	Shared Read	N/A	N/A
	The Raft	Realistic Fiction	Classroom Library	O	540
	How Butterflies Came to Be	Folktale	Leveled Reader	J, L	340, 440

Grade 2: Text Extensions

Use the following additional texts to extend your text sets.

UNIT 3 TEXTS	EXTEND YOUR TEXT SET				
TEXT SET 1	**TITLE**	**GENRE**	**TYPE**	**GR**	**LEXILE**
How do inventions affect our lives?	"Pedal Power"	Nonfiction	Shared Read	N/A	N/A
	The Sky is Full of Stars	Nonfiction	Classroom Library	N	570
	Wind Power	Nonfiction	Leveled Reader	J, K, M, P	440, 490, 550, 690
TEXT SET 2					
How does learning about the world help you to appreciate it?	"Alaska: A Special Place"	Nonfiction	Shared Read	N/A	N/A
	"Into the Sea"	Nonfiction	Shared Read	N/A	N/A
	"Lighting Lives"	Nonfiction	Shared Read	N/A	N/A
	"Families Work"	Nonfiction	Shared Read	N/A	N/A
	Bats: Creatures of the Night	Nonfiction	Classroom Library	K	510
	Volcanoes	Nonfiction	Classroom Library	I	380
TEXT SET 3					
How can characters in a story grow and change?	"Maria Celebrates Brazil"	Realistic Fiction	Shared Read	N/A	N/A
	"A Visit to the Desert"	Realistic Fiction	Shared Read	N/A	N/A
	"The Boy Who Cried Wolf"	Fable	Shared Read	N/A	N/A
	The Fire Cat	Realistic Fiction	Classroom Library	J	400
	Henry and Mudge: The First Book	Fiction	Classroom Library	J	460
	Fox and His Friends	Fiction	Classroom Library	J	200
	Where Are They Going?	Realistic Fiction	Leveled Reader	J, K	380, 440

Grade 2: Text Extensions

Use the following additional texts to extend your text sets.

UNIT 4 TEXTS	EXTEND YOUR TEXT SET				
TEXT SET 1	**TITLE**	**GENRE**	**TYPE**	**GR**	**LEXILE**
What makes different parts of the world unique?	"A Prairie Guard Dog"	Nonfiction	Shared Read	N/A	N/A
	"Tornado!"	Nonfiction	Shared Read	N/A	N/A
	"Dive Teams"	Nonfiction	Shared Read	N/A	N/A
	Volcanoes	Nonfiction	Classroom Library	I	380
	Rocky Mountain National Park	Nonfiction	Leveled Reader	H, J, L, O	320, 430, 540, 630
TEXT SET 2					
What are some themes in stories we read?	"The Boy Who Cried Wolf"	Fable	Shared Read	N/A	N/A
	"Why Fir Tree Keeps His Leaves"	Myth	Shared Read	N/A	N/A
	The Treasure	Fiction	Classroom Library	K	490
	The Cat and the Mice	Fable	Leveled Reader	D, F	180, 200
	The Dog and the Bone	Fable	Leveled Reader	J, K	320, 440
	The Spider and the Honey Tree	Fable	Leveled Reader	N	590
TEXT SET 3					
What can we learn by comparing and contrasting story events?	"Maria Celebrates Brazil"	Fiction	Shared Read	N/A	N/A
	"A Visit to the Desert"	Realistic Fiction	Shared Read	N/A	N/A
	Fox and His Friends	Fantasy	Classroom Library	J	200
	The Fire Cat	Fantasy	Classroom Library	J	400
	The Raft	Realistic Fiction	Classroom Library	O	540

Grade 2: Text Extensions

Use the following additional texts to extend your text sets.

UNIT 5 TEXTS	EXTEND YOUR TEXT SET				
TEXT SET 1	**TITLE**	**GENRE**	**TYPE**	**GR**	**LEXILE**
How can we overcome a challenge?	"The Art Project"	Realistic Fiction	Shared Read	N/A	N/A
	Keena Ford and the Field Trip Mix Up	Realistic Fiction	Classroom Library	N/A	620
	The Fire Cat	Fantasy	Classroom Library	J	400
	Magic Tree House #13: Vacation Under the Volcano	Fiction	Classroom Library	M	420
	A New Life in India	Realistic Fiction	Leveled Reader	J, L	440, 480
TEXT SET 2					
How can learning about the past help us?	*Pets at the White House*	Nonfiction	Classroom Library	I	470
	Tara and Tiree, Fearless Friends: A True Story	Nonfiction	Classroom Library	H	230
	Digging for Sue	Expository Text	Leveled Reader	M, P	550, 670
TEXT SET 3					
How can we achieve our goals?	"Little Flap Learns to Fly"	Fantasy	Shared Read	N/A	N/A
	The Eagle	Fantasy	Classroom Library	N/A	630
	The Sign Painter	Realistic Fiction	Classroom Library	N/A	250
	Gooney Bird and the Room Mother	Fiction	Classroom Library	Q	660

Grade 2: Text Extensions

Use the following additional texts to extend your text sets.

UNIT 6 TEXTS	EXTEND YOUR TEXT SET				
TEXT SET 1	**TITLE**	**GENRE**	**TYPE**	**GR**	**LEXILE**
How does a character's point of view help you understand the theme?	"A Visit to the Desert"	Realistic Fiction	Shared Read	N/A	N/A
	"Happy New Year!"	Realistic Fiction	Shared Read	N/A	N/A
	"A Difficult Decision"	Realistic Fiction	Shared Read	N/A	N/A
	Magic Tree House #13: Vacation Under the Volcano	Fiction	Classroom Library	M	420
	Henry and Mudge: The First Book	Fiction	Classroom Library	J	460
	Cowgirl Kate and Cocoa	Fiction	Classroom Library	K	400
TEXT SET 2					
What is the purpose for writing expository texts?	"Alaska: A Special Place"	Nonfiction	Shared Read	N/A	N/A
	"Visiting the Past"	Nonfiction	Shared Read	N/A	N/A
	Plants Grow!	Nonfiction	Classroom Library	N/A	430
	Where Do Polar Bears Live?	Nonfiction	Classroom Library	N/A	690
	Volcanoes	Nonfiction	Classroom Library	I	380
	Government Rules	Expository Text	Leveled Reader	H, J, K, M, P	370, 460, 490, 540, 670
TEXT SET 3					
What are different ways that authors share information?	"Magnets Work!"	Nonfiction	Shared Read	N/A	N/A
	"Lighting Lives"	Nonfiction	Shared Read	N/A	N/A
	"Tornado!"	Nonfiction	Shared Read	N/A	N/A
	Fire Fighter!	Nonfiction	Classroom Library	L	400
	The Sky is Full of Stars	Nonfiction	Classroom Library	N	570
	Life in an Ocean	Nonfiction	Classroom Library	G	290
	The Story of Ruby Bridges	Biography	Classroom Library	O	730
	Rudy Garcia-Tolson	Biography	Leveled Reader	G, I, K, M, P	290, 380, 470, 550, 640

Grade 3: Text Extensions

Use the following additional texts to extend your text sets.

UNIT 1 TEXTS	EXTEND YOUR TEXT SET				
TEXT SET 1	**TITLE**	**GENRE**	**TYPE**	**GR**	**LEXILE**
How do characters' wants and needs affect stories?	"Anansi Learns a Lesson"	Folktale	Shared Read	N/A	N/A
	"Nail Soup"	Folktale	Shared Read	N/A	N/A
	Stone Fox	Fiction	Classroom Library	P	550
	Tops and Bottoms	Trickster Tale	Classroom Library	M	580
	The Bear Who Stole the Chinook	Folktale	Leveled Reader	P	740
	The King of the Birds	Folktale	Leveled Reader	M, N	550, 600
TEXT SET 2					
How can problem solving lead to new ideas?	"Kids to the Rescue"	Expository Text	Shared Read	N/A	N/A
	"Bats Did it First"	Expository Text	Shared Read	N/A	N/A
	Moonwalk: The First Trip to the Moon	Informational Text	Classroom Library	O	550
	Inspired by Nature	Expository Text	Leveled Reader	I, L, M, O, Q	480, 570, 650, 660, 790
TEXT SET 3					
How do authors use details to explain the main idea?	"Every Vote Counts"	Expository Text	Shared Read	N/A	N/A
	"Earth and Its Neighbors"	Expository Text	Shared Read	N/A	N/A
	So You Want to Be President?	Informational Text	Classroom Library	S	730
	Susan B. Anthony: Fighter for Women's Rights	Biography	Classroom Library	J	530
	The Race for the Presidency	Expository Text	Leveled Reader	H, L, M, N, Q	330, 560, 710, 720, 890
	Protecting the Islands	Expository Text	Leveled Reader	H, L, M, N, Q	370, 560, 660, 720, 810

Grade 3: Text Extensions

Use the following additional texts to extend your text sets.

UNIT 2 TEXTS	EXTEND YOUR TEXT SET				
TEXT SET 1	**TITLE**	**GENRE**	**TYPE**	**GR**	**LEXILE**
How can we solve problems?	"Bruno's New Home"	Fantasy	Shared Read	N/A	N/A
	"Inchworm's Tale"	Folktale	Shared Read	N/A	N/A
	Cam Jansen #28: The Green School Mystery	Realistic Fiction	Classroom Library	N	490
	The Boxcar Children #54: The Hurricane Mystery	Realistic Fiction	Classroom Library	O	580
	A Chef in the Family	Realistic Fiction	Leveled Reader	N, O	440, 530
TEXT SET 2					
How is taking action an important thing to do?	"Room to Grow"	Narrative Nonfiction	Shared Read	N/A	N/A
	"Dolores Huerta: Growing Up Strong"	Biography	Shared Read	N/A	N/A
	Martin Luther King, Jr. and the March on Washington	Biography	Classroom Library	M	430
	Susan B. Anthony: Fighter for Women's Rights	Biography	Classroom Library	J	530
	Firefighting Heroes	Expository Text	Leveled Reader	K, N, O, P, R	520, 600, 610, 690, 780
TEXT SET 3					
How do people (characters) figure things out?	"The New Hoop"	Realistic Fiction	Shared Read	N/A	N/A
	The Boxcar Childen #1	Realistic Fiction	Classroom Library	O	490
	Cam Jansen #28: The Green School Mystery	Realistic Fiction	Classroom Library	N	490
	Melanie's Mission	Realistic Fiction	Leveled Reader	N, O	510, 590

Grade 3: Text Extensions

Use the following additional texts to extend your text sets.

UNIT 3 TEXTS	EXTEND YOUR TEXT SET				
TEXT SET 1	**TITLE**	**GENRE**	**TYPE**	**GR**	**LEXILE**
How can we use our unique characteristics to help others?	"Bruno's New Home"	Fantasy	Shared Read	N/A	N/A
	Amos & Boris	Fantasy	Classroom Library	O	810
	Duck's Discovery	Fantasy	Leveled Reader	L, M	410, 530
	Weaver of Rugs	Folktale	Leveled Reader	J, M	480, 520
TEXT SET 2					
How does exploring new ideas improve our world?	"Firsts in Flight"	Expository Text	Shared Read	N/A	N/A
	"Here Comes Solar Power"	Expository Text	Shared Read	N/A	N/A
	Benjamin Banneker: Pioneering Scientist	Biography	Classroom Library	O	550
	Moonshot: The Flight of Apollo 11	Informational Text	Classroom Library	N	990
	The Future of Flight	Expository Text	Leveled Reader	J, M, N, O, R	480, 600, 650, 690, 770
TEXT SET 3					
How does learning about events and people in history help us today?	"Mary Anderson's Great Invention"	Biography	Shared Read	N/A	N/A
	"Rocketing into Space"	Biography	Shared Read	N/A	N/A
	Susan B. Anthony: Fighter for Women's Rights	Biography	Classroom Library	J	530
	Moonwalk: The First Trip to the Moon	Informational Text	Classroom Library	O	550
	Life of a Homesteader	Expository Text	Leveled Reader	I, M, N, O, Q	440, 520, 560, 690, 850

Grade 3: Text Extensions

Use the following additional texts to extend your text sets.

UNIT 4 TEXTS	EXTEND YOUR TEXT SET				
TEXT SET 1	**TITLE**	**GENRE**	**TYPE**	**GR**	**LEXILE**
How do authors use a character's point of view to tell a story?	"The Dream Catcher"	Realistic Fiction	Shared Read	N/A	N/A
	"Sailing to America"	Historical Fiction	Shared Read	N/A	N/A
	Tops and Bottoms	Trickster Tale	Classroom Library	M	580
	Sarah, Plain and Tall	Historical Fiction	Classroom Library	R	560
	A Row of Lamps	Realistic Fiction	Leveled Reader	L, M	310, 410
TEXT SET 2					
How do authors organize texts to give information?	"Earth and Its Neighbors"	Expository Text	Shared Read	N/A	N/A
	"Rescue Dogs Save the Day"	Expository Text	Shared Read	N/A	N/A
	A Medieval Feast	Informational Text	Classroom Library	Q	840
	So You Want to Be President?	Informational Text	Classroom Library	S	730
	Bat Loves the Night	Informational Text	Classroom Library	M	560
	Destination Saturn	Expository Text	Leveled Reader	I, L, M, N, Q	440, 500, 660, 700, 780
TEXT SET 3					
How can being determined help you achieve your goal?	"The New Hoop"	Realistic Fiction	Shared Read	N/A	N/A
	Make Way for Dyamonde Daniel	Realistic Fiction	Classroom Library	N/A	620
	First Flight	Historical Fiction	Classroom Library	K	460
	The Salvage Crew	Realistic Fiction	Leveled Reader	N, O	610, 670

Grade 3: Text Extensions

Use the following additional texts to extend your text sets.

UNIT 5 TEXTS	EXTEND YOUR TEXT SET				
TEXT SET 1	**TITLE**	**GENRE**	**TYPE**	**GR**	**LEXILE**
How do we get what we need?	"The Big Blizzard"	Historical Fiction	Shared Read	N/A	N/A
	"Nail Soup"	Folktale	Shared Read	N/A	N/A
	Amos & Boris	Fantasy	Classroom Library	O	810
	Stone Fox	Fiction	Classroom Library	P	550
	Jungle Treasures	Folktale	Leveled Reader	L, N	560, 680
TEXT SET 2					
What can we do to help our community?	"Kids to the Rescue"	Expository Text	Shared Read	N/A	N/A
	"Room to Grow"	Narrative Nonfiction	Shared Read	N/A	N/A
	Martin Luther King, Jr. and the March on Washington	Biography	Classroom Library	M	430
	Lion Dancer: Ernie Wan's Chinese New Year	Expository Text	Classroom Library	N	540
	Judy Baca	Biography	Leveled Reader	G, L, K, M, P	310, 560, 610, 630, 750
TEXT SET 3					
How does technology change how we do things?	"Firsts in Flight"	Expository Text	Shared Read	N/A	N/A
	"Earth and Its Neighbors"	Expository Text	Shared Read	N/A	N/A
	Moonshot: The Flight of Apollo 11	Informational Text	Classroom Library	N	990
	The Future of Flight	Expository Text	Leveled Reader	J, M, N, O, R	480, 600, 650, 690, 770

Grade 3: Text Extensions

Use the following additional texts to extend your text sets.

UNIT 6 TEXTS	EXTEND YOUR TEXT SET				
TEXT SET 1	**TITLE**	**GENRE**	**TYPE**	**GR**	**LEXILE**
How are different types of fiction similar? How are they different?	"Juanita and the Beanstalk"	Fairy Tale	Shared Read	N/A	N/A
	"Jane's Discovery"	Historical Fiction	Shared Read	N/A	N/A
	The Lighthouse Family: The Storm	Fantasy	Classroom Library	O	700
	Stone Fox	Fiction	Classroom Library	P	550
	Why the Sea is Salty: A Scandinavian Folktale	Folktale	Leveled Reader	N, O	510, 570
TEXT SET 2					
How can we use information to solve problems?	"Here Comes Solar Power"	Expository Text	Shared Read	N/A	N/A
	"Bats Did It First"	Expository Text	Shared Read	N/A	N/A
	Benjamin Banneker: Pioneering Scientist	Biography	Classroom Library	O	550
	Inspired by Nature	Expository Text	Leveled Reader	I, L, M, O, Q	480, 570, 650, 660, 790
TEXT SET 3					
How can we learn from our mistakes?	"Anansi Learns a Lesson"	Folktale	Shared Read	N/A	N/A
	"Athena and Arachne"	Myth/Drama	Shared Read	N/A	N/A
	The Stories Julian Tells	Realistic Fiction	Classroom Library	O	520
	First Flight	Historical Fiction	Classroom Library	K	460
	Quarreling Quails	Folktale	Leveled Reader	H, K	290, 410
	A Gift for Mario	Folktale	Leveled Reader	R	800

Grade 4: Text Extensions

Use the following additional texts to extend your text sets.

UNIT 1 TEXTS	EXTEND YOUR TEXT SET				
TEXT SET 1	**TITLE**	**GENRE**	**TYPE**	**GR**	**LEXILE**
How do natural forces affect us?	"Animal Adaptations"	Expository Text	Shared Read	N/A	850
	"Wonders of the Night Sky"	Expository Text	Shared Read	N/A	880
	A River Ran Wild	Informational Nonfiction	Classroom Library	Q	670
	Planet Power	Narrative Nonfiction	Leveled Reader	N, Q, R, R, U	650, 700, 770, 850, 920
TEXT SET 2					
How do characters make decisions?	"The Fisherman and the Kaha Bird"	Folktale	Shared Read	N/A	800
	"Sadie's Game"	Realistic Fiction	Shared Read	N/A	850
	The House of Dies Drear	Realistic Fiction	Classroom Library	V	670
	Riding Freedom	Historical Fiction	Classroom Library	P	720
	The Prince Who Could Fly	Drama	Leveled Reader	P, Q	N/A
TEXT SET 3					
Why does the author choose a particular genre for a story?	"Words for Change"	Biography	Shared Read	N/A	820
	"The History of Money"	Expository Text	Shared Read	N/A	900
	Who Was Jackie Robinson?	Biography	Classroom Library	P	670
	A Day in the Senate	Narrative Nonfiction	Leveled Reader	L, O, P, Q, T	580, 680, 800, 820, 890
	The Bike Company	Expository Text	Leveled Reader	N, Q, R, S, V	570, 600, 710, 790, 860

Grade 4: Text Extensions

Use the following additional texts to extend your text sets.

UNIT 2 TEXTS	EXTEND YOUR TEXT SET				
TEXT SET 1	**TITLE**	**GENRE**	**TYPE**	**GR**	**LEXILE**
What can we learn about friendship from animal stories?	"The Dragon Problem"	Fairy Tale	Shared Read	N/A	740
	Mrs. Frisby and the Rats of NIMH	Fantasy	Classroom Library	V	790
	Putting on an Act	Realistic Fiction	Leveled Reader	K, O	440, 620
	Dolphin Cove	Realistic Fiction	Leveled Reader	T	780
	The Big One	Realistic Fiction	Leveled Reader	P, Q	530, 690
	The Badger and the Fan	Folktale	Leveled Reader	O, Q	530, 720
TEXT SET 2					
How are living things connected?	"Food Fight"	Persuasive Article	Shared Read	N/A	870
	Quest for the Tree Kangaroo	Nonfiction	Classroom Library	U	830
	The Moon and I	Nonfiction	Classroom Library	N/A	870
	The Forever Forest: Kids Save a Tropical Treasure	Nonfiction	Classroom Library	N/A	950
	Hornets	Expository Text	Classroom Library	N/A	760
	The Battle Against Pests	Persuasive Text	Leveled Reader	L, O, P, Q, T	660, 750, 770, 880, 910
TEXT SET 3					
How do authors use point of view in a story or poem?	"Sing to Me"	Narrative Poetry	Shared Read	N/A	N/A
	"A Telephone Mix-Up"	Historical Fiction	Shared Read	N/A	950
	The Birchbark House	Historical Fiction	Classroom Library	T	970
	Floozle Dreams	Fantasy	Leveled Reader	L, P	540, 670
	Krillville	Fantasy	Leveled Reader	U	810
	The Wolves of Yellowstone	Fantasy	Leveled Reader	Q, R	610, 740

Grade 4: Text Extensions

Use the following additional texts to extend your text sets.

UNIT 3 TEXTS	EXTEND YOUR TEXT SET				
TEXT SET 1	**TITLE**	**GENRE**	**TYPE**	**GR**	**LEXILE**
How can we help our friends overcome obstacles?	"The Dragon Problem"	Fairy Tale	Shared Read	N/A	740
	"The Time Specs 3000"	Fantasy	Shared Read	N/A	910
	Project Mulberry	Realistic Fiction	Classroom Library	T	690
	The Borrowers Afield	Nonfiction	Classroom Library	N/A	910
	The Little Prince	Fantasy	Classroom Library	X	710
	Krillville	Fantasy	Leveled Reader	U	810
TEXT SET 2					
How can perseverance help make change happen?	"Rescuing Our Reefs"	Narrative Nonfiction	Shared Read	N/A	810
	"The Great Energy Debate"	Narrative Nonfiction	Shared Read	N/A	910
	Happy Birthday, Martin Luther King	Biography	Classroom Library	L	800
	Saving San Francisco Bay	Narrative Nonfiction	Leveled Reader	K, O, P, Q, T	580, 690, 820, 850, 900
	A Day in the Senate	Narrative Nonfiction	Leveled Reader	L, O, P, Q, T	580, 680, 800, 820, 890
	Planet Power	Narrative Nonfiction	Leveled Reader	N, Q, R, R, U	650, 700, 770, 850, 920
TEXT SET 3					
In what ways can advances in science be helpful or harmful?	"Stephanie Kwolek: Inventor"	Biography	Shared Read	N/A	830
	"Your World Up Close"	Expository Text	Shared Read	N/A	860
	Toys: Amazing Stories Behind Some Great Inventions	Expository Text	Classroom Library	U	920
	Start Small, Think Big	Persuasive Text	Leveled Reader	J, N, O, Q, T	590, 660, 710, 780, 890
	The Inventive Lewis Latimer	Biography	Leveled Reader	M, P, Q, R, U	600, 630, 710, 800, 900

Grade 4: Text Extensions

Use the following additional texts to extend your text sets.

UNIT 4 TEXTS	EXTEND YOUR TEXT SET				
TEXT SET 1	**TITLE**	**GENRE**	**TYPE**	**GR**	**LEXILE**
How do authors convey factual information differently?	"Judy's Appalachia"	Biography	Shared Read	N/A	830
	"The Great Energy Debate"	Narrative Nonfiction	Shared Read	N/A	910
	Horses	Expository Text	Classroom Library	R	930
	The Forever Forest	Narrative Nonfiction	Classroom Library	S	950
	George's Giant Wheel	Narrative Nonfiction	Leveled Reader	J, N, O, P, S	490, 550, 610, 810, 910
	Extreme Animals	Expository Text	Leveled Reader	K, O, P, Q, T	550, 590, 680, 830, 890
TEXT SET 2					
How does the past impact a character's actions?	"The Ant and the Grasshopper"	Drama	Shared Read	N/A	N/A
	"Sadie's Game"	Realistic Fiction	Shared Read	N/A	850
	M.C. Higgins the Great	Realistic Fiction	Classroom Library	X	620
	The House of Dies Drear	Realistic Fiction	Classroom Library	V	670
	Nonna's Recipes	Historical Fiction	Leveled Reader	R	510, 740
TEXT SET 3					
How can we succeed at what we try to accomplish?	"Freedom at Fort Mose"	Historical Fiction	Shared Read	N/A	1000
	Because of Winn-Dixie	Realistic Fiction	Classroom Library	R	610
	Mrs. Frisby and the Rats of NIMH	Fantasy	Classroom Library	V	790
	The Adventures of Sal Fink	Tall Tale	Leveled Reader	M, P	600, 650

Grade 4: Text Extensions

Use the following additional texts to extend your text sets.

UNIT 5 TEXTS	EXTEND YOUR TEXT SET				
TEXT SET 1	**TITLE**	**GENRE**	**TYPE**	**GR**	**LEXILE**
How are characters in different stories alike and different?	"Remembering Hurricane Katrina"	Realistic Fiction	Shared Read	N/A	800
	"A Telephone Mix-Up"	Historical Fiction	Shared Read	N/A	950
	The Accidental Hero	Fiction	Classroom Library	N/A	780
	The Little Prince	Fantasy	Classroom Library	X	710
	Mabuhay	Historical Fiction	Leveled Reader	M, Q	530, 580
TEXT SET 2					
How do inventors use their knowledge to help others?	"Food Fight"	Persuasive Text	Shared Read	N/A	870
	George's Giant Wheel	Narrative Nonfiction	Leveled Reader	J, N, O, P, S	490, 550, 610, 810, 910
	Start Small, Think Big	Persuasive Text	Leveled Reader	J, N, O, Q, T	590, 660, 710, 780, 890
TEXT SET 3					
How can learning about the past help you understand the present?	"Words for Change"	Biography	Shared Read	N/A	820
	"The History of Money"	Expository Text	Shared Read	N/A	900
	A River Ran Wild	Informational Nonfiction	Classroom Library	Q	670
	Jacob Riis: Champion of the Poor	Biography	Leveled Reader	L, O, P, Q, T	610, 610, 650, 790, 870
	Planet Power	Narrative Nonfiction	Leveled Reader	N, Q, R, R, U	650, 700, 770, 850, 920

Grade 4: Text Extensions

Use the following additional texts to extend your text sets.

UNIT 6 TEXTS	EXTEND YOUR TEXT SET				
TEXT SET 1	**TITLE**	**GENRE**	**TYPE**	**GR**	**LEXILE**
What can we learn about ourselves from reading about the past?	"The Fisherman and the Kaha Bird"	Folktale	Shared Read	N/A	800
	"The Time Specs 3000"	Fantasy	Shared Read	N/A	910
	M.C. Higgins the Great	Realistic Fiction	Classroom Library	X	620
	A Better Way	Historical Fiction	Leveled Reader	U	790
TEXT SET 2					
How do ideas change over time?	"Judy's Appalachia"	Biography	Shared Read	N/A	830
	"Food Fight"	Persuasive Article	Shared Read	N/A	870
	Happy Birthday, Martin Luther King	Biography	Classroom Library	L	800
	Who Was Jackie Robinson	Biography	Classroom Library	P	670
	Nellie Bly: Reporter for the Underdog	Biography	Leveled Reader	L, O, P, Q, T	580, 680, 730, 790, 880
TEXT SET 3					
How do our experiences shape us?	"Remembering Hurricane Katrina"	Realistic Fiction	Shared Read	N/A	800
	"The Time Specs 3000"	Fantasy	Shared Read	N/A	910
	Riding Freedom	Historical Fiction	Classroom Library	P	720
	Project Mulberry	Realistic Fiction	Classroom Library	T	690
	The Little Prince	Fantasy	Classroom Library	X	710
	The Final	Realistic Fiction	Leveled Reader	U	800

Grade 5: Text Extensions

Use the following additional texts to extend your text sets.

UNIT 1 TEXTS	EXTEND YOUR TEXT SET				
TEXT SET 1	**TITLE**	**GENRE**	**TYPE**	**GR**	**LEXILE**
How can a character's ideas evolve?	"A Reluctant Traveler"	Realistic Fiction	Shared Read	N/A	770
	"Miguel in the Middle"	Realistic Fiction	Shared Read	N/A	890
	Frindle	Realistic Fiction	Classroom Library	R	830
	Granny Torelli Makes Soup	Realistic Fiction	Classroom Library	S	810
	Snap Happy	Realistic Fiction	Leveled Reader	S, U	550, 810
TEXT SET 2					
How can your environment impact your ideas?	"Growing in Place: The Story of E. Lucy Braun"	Biography	Shared Read	N/A	690
	"Frederick Douglass: Freedom's Voice"	Biography	Shared Read	N/A	830
	"Words to Save the World: The Work of Rachel Carson"	Biography	Shared Read	N/A	980
	My Librarian is a Camel	Informational Text	Classroom Library	Q	980
	The Power of a Team	Expository Text	Leveled Reader	O, R, S, T, W	670, 740, 800, 900, 1010
	Jane Addams: A Woman of Action	Biography	Leveled Reader	O, R, S, T, W	630, 700, 710, 910, 1000
TEXT SET 3					
How do you determine an author's point of view?	"What was the Purpose of the Incas' Strange Strings?"	Persuasive Article	Shared Read	N/A	920
	"Power from Nature"	Expository Text	Shared Read	N/A	910
	"Should Plants and Animals from Other Places Live Here?"	Persuasive Article	Shared Read	N/A	930
	We Are the Ship: The Story of Negro League Baseball	Informational Text	Classroom Library	W	900
	The Delta	Expository Text	Leveled Reader	O, R, S, U, X	680, 780, 830, 890, 1020

Grade 5: Text Extensions

Use the following additional texts to extend your text sets.

UNIT 2 TEXTS	EXTEND YOUR TEXT SET				
TEXT SET 1	**TITLE**	**GENRE**	**TYPE**	**GR**	**LEXILE**
How do the actions of people long ago affect what happens today?	"Fantasy Becomes Fact"	Biography	Shared Read	N/A	800
	"Frederick Douglass: Freedom's Voice"	Biography	Shared Read	N/A	830
	So You Want to be an Inventor	Expository Text	Classroom Library	P	840
	Save This Space!	Narrative Nonfiction	Leveled Reader	M, Q, R, S, V	490, 750, 730, 960, 980
	Snapshot! The Story of George Eastman	Biography	Leveled Reader	M, Q, R, S, V	580, 760, 640, 860, 960
TEXT SET 2					
How important is motivaton and planning when working to achieve a goal?	"A Fresh Idea"	Realistic Fiction	Shared Read	N/A	760
	The Midnight Fox	Realistic Fiction	Classroom Library	R	970
	Parker's Plan	Realistic Fiction	Leveled Reader	M, Q	500, 680
	Can-do Canines	Realistic Fiction	Leveled Reader	R, S	570, 790
TEXT SET 3					
What can you do to get the information you need?	"Miguel in the Middle"	Realistic Fiction	Shared Read	N/A	890
	"The Bully"	Realistic Fiction	Shared Read	N/A	850
	Granny Torelli Makes Soup	Realistic Fiction	Classroom Library	S	810

Grade 5: Text Extensions

Use the following additional texts to extend your text sets.

UNIT 3 TEXTS	EXTEND YOUR TEXT SET				
TEXT SET 1	**TITLE**	**GENRE**	**TYPE**	**GR**	**LEXILE**
How can new experiences change the way we think?	"A Fresh Idea"	Realistic Fiction	Shared Read	N/A	760
	"The Day the Rollets Got Their Moxie Back"	Historical Fiction	Shared Read	N/A	900
	SeeSaw Girl	Historical Fiction	Classroom Library	Q	810
	The Secret Garden	Novel	Classroom Library	R	710
	Alice's Adventures in Wonderland	Fantasy	Classroom Library	Z	980
	Enemy or Ally	Realistic Fiction	Leveled Reader	T, U	700, 840
TEXT SET 2					
How do authors organize information in a text?	"A Life in the Woods"	Narrative Nonfiction	Shared Read	N/A	740
	"Creating a Nation"	Expository Text	Shared Read	N/A	690
	"Forests on Fire"	Expository Text	Shared Read	N/A	960
	Arctic Lights, Arctic Nights	Expository Text	Classroom Library	Q	890
	What About Robots?	Expository Text	Leveled Reader	M, Q, R, S, V	600, 740, 760, 840, 990
	Mars	Expository Text	Leveled Reader	P, R, S, U, X	680, 700, 700, 900, 970
TEXT SET 3					
What can we learn from reading about the past?	"Frederick Douglass: Freedom's Voice"	Biography	Shared Read	N/A	830
	"Words to Save the World: The Work of Rachel Carson"	Biography	Shared Read	N/A	980
	When Washington Crossed the Delaware	Expository Text	Classroom Library	S	860
	Why Don't You Get a Horse, Sam Adams?	Biography	Classroom Library	R	800
	Roberto Clemente	Narrative Nonfiction	Classroom Library	K	800
	The Bill of Rights	Expository Text	Leveled Reader	M, Q, R, S, V	600, 820, 840, 920, 1000

Grade 5: Text Extensions

Use the following additional texts to extend your text sets.

UNIT 4 TEXTS	EXTEND YOUR TEXT SET				
TEXT SET 1	**TITLE**	**GENRE**	**TYPE**	**GR**	**LEXILE**
How can point of view influence how you interpret a story?	"Whitewater Adventure"	Realistic Fiction	Shared Read	N/A	760
	"Survivaland"	Fantasy	Shared Read	N/A	790
	"Shipped Out"	Historical Fiction	Shared Read	N/A	810
	Bud, Not Buddy	Historical Fiction	Classroom Library	U	950
	Dancing the Flamenco	Realistic Fiction	Leveled Reader	S, T	510, 790
TEXT SET 2					
How does the author's perspective influence how he/she shares information?	"Are Electronic Devices Good for Us?"	Persuasive Article	Shared Read	N/A	900
	"What was the Purpose of the Inca's Strange Strings?"	Persuasive Article	Shared Read	N/A	920
	Volcano: The Eruption and Healing of Mt. St. Helens	Expository Text	Classroom Library	U	830
	The Power of a Team	Expository Text	Leveled Reader	O, R, S, T, W	670, 740, 800, 900, 1010
	The Great Plains	Expository Text	Leveled Reader	P, S, T, U, X	680, 760, 830, 910, 1020
TEXT SET 3					
How do you express something that is important to you?	"A Simple Plan"	Poetry	Shared Read	N/A	N/A
	"To Travel"	Poetry	Shared Read	N/A	N/A
	Bud, Not Buddy	Historical Fiction	Classroom Library	U	950
	Hard Times	Historical Fiction	Leveled Reader	S, U	520, 830

Grade 5: Text Extensions

Use the following additional texts to extend your text sets.

UNIT 5 TEXTS	EXTEND YOUR TEXT SET				
TEXT SET 1	**TITLE**	**GENRE**	**TYPE**	**GR**	**LEXILE**
How can people adapt to difficult situations?	"Whitewater Adventure"	Realistic Fiction	Shared Read	N/A	760
	"The Bully"	Realistic Fiction	Shared Read	N/A	850
	The Midnight Fox	Realistic Fiction	Classroom Library	R	970
	Welcome to the Wilds	Fantasy	Leveled Reader	W	890
	The Victory Garden	Historical Fiction	Leveled Reader	X	900
	Enemy or Ally	Realistic Fiction	Leveled Reader	T, U	700, 840
TEXT SET 2					
How do changes in the environment and technology affect living things?	"Gulf Spill Superheroes"	Expository Text	Shared Read	N/A	860
	"Power from Nature"	Expository Text	Shared Read	N/A	910
	So You Want to be an Inventor	Expository Text	Classroom Library	P	840
	The Delta	Expository Text	Leveled Reader	O, R, S, U, X	680, 780, 830, 890, 1020
TEXT SET 3					
How do natural events and human activities help and hurt our environment?	"Words to Save the World: The Work of Rachel Carson"	Biography	Shared Read	N/A	980
	Save This Space!	Narrative Nonfiction	Leveled Reader	M, Q, R, S, V	490, 750, 730, 960, 980
	Norman Borlaug and the Green Revolution	Biography	Leveled Reader	N, Q, R, S, V	580, 740, 770, 900, 940
	Ocean Threats	Expository Text	Leveled Reader	P, R, S, U, X	730, 830, 870, 950, 990

Grade 5: Text Extensions

Use the following additional texts to extend your text sets.

UNIT 6 TEXTS	EXTEND YOUR TEXT SET				
	TITLE	GENRE	TYPE	GR	LEXILE
TEXT SET 1					
How can working together help us solve problems?	"A Fresh Idea"	Realistic Fiction	Shared Read	N/A	760
	"Miguel in the Middle"	Realistic Fiction	Shared Read	N/A	890
	Masterpiece	Fantasy	Classroom Library	U	700
	In Drama Valley	Fantasy	Leveled Reader	S, T	600, 790
	Welcome to the Wilds?	Fantasy	Leveled Reader	W	890
	Hard Times	Historical Fiction	Leveled Reader	S, U	520, 830
TEXT SET 2					
How can an environment shape its inhabitants?	"A Life in the Woods"	Narrative Nonfiction	Shared Read	N/A	740
	"Frederick Douglass: Freedom's Voice"	Biography	Shared Read	N/A	830
	Roberto Clemente: Pride of the Pittsburgh Pirates	Narrative Nonfiction	Classroom Library	K	800
	Volcano: The Eruption and Healing of Mt. St. Helens	Expository Text	Classroom Library	U	830
	The Anasazi	Expository Text	Leveled Reader	O, R, S, T, W	740, 810, 830, 900, 1010
TEXT SET 3					
What can our connections to the world teach us?	"A Simple Plan"	Poetry	Shared Read	N/A	N/A
	Snap Happy	Realistic Fiction	Leveled Reader	S, U	550, 810
	Welcome to the Wilds	Fantasy	Leveled Reader	W	890